D0046484

RENEWALS 458-4574
DATE DUE

The Regulation of Science and Technology

Studies in Regulation

General Editor: **George Yarrow**, Director, Regulatory Policy Institute and Regulatory Policy Research Centre, Hertford College, Oxford

Government regulation of business activity is a pervasive characteristic of modern economies, including those most committed to free markets. For good or ill, regulation has far-reaching implications for economic performance, and understanding the processes at work is an important task for anyone seeking to analyse the determinants of performance. Quite frequently, however, analysis is restricted to a very specific aspect of business activity or to a particular sector of the economy, an approach that serves to limit the insights into regulatory issues that may be gained.

A guiding principle behind this series of books is that regulatory processes exhibit a number of common features that are likely to manifest themselves in a range of different circumstances. A full understanding of the motives for and effects of regulation therefore requires study of these common features, as well as the specifics of particular cases of government interventions. Thus, it is possible to learn something relevant about, say, the regulation of utilities from the study of financial services regulation, or about industrial policy from the study of environmental regulation.

This focus on regulatory processes in general, as well as on specific aspects of particular interventions, also points to the value of interdisciplinary analysis. Policy formulation, development and implementation each have political, legal and economic aspects, and the boundaries between traditional academic disciplines can be obstacles to progress in regulatory studies. In this series, therefore, a wide range of different perspectives on regulation and on regulatory processes will be presented, with the aim of contributing to the development of new insights into important policy issues of the day.

Titles include:

Bill Bradshaw and Helen Lawton Smith (*editors*)
PRIVATIZATION AND DEREGULATION OF TRANSPORT

Helen Lawton Smith and Nick Woodward (*editors*)
ENERGY AND ENVIRONMENT REGULATION

Helen Lawton Smith (*editor*)
THE REGULATION OF SCIENCE AND TECHNOLOGY

Studies in Regulation
Series Standing Order ISBN 0–333–71498–9
(*outside North America only*)

You can receive future titles in this series as they are published by placing a standing order. Please contact your bookseller or, in case of difficulty, write to us at the address below with your name and address, the title of the series and the ISBN quoted above.

Customer Services Department, Macmillan Distribution Ltd, Houndmills, Basingstoke, Hampshire RG21 6XS, England

The Regulation of Science and Technology

Edited by

Helen Lawton Smith
Reader in Local Economic Development
Centre for Local Economic Development
Coventry Business School
Coventry University

Research Director
Oxfordshire Economic Observatory
School of Geography and the Environment
Oxford University

palgrave

First published 2002 by
PALGRAVE
Houndmills, Basingstoke, Hampshire RG21 6XS and
175 Fifth Avenue, New York, N.Y. 10010
Companies and representatives throughout the world

PALGRAVE is the new global academic imprint of
St. Martin's Press LLC Scholarly and Reference Division and
Palgrave Publishers Ltd (formerly Macmillan Press Ltd).

ISBN 0–333–79045–6 hardback

This book is printed on paper suitable for recycling and
made from fully managed and sustained forest sources.

A catalogue record for this book is available
from the British Library.

Library of Congress Cataloging-in-Publication Data
The regulation of science and technology / edited by Helen Lawton
Smith
        p. cm. — (Studies in regulation)
    Includes bibliographical references and index.
    ISBN 0–333–79045–6
        1. Science and state—Great Britain. 2. Technology and state-
–Great Britain. 3. Science and law—Great Britain. 4. Technology
and law—Great Britain. I. Lawton Smith, Helen. II. Series.

Q127.G7 R44 2001
338.941'06—dc21
                                                        2001021727

10   9   8   7   6   5   4   3   2   1
11 10 09 08 07 06 05 04 03 02

Printed and bound in Great Britain by
Antony Rowe Ltd, Chippenham, Wiltshire

Contents

Notes on the Contributors

John Abraham is Professor of Sociology and Co-director of the Centre for Research in Health And Medicine (CRHAM) at the University of Sussex where he teaches and researches in sociology and politics of science, technology and medicine. His books include: *Science, politics and the pharmaceutical industry: controversy and bias in drug regulation; The therapeutic nightmare: the battle over the world's most controversial sleeping pill*; and (with Graham Lewis) *Regulating medicines in Europe*.

Nick Bloom is a senior research economist at the Institute for Fiscal Studies, having joined in 1996 on completion of an M.Phil. at Oxford University. His research focuses on the behaviour of investment under fixed costs and irreversibilities in the presence of uncertainty, empirical models of research and development expenditure, and the pharmaceutical industry.

David R. Charles is a Principal Research Associate in the Centre for Urban and Regional Development Studies, University of Newcastle and Co-ordinator of a research group on Innovation, Learning and Knowledge. He has research interests in the areas of organisational change, technology policy and urban and regional development. Recent and current projects include work on university institutional relations with their local regions, graduate labour markets, regional cluster policies, the competitiveness of cities in the knowledge economy, and the management of intellectual property by university spin offs. He is currently co-ordinating international EU projects on universities and regional development, and on the evaluation of regional innovation and technology transfer strategies.

Lucy Chennells is a senior research economist at the Institute for Fiscal Studies having joined in 1993 from the Fiscal Affairs division of the OECD. Her research interests include UK and international corporate tax, company dividend behaviour and shareholder composition, and the effects of technology on wages.

Richard Darton joined the Amsterdam research laboratory of Shell in 1975, and subsequently worked in Shell's Oil and Gas, and Chemicals

Manufacturing functions. Since 1991 he has been teaching and researching in chemical engineering at the University of Oxford, Department of Engineering Science. He is Editor-in-Chief of *Chemical Engineering Journal*, and is a founder member of the Oxford Centre for Environmental Biotechnology.

Paul A. David is Professor of Economics at Stanford University, and also is Senior Research Fellow of All Souls College, Oxford. He also is a Senior Fellow of Stanford University's Institute for Economic Policy Research (SIEPR), where he leads the High Technology Impact Program, and is Professorial Fellow of the Economics of Science and Technology at the Maastricht Economic Research Institute on Innovation and Technology (MERIT), in the Rijksuniversiteit Maastricht. David was elected a Fellow of the International Econometrics Society (1975), a Fellow of the American Academy of Arts and Sciences (1979), and an Ordinary Fellow of the British Academy (1995). He has served as (elected) Vice-President, and President of the Economic History Association, and presently is an elected Member of the Council of the Royal Economics Society. He has been a Visiting Professor of Economics at Harvard University, the Pitt Professor of American History and Institutions at the University of Cambridge, Visiting Professor in the Economics of Science and Technology at the University of Paris-Dauphine. He has served as consultant to the United Nations Commission on Trade and Development, the United Nations University Institute on New Technologies, the World Bank, the Organization for Economic Cooperation and Development, various EC Directorates of the European Union, the US National Academy of Sciences' National Research Council, the US National Science Foundation, the Economic and Social Research Council (UK), the German Monopolies Commission, the Rockefeller Foundation, Leverhulme Trust, and other public and private organisations.

Rachel Griffith is Senior Research Economist and Programme Co-ordinator in the corporate sector at the Institute for Fiscal Studies. She joined the IFS in 1993 having previously worked for a small investment research firm. She is an Honorary Research Fellow of University College, London and was visiting professor at University of California at Los Angeles for the academic year 1999/2000. Her research focuses on empirical investigation of the impact that foreign investment and the presence of foreign firms has on economic performance and productivity. She also looks at the factors influencing multinational firm's location choices and the design and implementation of technology policy and the impact of tax in determining where firms locate.

Sir Douglas Hague was one of the founders of the Manchester Business School, where he was deputy director from 1978 to 1981 and remains a visiting professor. Following membership of the Price Commission he was a personal economic advisor to Mrs Margaret Thatcher from 1967 to 1979, an adviser to the Prime Minister's Policy Unit from 1979 to 1983 and was Chairman of the Economic and Social Research Council from 1983 to 1987. He is an Associate Fellow of Templeton College, Oxford and is also Chairman of Oxford Strategy Network. Following publication of *Beyond Universities*, Sir Douglas is researching into the way higher education is likely to develop in the next decade.

Alan Irwin is Professor of Sociology in the Department of Human Sciences, Brunel University. He is author of *Risk and the Control of Technology and Citizen Science* and co-editor (with Brian Wynne) of *Misunderstanding Science?* He has published papers in numerous journals and edited collections. Currently, his research interests are in environmental sociology, science and its publics and regulatory policy.

Helen Lawton Smith is Reader in Local Economic Development, Centre for Local Economic Development, Coventry University. She was previously Research Director (1992–1995) then Director of Science Policy Studies (1992–1998) at the Regulatory Policy Research Centre, Hertford College, Oxford. She is Senior Research Associate at the School of Geography and the Environment, Oxford University and a Research Associate at the Centre for Business Research, University of Cambridge. Her research interests include the geography of innovation and the economic governance of innovation systems. Her books *Technology Transfer and Industrial Change in Europe* and *Privatisation and Deregulation of Transport* (with Bill Bradshaw) are published by Macmillan – now Palgrave.

John Lovering worked in a community-based employment initiative in North Wales after studying Economics at Bangor. In 1982 he took up a research post at the School for Advanced Urban Studies at the University of Bristol, where he remained for ten years. After a spell at the Geography Department at Liverpool University, he was appointed Professor of Geography at Hull University in 1994. Since 1996 he has been based in the Department of City and Regional Planning, Cardiff University, where he heads a new degree in Geography and Planning. His main research interests lie in the geography of economic development, the role of labour markets in economic development, and social inequalities in the historical and recent development of the Welsh economy, devolution and the new political-economy of Wales, globalisation, transnational enterprise and the State, the relationship between defence spending and regional/national development and the restructuring of the defence industry at the UK, European and global levels. He has undertaken research funded by a range of academic and practitioner bodies including the British Economic and Social Research Council, the European Commission, United Nations University, the US Council of Foreign Relations, Bonn International Centre for Conversion, trades unions, local authorities and Training and Enterprise Councils. He also gives talks to local community-based organisations on defence and war issues, on globalisation and unemployment and on the Welsh economy. He is currently writing a book on war and the arms industry entitled *The Means of Destruction*.

Erik Millstone is a Senior Lecturer in the Science and Technology Policy Research Unit at Sussex University. Since 1974 he has been researching the role of scientific evidence and scientific expertise in regulatory policy-making. The initial focus was on a UK–US comparison of policies to regulate toxicological hazards from food additives and contaminants. In the 1980s the focus of the comparisons extended to take into account the role of EC/EU bodies and since 1992 that has been extended to examine the role of global bodies, especially those convened under the auspices of the World Health Organisation. His interests have also expanded to include non-food policy issues such as lead pollution. He is currently engaged on a European Commission funded project to examine the history of BSE policy-making in several EU member states and at the European Commission, to learn lessons for food safety policy-making in the EU. He is the author of *Food Additives Lead and Public Health*, co-author of *Our Genetic Future: the science and ethics of genetic technology* and *Health and Environmental Impact Assessment*.

John Mulvey After nearly forty years of research in particle physics, during which he spent three years on the Board of Directors and was Chairman of several international committees, John Mulvey retired from Physics at Oxford in 1990 to open the first office of the Save British Science Society (SBS), of which he was a founder member. He retired again, from the post of Director of SBS, in 1998 but continues to help as a member of the SBS Executive Committee.

Gerald Paterson read physics at Hertford College, Oxford and qualified as a Chartered Patent Agent before reading for the Bar at Gray's Inn. He practised at the Patent Bar from 1966 to 1985, when he was appointed a member of the enlarged Board of Appeal and of the Boards of Appeal of the European Patent Office in Munich. He became Chairman of Boards of Appeal in 1990 and retired in 1997.

Henry Rothstein is currently a Research Officer in the Department of Government at the London School of Economics. He was previously a Research Fellow at the Centre for Research into Innovation, Culture and Technology (CRICT), Brunel University whilst undertaking the research discussed in this book. His research interests include the role of science in regulatory policy and the mechanics and dynamics of risk regulation regimes across a wide spectrum of policy domains. He has published widely on these topics in a number of journals, most recently including *Risk Management: an International Journal* and *Health, Risk and Society* and in edited volumes including R. Bal and W. Halffman (eds) *The Politics of Chemical Risk: Scenarios for a Regulatory Future*.

John Van Reenen was educated at Queens' College Cambridge and the London School of Economics, and is a Professor of Economics at University College, London and a Research Fellow at the Institute of Fiscal Studies and CEPR. He is an editor of the *Review of Economic Studies, European Economic Review* and *Journal of Industrial Economics* and has written over forty papers on the economics of innovation, labour markets, industries and other issues. In 1998 he was visiting professor in Berkeley, University of California.

I
Introduction

1
The Context for Science and Technology Regulation

Helen Lawton Smith

Introduction

This book sets out to explore and comment on the complexity of the regulatory processes governing the production, ownership and exploitation of science and technology. The chapters are mainly updated versions of papers presented at a seminar held in March 1996 organised by the Regulatory Policy Research Centre, Hertford College as one of the Regulatory Policy Seminar series funded by the Economic and Social Research Council (award no. R45126440395), and supported by Coventry Business School, where it was held. Two additional chapters (by David Charles and Henry Rothstein and Alan Irwin) have been included. The purpose of the seminar was to bring together a range of perspectives on the ways in which science and technology is regulated and brought together academics, policy makers, industrialists, and representatives from pressure groups. The key theme was the inseparability of the political-regulatory climate, the kind of science and technology research conducted in universities and in industry, the way that research is utilised by industry, and the intent to which it is used by actors within the regulatory system to support particular positions.

Background

In the UK, under successive Conservative governments from 1979 to 1997 the political focus was on the exploitation of the science base. The policy approach in this period has been labelled 'policy for technological innovation' and is reputed to be commonly regarded as the third phase of postwar science and technology policy, having replaced the so-called 'policy for science' approach of the 1950s and

1960s and its successor, the 'science in policy' approach of the 1970s. What differentiates the third phase from that of its predecessors is the explicit expectation by government that universities (and national laboratories) assume centre stage in the promotion of economic growth. Exploiting the potential of the 'Triple Helix' (Etzkowitz, 1994, 139) of university-industry-government is increasingly regarded as an important part of policies designed to achieve the goal of wealth creation (Blankenburg, 1998, 2). This process, combined with a decline in government support for science relative to other countries, was so extensive in the UK that 1986 saw the creation of a pressure group Save British Science (SBS), formed by two Oxford academics, in dismay at what they saw as the threat to long-term research. This was the year that the Prime Minister, Mrs Margaret Thatcher, was refused an honorary degree from Oxford University because of her attitude towards science and education funding of the universities. Indeed, the first decade of Conservative governments saw a decline of the government's share of funding for research in universities from 81 per cent to 72 per cent, with a respective increase in income from charities, industry and overseas sources (SBS, 1994).

The basic principle of exploitation recorded in official publications, was enacted by direct intervention in the market for information by mechanisms designed to encourage technology transfer out of public sector research institutions (universities and national laboratories), and by the restructuring of major sectors of the science base. The ending of British Technology Group's right of first refusal of inventions arising from publicly funded research in universities in 1983 was a milestone in that it gave universities more independence to exploit the intellectual property generated by their researchers.

The principle of exploiting rather than only developing technology was laid down in the 1988 White Paper 'DTI – the department for enterprise'. The White Paper contained three central concepts (Walker 1993, 184). One was 'open market', which in practice meant that 'competition policy' came to form the core of the government's industrial policy. The second concept was 'enterprise'. Lack of enterprise was identified as having played a major part in the relative decline of the British economy (DTI, 1988, 1). The third was that the government's support for innovation should be constrained in expenditure terms. The White Paper argued that the emphasis should be placed on achieving greater value-for-money by raising the efficiency with which resources were used, not least by making their allocation conditional on recipients satisfying strict performance criteria. Walker argues that this meant that in relation to science, to education, to R&D, and all other areas where the state played a part in the innovation system, assessment of performance was based on demonstrable returns, and that long-term projects with uncertain paybacks were rationed. Walker therefore concludes that the government's attitude towards science and technology prioritised productivity and cost reductions before expansion and creation of new capabilities, even where, as in education, there was a historic tendency towards under-investment. This marked changes in the representation of society's value of science and technology.

Mechanisms designed to encourage industry and academic links underwent radical change in both the UK and in Europe. In the UK they were rationalised through changes in both the programmes available and in the emphasis in the research councils, which themselves were reorganised in 1994. The ALVEY Programme was introduced in 1983 and constituted the single largest UK IT policy initiative in the 1980s costing the public purse some £200 million, with industry contributing an estimated £150 million. It was sponsored by the DTI, SERC and MoD. One of its main aims was to improve the competitiveness of the UK IT sector. One of its main achievements was in fortifying the research community, and in nurturing links between academia and industry (HMSO, 1991, i). ALVEY was the last large-scale national research programme. From September 1993, LINK became the only national collaborative R&D mechanism. Although LINK was intended to bridge the gap between industry and academia, at its inception it was anticipated that it would be unlikely to generate the gains of ALVEY in fostering closer links between the industrial and academic communities because it was another fragmented initiative (Georghiou *et al.*, 1992). The UK's strategy has been instead to provide increased levels of funding to the EC to support programmes such as ESPRIT (information technologies) and BRITE-EURAM (materials). Moreover, the greater availability of funding at the European rather than the national level has resulted in the UK having the largest number of collaborative links of any member state (Georghiou *et al.*, 1992). The budget for science programmes run by the EC rose sharply over the period 1985 to 1997 as the EU sought first to overcome declining competitiveness of key sectors such as IT and the widening gap between Europe and US/Japan and more recently as a result of a greater emphasis on social objectives (see chapter by Charles this book).

During the 1980s and 1990s the government encouraged inward investment as an economic growth strategy rather than supporting indigenous industry. This policy was associated with a decline in investment in R&D and a reduction in some sectors in the levels of funding research in universities and national laboratories. During the 1980s and 1990s compared to the UK, industry in Germany and the US was spending more than twice as much on developing new ideas and technology for every member of the labour force. France was spending twenty per cent more than the UK, but was still short of the US, Germany and Japan. In the year 1990 to 1991 for example, UK industrial spending on R&D fell by 10 per cent in real terms, while in France during the 1980s the percentage increased (Save British Science 1994 4). According to Walker (1993, 186) what has been lost in the move from the 'mission-oriented' approach of supporting big-science that Britain shared with France and the United States to that of emphasising exploitation – the 'diffusion-oriented' approach – has been the failure to recognise the 'importance of building strong technological capabilities'. This is manifest in the country's failure to invest in strategic areas. The UK has neither 'shown little appetite for the investments required for the heavy investments required to maintain strong indigenous industries' nor been willing 'to play a part in identifying and supporting technologies which have a strategic value'. Examples of lack of commitment to supporting a domestic electronics industry were the sale of INMOS to SGS-Thomson and ICL to Fujitsui. Walker states that these illustrate Britain's 'unconcern over the fate of its remaining semiconductor and large scale computer capabilities'.

Although most inward investment in that decade was in production and service activities, there was an inflow of Japanese, US and European R&D centres into the UK attracted by the potential rewards of interaction with centres of excellence. These include Sharp and Rand Information Systems Ltd to Oxford and Microsoft to Cambridge. Thus the map of scientific and engineering research was changing as a result of decisions made by foreign industry rather than UK industry to collaborate with the science base.

In the late 1980s the UK began a series of changes to the structure of the higher education system (See David *et al.*, 1995, 36). The turning point in the process of change of the funding system was the Education Reform Act (1988). The Act created two new funding Agencies, the Universities Funding Council (UFC) and the Polytechnic and Colleges Funding Council (PCFC). These modified the 'logic' of higher education funding. The two agencies were created as 'buyers of academic services'. In 1993, the UFC and PCFC were merged into a single Higher Education Funding Council (HEFC) with separate agencies for England, Scotland

and Wales. At the same time the higher education sector was transformed with 39 polytechnics and colleges being granted university status. Other institutions subsequently became universities. Under the old system in 1993, there were 74 different universities including the colleges of London University (David *et al.*, 1995, 36). Now there are 120. A general trend was the growth of researchers appointed to short-term contracts in both universities and national laboratories. At the same time pay in the university sector, although not in national laboratories, fell behind pay for equivalent work in industry.

The 1990s saw further radical changes in the UK's science base and in the regulatory system. The 1993 White Paper 'Realising Our Potential: A Strategy for Science, Technology and Engineering', not only formalised the rhetoric through which the debate about science and technology was being discussed with its focus on exploitation of research but also announced the Technology Foresight Programme and the review of a historically important component of the science base, the government laboratories. The Foresight Programme was established in 1994 and the Report on the Multi-Departmental Scrutiny of Public Sector Research Establishments was published in the same year. This provided the framework for further privatisation of national laboratories, for example the National Engineering laboratory in 1995 and AEA Technology, the commercial operation of the UKAEA in 1996, and rationalisation of other laboratories. Measures to make research in government laboratories more commercial have their parallel in other countries, including the USA (see Etzkowitz and Stevens, 1995; Branscomb, 1993), Belgium (Van Dierdonk *et al.*, 1990) and France (Chesnais, 1993).

The UK Foresight programme is managed by the Office of Science and Technology in the Department of Trade and Industry. In 1995 the first set of visions and recommendations for action were published. This was followed by four years of development and implementation. A new round of Foresight began on 1 April 1999. The purpose of Foresight is to:

- develop visions of the future – looking at possible future needs, opportunities and threats and deciding what should be done now to make sure that we are ready for these challenges.
- build bridges between business, science and government, bringing together the knowledge and expertise of many people across all areas and activities; in order to increase national wealth and quality of life.

Reorganisation within the science base also resulted from the great wave of a different kind of regulation – or deregulation – that of privatisation. In the decade from 1979, almost half the UK's state-owned industrial sector was sold, over 700 000 workers moved to the private sector and over £25bn of shares sold as privatisation issues (Hoare, 1997, 254). Comprising part of the state-owned sector was the R&D laboratories of the utilities – gas, water, electricity, telecoms, which had long interacted with universities and national laboratories. The long term implications of the privatisation process on the relationship between universities and the privatised companies are yet to be analysed.

The regulatory system itself was also changing. For example, there was a centralisation of regulation of science and technology. In 1992 responsibility for co-ordination was brought together with the creation of the Office of Science and Technology (OST) in the Cabinet Office, headed by the Chief Scientific Adviser. The Office has responsibility for the Science Budget. This includes support for the five research councils. The Chancellor of the Duchy of Lancaster then provided science and technology, as a single entity, with its first cabinet representation since the 1960s. Overall Cabinet responsibility remained with the Prime Minister. A further aspect of these changes was that the new Office took on responsibility for the Science Budget. This responsibility was short-lived. In 1995, the Department and Trade and Industry, took overall control of the Science Budget. While the transfer of the control of spending on science to the OST within the Cabinet Office 'brought it to a more central position in the government and increased its importance to decisions in almost all sections of policy' the removal of the Office to the DTI was seen by SBS as being 'Reduced to the ranks'. The change meant that instead of the OST being engaged in a constructive dialogue with a Ministry that SBS believed was listening, it was 'banished to a corner of the DTI, a Department with an appalling record in the understanding of the research process and its management' (SBS, 1995, 1). Part of the problem identified by SBS was that in the 1980s and 1990s there was little political representation of the science and technology community in government and not where it mattered, few government ministers had science degrees.

An assessment of the changes within higher education was undertaken by The Dearing Committee. This was appointed in 1996 to advise on the long term development of higher education. In the Report (1997) the Committee expressed their concern that the long term well-being of higher education should not be damaged by the needs of the short term. They were particularly concerned about planned further reductions in the amount of funding for higher education. If these are projected forward, it will have been halved in 25 years. The Report argued that this would damage both the quality and effectiveness of higher education. Concern was expressed about some other immediate needs, especially in relation to research. It recommended that students contribute to university fees. This measure was adopted in 1998, to considerable protest from inside and outside the universities.

At the European level EU decisions on technical standards, market entry and competition were having a dramatic effect on the competitive environment of industry. In this context, new technical, institutional and market arrangements were reshaping the terms and conditions under which firms appropriate the resources of national laboratories and universities. The 1990s also saw the expansion of global regulatory agencies (see for example chapters by Millstone and Abraham in this book).

The legacy of the Conservative government is a decline in national R&D spending. In September 1999 the OECD's publication *The Science, Technology and Industry Scoreboard: Benchmarking the Knowledge-based Economies* showed that Britain is continuing to invest less than other industrialised countries. While sustained economic growth has

Table 1.1: Key policy initiatives

1983	Ending of BTGs right of first refusal of inventions arising from publicly funded research in universities
1986	Formation of Save British Science
1988	Education Reform Act – created two new funding agencies Universities Funding Council (UFC) and Polytechnics and Colleges Funding Council (PCFC)
1987	Single European Act
1988	White Paper 'DTI – the department for enterprise'
1988	Next Steps initiatives creation of executive agencies to bring efficiency into government laboratories
1993	White Paper *Realising Our Potential*
1993	Merger of UFC and PCFC to form HEFC, 'New universities' created.
1994	Technology Foresight Programme
1994	Multi-departmental scrutiny of Public Sector Research Establishments
1997	Dearing Report *Higher Education in the Learning Society*
1998	White Paper *Our Competitive Future*
1999	Sainsbury Report *Biotechnology Clusters*
1999	RDAs established 1 April
1999	Independent Review of Higher Education Pay and Conditions (The Bett Report)

prompted most countries to increase the proportion of national income invested in R&D, it appears to have the opposite effect in Britain. R&D spending continued to fall, reaching 1.9 per cent of GDP in 1997, down from 2 per cent in 1995 and 2.2 per cent in 1993. The average for OECD countries is 2.2 per cent of GDP. The figure was higher for Sweden (almost 4 per cent) and for Finland, Korea and the United States (almost 3 per cent). However, some other large economies also saw a decline, including Germany and France (*Guardian* 29 September 1999). While government funding of the science base declined under the Conservatives, charities increased their level of funding. For example the Wellcome Trust funds some £300 million research in universities each year, most going to Oxford and Cambridge. The Trust has additionally provided some £100 million in building the Sanger Centre in Cambridge.

The prime litmus test of conditions within the science base, the scientific labour market, has been undergoing structural change with evidence of a new brain drain. This is due in part to the diminishing rewards and career prospects in academia plus the cutback in research funding. In the mid-1990s the UK topped European countries in the number of professionals emigrating to the US, around a quarter of whom went to California, New York State and Massachusetts, attracted by the scientific pull of centres of excellence in these locations (Mahroum, 1998). The situation was summarised in the *Guardian* 24 September 1999, 3: 'Poor salaries, a lack of research funding and less-than-modern facilities have contributed to low morale in Britain's academic and scientific communities. The lack of a proper career infrastructure has led to the loss of key people, leaders and high flyers. In 1994, five of the country's 10 top geneticists left London for jobs abroad'. These issues were to a limited extent addressed by the Bett Report (1999), which recommended a £450 million boost to academic earnings.

To illustrate the range of ways in which science and technology is regulated and to provide a lead-in to the themes discussed in the book, I turn to the pharmaceutical industry. This sector has been intimately involved in regulatory processes determining the production, ownership and exploitation of science and technology in the UK as the following examples of interaction illustrate.

First, Sir Richard Sykes, chair of Glaxo Wellcome (GW) was interviewed on the Radio 4 *Today* programme, 4 October 1999. He accused the government of fostering an environment antagonistic to the pharmaceuticals sector. At issue was the refusal of HM government's National Institute for Clinical Excellence (NICE) to recommend that their influenza drug Relenza be prescribed on the NHS. He issued a veiled threat to the government. At issue was the fact that GW spent more than 50 per cent of its research budget while deriving only six per cent of its sales, in the UK. Sir Richard said that 'these factors call into question the attractiveness of the UK to a global company'. The company also suggested that others in the sector might also consider moving out of the UK. These threats amounted to a disingenuous attempt to thwart the regulators' (*Guardian,* 5 October 1999, 28). GW was also joined in protest by Astra Zeneca and SmithKline Beecham, the other members of the British Pharma Group, in protesting to the government. This event follows close on a decision by the Secretary of State at the Department of Environment, Transport and the Regions (DETR) to reject the Wellcome Trust's proposal for a 40 000 sq. meter development at Hinxton Hall in rural Cambridgeshire, although an incubation centre and grow-on space for new firms would be allowed. Although GW and the Wellcome Trust are separate entities, pharmaceutical companies such as GW are concerned that the decision would signal a lack of commitment to science (*Guardian,* 13 September 1999, 5). NICE was first welcomed by the industry because it was an agency responsible for making the health system more scientific and evidence based, ensuring an end to waste (*Observer* 10 October 1999). The Relenza incident and the Hinxton Hall issue are important because it signifies the kinds of messages that an industry will try to use to exert pressure on government and the value placed on communication with government through the mass media. In this instance pressure was resisted.

Second, the industry by necessity has to make sunk investments in research and development. It is also subject to price regulation in the form of the Pharmaceutical Price Regulation Scheme (PPRS). In 1993 a 2.5 per cent price reduction was agreed between the industry and government. The issue here is that the pharmaceutical companies have to be confident of recovering this expenditure through a pricing regime which allows mark-ups over marginal costs, otherwise the investible funds will dry up (Cave and Towse, 1997).

Third, the need for economies of scale for R&D in the pharmaceutical industry have brought the industry into conflict with European Competition policy. As indicated above, one of the key features of the industry is its R&D intensity – it is the UK's largest investor in R&D

and has a very high level of external research links. Kelly and Hadden (forthcoming) have pointed out that,

> ... joint ventures can give rise to extremely complex issues of product definition and assessment of the competitive impact of the transaction. This is particularly true with regard to overlaps in R&D where competition authorities are obliged to deal with nebulous concepts such as future markets. While previous Commission decisions and decisions of other competition authorities can give some guidance to the approach that might be taken in future mergers, it is sometimes difficult to determine what their approach might be in a given situation. This is complicated by the fact that at the European level, the desire to create a single market and to promote European champions may introduce a political element into the decision making process, the effect of which can be difficult to predict as companies such as British Airways and American Airlines found to their cost.

Further regulation of the industry includes, financial, in the form of rules governing raising capital on markets, harmonisation of regulations, for example, the ICH (International Committee on Harmonisation) and other forms discussed in chapters in this book including intellectual property (Paterson), health care (Abraham) and environmental regulation (Millstone).

The new realities

The election of a Labour Government on 1 May 1997 brought a greater commitment to funding science and technology. The Comprehensive Spending Review (CSR) announced on 31 July 1998 contained an allocation of £1.4 billion of new money, including £400 million from the Wellcome Trust. Most of the money (£700 million) was to go to the Office of Science and Technology, essentially the Research Councils (SBS, 1998, 1). In the SBS Winter newsletter 1999 in a marked contrast in tone with newsletters published under Conservative governments, SBS stated 'We genuinely appreciate the Government's recognition that British Science needs new investment'. SBS, however, also feel that the battle is not yet won as there remain problems of funding infrastructure, competitive salaries and the indirect costs of Research Council Grants. The CSR was also welcomed by industry (see for example SmithKline Beecham, 1998, 3).

Other new agendas under the Labour government, include promotion of particular sectors in general and clusters of firms in particular. There is now a spatial dimension to science policy. The Scotland Act and the Government of Wales Act will give new powers to respectively, the new Parliament and Assembly over science and education policy, but the new role of Regional Development Agencies will also be important for science (SBS, 1999b, 1). Although money promised for science and technology was already announced in the CSR, a Science and Technology Champion is to be appointed, whose job it will be to promote the understanding of science in government. The Liberal Democrats who share power in Scotland have set a target of 0.4 per cent of the Scottish GDP to be invested in the science base, which would be a rise of 0.02 per cent representing about £11 million Scotland.

The formation of clusters of high-technology firms such as those in Oxfordshire and Cambridgeshire are key themes in the Competitiveness White Paper *Our Competitive Future: Building the Knowledge Driven Economy* (DTI, 1998, chapter 5) and in the Sainsbury Report *Biotechnology Clusters* – Report of a team led by Lord Sainsbury, Minister for Science (the science and technology champion). RDAs were introduced with a specific remit for excellence, thereby changing the regional map of innovation policy. The themes of entrepreneurship, innovation and cluster formation are emphasised by the respective RDAs SEEDA (1999, para. B1.14) and EEDA (1999, 11). In defining the role of the regional strategies of the RDAs, the DETR (1997, para. 4.13) stated that 'the strategy will support and enhance national policies in ways which meet regional needs ... much of the work of the RDA and other local and regional partners will follow the framework of the strategy, to ensure the greatest possible coherence'. The DETR (1999) has subsequently identified the fundamental purpose of the regional strategies as being to improve economic performance and to enhance the region's competitiveness. In terms of the relationship with localities, the DETR (1999b) has stated that 'there was no intention that RDAs would take powers away from localities, all the powers which RDAs have been given come from above, or had been carried out at the regional level already. It was not envisaged that the RDAs would take powers away from local authorities or would interfere at local level' (Waters and Lawton Smith, 1999).

The 1998 budget announced the 'merging of the enterprise investment scheme and capital gains tax reinvestment relief in order to provide more generous, more efficient and better targeted help to encourage venture capital in Britain'. The 1999 budget introduced a new enterprise grant, enterprise incentives for managers, and a new research and development tax credit targeted to small businesses.

In Europe, the Fourth Framework has been succeeded by the Fifth Framework. The Fifth Framework (1998–2002) differs from its predecessors in that it has been conceived to solve problems and to respond to major economic challenges facing the European Union. Priorities have been chosen according to three principles:

- European 'Value Added' and the subsidiary principle, for example to reach a critical mass or contribute to solving problems of a European dimension.
- Social Objectives, such as quality of life, employment or protection of the environment in order to meet the expectations and concerns of the Union's citizens.
- Economic development and scientific and technology prospects in order to contribute to the harmonious and sustainable development of the European Union as a whole.

(The European Commission, 1999)

The book

The chapters in the book cover different kinds and domains of regulation of science and technology. As well as through technology, policy government intervention in the conduct and exploitation of science and technology results from regulations covering health and safety, legal ownership of intellectual property, regulation for ethical purposes, competition policy and regional/local economic development. Each can have a direct impact on scientific and engineering activities in both the public sector and in industry. The chapters raise a number of issues about the implications and consequences of the different forms of regulation directly for the science base, industry, the consumer and in analytical terms about processes of regulation.

The major issues in this book can be summarised as encompassing:

- accountability
- ownership of intellectual property
- the public interest, how it is defined and represented
- the balance between the interests of industry, the science base and the consumer

- problems of measurement as a basis for determining policy
- regulatory capture lack of protection for the consumer
- the proper role of institutions – regulatory, governments, transnational bodies etc.

The issues

The chapters in the first section cover what might be broadly described as technology policy. At a basic level, technology policy has been defined by Stoneman (1987, 4–5) as 'a set of policies involving government intervention in the economy with the *intent* of affecting the process of technological innovation'. The link between innovation, technology and technology policy is expressed by Roobeek (1990, 14). She argues that innovation potential hinges on the capability to combine and integrate developments from diverse sciences and sections of industry, and that as a result economic growth has come increasingly to rest on systematised technological and scientific fundamental research. Thus the state has a role to play in (a) overcoming industry's short-term horizons, (b) generating external effects arising from an extensive scientific infrastructure (c) subsidising very expensive but strategically important research (d) gearing science and educational systems to meet current needs and (e) overcoming problems of non-allocation for fundamental research arising out of failures of market forces. These activities reduce the risk to industry of the uncertainties of longer term research investment (see Rosenberg 1990, 165). However, evidence suggests that some fields of the economy are more susceptible to government control than others (Roobeek 1990, 22). This book tends to suggest that balance has been the other way round, that government has been more susceptible to influence by some sectors rather than by others.

Paul David in his overview chapter encapsulates the major political and economic processes shaping the production and use of science and technology. He highlights the cumulative nature of technology and presents the economic justification for regulating the supply of basic research. His chapter reviews the whole question of the purpose of the knowledge infrastructure – universities and national laboratories, the role of the scientist and engineer, and the assumptions made about what science and technology are for. He identifies problems associated with focusing on short-term economic performance goals in reshaping the innovation process. He provides a critique of linear models of technology push and market pull, with reference to the 1993 White Paper

Realising Our Potential and the Technology Foresight Programme. His bottom line is that there needs to be a better balance between competing objectives of short-run exploitation and long-run regeneration of the science and technology base. This calls for support of the science base infrastructure for vigorous 'open science' exploration, while at the same time, creating the financial conditions and intellectual property rights protections that enable business to invest profitably in the conduct of commercially orientated R&D.

John Mulvey, an academic in the nuclear physics department, and Denis Noble, an academic in the physiology department in the University of Oxford, took the first steps that led to founding of SBS in 1986. Not surprisingly Mulvey's chapter is concerned with the paradigm shift in government policy. This is the implicit trust that, left to themselves scientists would advance science and technology in the most effective and most efficient way, has been withdrawn. However, the consequence of that – the challenge for governments in delivering better value for money based on the intention of increasing efficiency – is how to set a value on research which has been done and which might be done in the future. His theme is the impossibility of valuing the benefits of long term research and he supports his arguments with examples of breakthroughs from research that had no obvious paybacks at the time, even to the researchers involved. He expresses frustration from within the system under the Conservatives at the system itself – and the ways it defines the public interest as being meeting a series of short-term goals. Like Richard Darton (see below) he recognises some merit in the Technology Foresight Programme, in the potential for bringing together scientists and engineers working in different disciples in a range of institutions, stimulating ideas and fresh lines of enquiry and to form networks. However, Mulvey criticises the politicians for seeing 'Foresight as "the street lamp" illuminating the area of pavement where the dropped gold coin is most easily found ...'.

Sir Douglas Hague looks ahead to what the system may be like in the next century. He begins by identifying four trends which he believes will transform universities in the next century, the rising demand for highly-skilled people, cost pressures, the transforming effects of the use of information and communication technologies (ICT) and the general rise in the supply of graduates in developed countries. He then discusses the main challenges to universities arising from those trends, particularly the ways in which the rising costs of research might be managed. He raises the question, what higher educational system will there be to regulate? He, like the previous authors, hopes that universities will be allowed to concentrate more on basic rather than applied research. He raises the possibilities of alternatives to a pure university system created by ICT, such as corporate and commercial universities, as have been introduced for example by Unipart in Oxford. In his third section, he presents his views on the challenges to the regulators, particularly the problems associated with the expansion of higher education. He cites the Open University as the prime example of how large numbers of students can receive a high quality education through distance learning methods. He argues that there is scope for an increase in the size of institutions and for there to be a reduction in their number. Referring to the Dearing Report he questions the existing basis for funding universities and criticises Dearing for not helping to resolve the issue of how an increase in the population of universities will automatically increase the productivity of the UK. He identifies the main barrier to increasing interaction as being one of conflicting cultures of universities with those of industry. He concludes by turning his question around by asking whether any regulatory system for higher education will remain by the year 2010.

Richard Darton examines public policy towards science and engineering from the point of view of process industries, which include pharmaceutical companies and petro-chemical companies such as Shell. This group of industries is important because it is highly reliant on technology and has a dominant position in funding R&D in the UK. While Sir Douglas Hague highlights the difference in culture between universities and industry, Darton focuses on the differences in objectives between those of industry, of competitive edge and profitability, and those of universities. He describes how intense commercial pressure has resulted in companies downsizing their R&D efforts and relying more on external sources such as universities, which in turn has weakened the basic difference between commercial and publicly funded research. This convergence, as Darton points out, has been enshrined in the Foresight Programme and has been welcomed by the process industries. While there are differing views about how far this process should go, there are in his view some benefits to the Programme, including shedding light on the strengths and weaknesses of the science and engineering base. A result of this might be greater provision of funding to strengthen the UK's academic process engineering capability.

Darton asks an interesting question – what if the UK were to start anew spending £3.1 billion on research each year? In answering, he suspects that there would be a much smaller role for the individual university professor or lecturer as principal investigator managing a small grant. More research would be undertaken in research units, centres of institutes which would develop as centres of excellence and continuity in the research process. The downside of that would be that the enthusiasm of young researchers would be lost as would the link between teaching and research. Moreover, there are costs to such centres, including the necessity of tracking policy and spending decisions, and trying to influence them, and the loss of innovation when commercial decisions made by the paymasters – industry – override the advantages of collaborative research. Darton also highlights the critical issues of the relationship between the location of industrial R&D, the availability of skilled labour and government policy, and the support for joint R&D projects involving foreign owned firms in the UK. He like Paul David, John Mulvey and Sir Douglas Hague, points to the dangers of falling investment in the science and engineering base.

The international context

Chapters in the second section examines the development of regulatory ensembles at different geographical scales, ranging from the national to the global. David Charles' chapter traces the development of EC support for innovation and its relationship with policies for reducing regional economic disparities. His chapter encompasses themes of jurisdiction, accountability and social welfare which are included in the policy making process. He highlights the change in emphasis away from spatial policies in the Framework Programmes which were purely designed to support science and technology to the most recent objectives that find resonance with the needs of the cohesion countries (Spain, Portugal, Greece and Ireland). He discusses the continuing policy conflicts within the different jurisdictions within the EC regulatory system, for example EC Competition Policy versus the reality of the way science and technology is increasingly undertaken – through collaboration.

The chapter deals with the evolution of policy priorities from the early 1980s when the Framework Programmes began, to current initiatives. He makes the point that the more cohesion-friendly objectives of the recent framework Programmes are still not altogether complementary to the Structural Funds. Charles discusses the transition from national sovereignty in industrial and technology policies to the ascendancy of the EU, the EU's response to the technology gap that emerged between Europe and Japan especially in information technologies (IT) in the early 1980s, the changing priorities and associated orientation of scientific and social research and the dramatic increase in the budget for the Framework Programmes. He charts the growth of Structural Fund programmes such as STRIDE 1990 which was designed to upgrade technological capacity in less favoured regions. He highlights the significance of the Single European Act of 1987. This introduced a new section on Research and Technological Development (RTD). It was the point at which the European Community had a formal legitimate basis for handling matters related to R&D. From then there was the basis for co-ordination of research policy in individual member states, and for a more cohesion friendly policy. The parallel growth of the RTD elements in the Structural Funds is a compensatory measure, and which should be seen as a different policy domain and one in which there may exist some conflicts with RTD policy. Finally he identifies possible future trends with EU RTD programmes, one of which is the erosion of national innovation systems in favour of regionalised systems and international networks. He concludes that the effect of EU policies is that of a pincer movement. The Framework Programmes encourage international links, and Structural Funds encourage regionalisation.

Gerald Paterson begins with a justification of the patenting system as a means of regulating the production of new knowledge. This is that patenting systems are designed to encourage technical research and development by granting a monopoly position for a period of years. This in principle means that researchers are more likely to make their inventions public and the availability of that information provides a basis for further research and development. and traces the development of the harmonisation of European patent laws and illustrates the practical application of European patent law to biotechnology. He shows that in politically sensitive areas of research, such as biotechnology, issues of morality and ethics are grounds for appeal against patents and so by extension have implications for the judgements made by scientists in the universities on what research is viable in the context of current and potential regulation. This point is made explicitly when the more 'generous and more certain' patent laws on the patentability of living organisms in the US are compared to those in Europe. Paterson makes the point that this generosity has been of considerable benefit to the American biological and pharmaceutical industries, producing increasing levels of R&D in these industries. The knock-on effect is increased levels of collaboration with the university sector.

Looking at the industry in its historical context and quoting another author, the main elements which contributed to the development of the industry in the US were technical: the ability to recombine, engineer or to manipulate DNA; a regulatory environment that encouraged the rapid application of research to applied problems as well as changes in the patent laws directed at encouraging the commercialisation of inventions in both industrial and academic settings; and the eventual dovetailing of government funded research with venture capital looking for investments to form an expanded base for molecular biological research and development (Rabinow, 1996, 19).

However, not all patenting is seen to be desirable because of the potential to limit dissemination of fundamentally important scientific knowledge. The prime example of this is research on DNA in the UK's Human Genome Project. Researchers are pledged to disseminate findings publicly and freely, a commitment insisted upon by John Sulston, Director of the Sanger Centre in Cambridge University. The Sanger Centre posts its results immediately on the Internet. Attempts by US drugs companies to privatise the knowledge by patent have been beaten off (*Observer* leader comment 3 October 1999, p. 28). The issue of regulation for ethical purposes is discussed by Claire Foster and Tom Wilkie in Abraham, Lawton Smith and Towse (forthcoming, Palgrave).

Nicholas Bloom, Lucy Chennells, Rachel Griffith and John van Reenen tackle the complex issue of how to measure the impact of tax regimes on the cost of R&D. They examine fiscal incentives to encourage R&D in eight countries, Australia, Canada, France, Great Britain, Germany, Italy, Japan and the US, between 1979 and 1994. The chapter places the analysis within a Schumpetarian framework which links faster economic growth with the introduction of new technologies, and discusses why R&D might be under-provided in market economies. The authors review the methodological issues associated with measuring the impact of tax on the cost of R&D. The difference between this and other studies is that it makes international comparisons over periods of time, whereas others have only considered the time series profile of one country or international comparisons at one point of time.

They report four main findings. First, there appears to be substantial differences in the cost of R&D between countries at any given point in time. Second, there has been a general trend towards more generous tax treatment of R&D (intangibles). Some countries have moved more rapidly than others because of differences in opinion about whether it is appropriate to encourage the development of a strong national R&D base in the context of evidence of strong international spillovers. Third, there has been an increasing diversity in the cost of R&D between countries. Finally, they use several stylised tax systems applied to a sample of firm level data to illustrate the substantial within-country heterogeneity that can arise from differences in design and implementation. They show that the impact of an incremental tax credit is significantly affected by the way the base is calculated, and that the benefits of tax credits are highly concentrated among a few firms.

Henry Rothstein and Alan Irwin's chapter is about the shaping of regulatory processes. They provide the sharpest example of the way regulatory theory and practice has developed over the last 30 years. They identify the evolution of regulation as a broader process of Europeanisation. They place their argument within the context of a society increasingly concerned with risk. Taking the example of a study of the pesticides industry, they 'illustrate the variety of activities and institutions that have evolved to meet regulatory demands'. These include the huge demand for information from every part of the process, and the interconnection of a range of institutions, academia, business and government. They say that the development of regulatory science represents an important field of changing 'knowledge relations' a field made all the more important by the ubiquitous character of contemporary risk concerns. Their chapter shows that the changing regulatory environment has stimulated patterns of scientific and policy activities often characterised by high degrees of hybridity as well as dominant patterns of cross-institutional working within and between national, European and global frameworks. They stress the role of informal relationships and trust in the practice of regulation as a component of the interconnection between cultural and technical assumptions in this field of scientific practice. They highlight tensions between the universalising tendencies of the European policy framework on the basis of science and the local conditions of regulatory implementation and practice. They consider the consequent problematic implications for transparency and accountability.

Regulation in practice

The chapters in the third section demonstrate the political dimensions to the forms that regulation takes in the UK and compares this with the situation in other countries. A particular theme is the distinctiveness of UK and EU regulatory systems.

Erik Millstone's chapter concerns the development of global regulatory systems. This is illustrated by a case study of a particular area of regulatory policy – that of environmental and consumer protection regulation. The driving force for the increasing spatial scale of regulation is different to that of pesticides, in this case it is trade liberalisation. Associated with the expansion of regulatory processes is a progressive shift from relatively well resourced to poorly resourced organisations and a decline in accountability. A key event was the signing of the Single European Act in 1987. Until then responsibility lay at national government level. Since then, Millstone argues, institutional mechanisms with which to check the decisions and actions of international institutions have not yet been developed, although they may be emerging.

Using the examples of toxic hazards and saccharin, Millstone argues that regulatory judgements in public health and environmental policy cannot be based purely on scientific considerations. The chapter analyses the changing ways in which regulatory policies are decided, and how international differences in regulatory systems are accounted for. After describing the structure of European institutions and the post-GATT global regime, Millstone compares regulatory processes in the UK less favourably to those which exist in the US. Twin themes of the chapter are the potential for regulatory capture by industry in Europe and the weakening of consumer protection at all spatial scales from the national to European to the global. Bodies such as CODEX and the WTO, which operate at the global scale, as in the case of the pharmaceutical industry described in the chapter by Abraham, are dominated by industry representatives. As a result there is a democratic deficit arising from the absence of checks and balances, which brings many risks both to public and environmental health and to public support for trade liberalisation and multinational agreements. This in turn decreases.

The failings in the international regulatory system are compounded by the knock-on effect on the relationship between the science base and the regulatory system as a result of the shift in responsibility from national to EC institutions. Although the UK devotes far fewer resources to commissioning and analysing existing research than the US, those resources are considerably greater than those in some EC bodies, for example the Scientific Committee for Food. The lack of funding diminishes the opportunity to finance independent and critical research. Moreover, the committees themselves may represent the interests of business. Millstone's chapter ends on a slightly more optimistic note for two main reasons. First he argues that political change can make a difference. He is more optimistic about the potential for food chemical safety under the new Labour government than under previous Conservative governments with the establishment of the Food Standards Agency, which in principle operates within a freedom of information regime. Second, the EC like the UK has accepted the necessity for separating industry sponsorship from regulation and as a result, in Europe at least, food safety standards are likely to rise. However, this trend will be at odds with the global regime.

John Lovering, like Erik Millstone, discusses the issue of accountability in his chapter on the growing influence of transnational industrial – governmental networks in the defence industry. The importance of the defence industry in the context of the regulation of science and technology is that defence spending is a major element in the science and technology activities of some industrialised countries – notably the UK, France and the USA. Lovering identifies the major changes in the defence industry in the post-cold war era, particularly the reduction in government defence spending, the lack of the realisation of the dual-use civil military convergence and the re-emergence of specialised defence companies, the transformation of the defence industry through the development of transborder (European and US) companies and 'new model' cross border collaborations. The defence industry is therefore no longer nationalised and, as a result, the relationship between defence companies and governments are changing. The key theme which Lovering develops is summarised in the sentence:

> The overall effect, I suggest, is that a significant part of the European S&T effort is moving beyond the regulatory influence of any accountable body, and in particular the elected polities which supposedly represent the peoples whose taxes find their way into this new network of actors.

He supports his arguments by tracing the restructuring of the defence industry and the efforts of national governments and the European Commission to develop a European policy and framework for action. He identifies the distinctiveness of the contemporary European defence industry as being rooted in the absence of both a powerful unitary state, and a cultural and corporate consensus. This contrasts sharply with its major competitor, the USA. He identifies the major organisations that have either sought to regulate the industry and failed because of those characteristics, for example the Western European Armaments Group (WEAG), and the location of the real source of power which led to transformation in the industry power – that of the companies themselves. The outcomes of the process of power realignment for the greater science base (industrial and public sector) at the national and European level is that companies can chose how best to exploit their technological capabilities and the skills of their workforce. This choice may lead to a small sub-set of high-technology defence-dual-use companies based in a small number of key locations in Europe's relatively advantaged regions, interacting with a co-ordinated network of European research laboratories. Moreover, the growth of collaboration is such that defence R&D is now 'more internationalised' than is civil R&D: overseas funds account for around less than one seventh of all business expenditure on civil R&D in Britain, but almost a quarter in defence R&D.

Abraham's chapter also focuses on the political and economic factors involved in the evolution of regulation. His objective is to provide a historically grounded assessment of modern medicines regulation in Britain. Whilst the safety of medicines is the overriding principle on which the regulatory system has evolved since the nineteenth century, the interests of the pharmaceutical industry rather than those of the consumer have dominated the policy making process. The basic issue is the conflict of interest between scientific advance and well-being of the industry on the one hand and the control over the use of powerful drugs in the interest of public safety on the other. In order to explain how technological risk has been subsumed into other priorities, Abraham takes a political economy approach examining where in the British state regulatory policy is made and the interactions between the state, capital and industrial interest. He draws on three theories of how the state regulates industrial activity: Bernstein's life-cycle theory of regulatory commissions (public interest theory), Marxist theories of regulation (regulation as an instrument of class oppression) and corporatist theory (the role of the state as defined in relation to the power of organised groups).

In tracing the development of regulation, Abraham argues that the legacy of the introduction of the Official Secrets Act of 1911 is the principle of secrecy which has characterised British medicine regulation ever since with significant consequences for the conditions under which governments have constructed regulatory policies. Issues of safety began to emerge in the political arena from the early 1920s. It was not until the 1960s that there were any regulatory controls on the testing of new drugs. These pre-dated the Thalidomide tragedy of 1962, but failed to prevent other failures most notably Eraldin in early 1980s. From the 1960s a series of Committees have advised on a range of issues such the Sainsbury Committee on the relationship between the pharmaceutical industry and the NHS (1967). Successive governments have resisted the idea of independent bodies, preferring self-regulation which has continued into the present day in the form of the Medicines Control Agency (MCA). During the 1970s the industry maintained its strategic influence over the DHSS but a tightening of the regime meant that there was less carte blanche acceptance of the industry's claims for efficacy and safety. Since then the range of regulatory mechanisms has been increasing at both the national, European and international scales. However, Abraham found evidence even in the 1990s that the pharmaceutical industry has been successful in obtaining the kind of regulatory authority in the UK that it campaigned for throughout the 1980s and that far from transparency increasing, secrecy makes it difficult for even determined observers to assess the nature and effects of regulatory changes designed to protect the public interest. This has led Abraham to favour the corporatist approach in explaining medicine regulation because there is evidence of regular bargaining between organised interests (in this case the pharmaceutical industry) and the state about the extent of regulation. He finds that there is little difference between the behaviour of the three main political parties over their period in office, all have been willing to compromise consumers' interests in the face of opposition from the pharmaceutical industry. He therefore acknowledges the validity of the Marxist view that parliamentary parties can have only minimal political impact relative to the power of the more enduring machinery of the state and capitalist interests. He also argues that the MCA potentially presents an example of regulatory capture as it is run as a business funded by the pharmaceutical industry rather than one of structural change.

Conclusions

What can be learned about processes of regulation from the chapters of the book? The first answer to this question is that we find that the range of regulatory mechanisms which have an impact on the production, ownership and exploitation of science and technology extends from the kinds of technology policies at national and European levels discussed by Paul David and David Charles to the forms of regulatory processes inherent in the relationship between the state, industry and the state funded research sector as discussed by Rothstein and Irwin, and Millstone.

The second is that there are, in evidence, processes of different kinds. Regulation is shown to be an outcome of political processes which are everything to do with ideology. This is the thread which ties the chapters together. Each of the chapters comment on the objectives and the mechanisms either in practice or which could be employed, under different kinds of political/economic regimes. For example, Bloom, Chennells and Griffith in their chapter on the impact of tax regimes on the cost of R&D point out that some countries believe that a strong domestic science base is crucial to economic success while others 'free-ride' on scientific research undertaken in other countries. The form that regulation takes is also an outcome of informal social processes involving networks on the one hand and the development of regulatory cultures on the other. I would say that Rothstein and Irwin are definitely in the camp of 'informal social process, networks and the development of regulatory cultures' while Abraham's chapter emphasises the latter. These three chapters echo earlier work by Hancher and Moran (1989, 291) who pointed out that networks comprise varying intensities of formality. They draw on 'network theory which demonstrates the significance of policy communities and networks within which "elite coalitions" allocate issues to particular arenas, manage the policy agenda, and allocate the range of participants allowed into decision making'. Power is, therefore, exerted through the representation of different groups in the policy making process which decide the allocation of resources to technological fields. In striking contrast to these chapters which in different ways illustrate processes operating internally within regulatory regimes, Lovering provides an example of extra-governmental process with the powerful defence companies challenging political control.

The third answer is that regulation is a response to different kinds of risk. These include:

- technological (Abraham and Lovering)
- safety (Abraham, Rothstein and Irwin, and Millstone).

Technological risks arise from scientific advance in the sense that while technical solutions can be found to solve particular problems (drugs, defence equipment), risks are caused by those technological advances. This is because they create other possibilities that need to be regulated. Risks to safety are the risks to consumers individually or collectively from environmental effects as a by-product of technological developments – for example posed by insufficient control over the use of potentially dangerous chemicals.

Indeed, several chapters show that the consumer is not necessarily the beneficiary of the changes in regulations which in principle are designed to overcome risk. Improved safety is sometimes a secondary consideration. This is because of another process which involves the interaction and interdependence of different interest groups. In this process it is the industry which 'captures' or negotiates with the regulators which gains most, often at the expense of the interests of the consumer. The close relationship between industry and regulators is discussed by Abraham and Millstone, who also point to secrecy and a lack of transparency within the process. Millstone sees the examples he cites as illustrative of specific institutional and political factors as key to accounting for international differences. He argues that one of the defining characteristics of British institutional structures has been that typically the responsibilities for regulating and sponsoring particular industrial sectors are invested in one and the same department. This point is also made by Abraham.

This issue raises the question of accountability, which Rothstein and Irwin, Millstone, Lovering and Abraham discuss. Their chapters illustrate just who is part of the regulatory process. They show that the balance between business and government is not always even, and that the academic community – the group which is on the receiving end of the regulation of science and technology and which might have an independent view of the direction in which regulations should go – is very often excluded from the process. According to Lovering, the defence industry has been able to prevent widespread public cynicism on defence spending in the UK in the post cold-war era. The transnational collaborations and agreements which tie companies and activities serve to de-politicise defence spending by overcoming the primary risk – that of political process – by which politicians have to convince the electorate of the necessity of maintaining a level of spending in the absence of an agreed military threat to UK security. Millstone argues that the greater the involvement of democratic institutions in policy making, the greater the degree of openness and accountability, and the more likely it will be that public policy will prudently protect public health.

The fourth answer is that there is a process by which a demand for regulation is created through the process of globalisation of markets and trade liberalisation (Millstone). Associated developments are the Europeanisation and globalisation of regulation (Charles, Paterson, Rothstein and Irwin, and Lovering). The locus of power shift on the direction of scientific and engineering, appears to be moving away from the nation state. Sometimes this has beneficial effects but more often detrimental affects. While Millstone highlights the adverse effects of Europeanisation resulting from the lowering of standards, Charles shows that the EU is sometimes far more concerned with the redistributive effects of science and technology policies than the UK. On the other hand, Millstone too showed that the EU can act in the public interest when national governments have failed to respond to risks posed by toxic hazards and food additives.

There are a number of outcomes to these processes. First the changes which the regulatory processes bring about, or respond to, construct and create a demand for new skills. For Sir Douglas Hague, like Paul David, a key issue for the UK competitiveness is the need to maintain a highly skilled labour force. However, the UK's technology policies have had an adverse effect on the academic scientific labour market, which was the reason why the Bett Report was commissioned. This in turn has the potential to impact on the location of industrial R&D and on industry's relationship with the science base. This is particularly significant in the defence industry (Lovering). Second is the development of regulatory institutions as brokers of information and influence. This was discussed by Millstone, Rothstein and Irwin, and Abraham. Third, in spite of the sentiments expressed in documents such as the 1993 White Paper about benefits to society at large, regulation can work to the detriment of the public interest when defined as the commitment to a strong independent science base. Regulation has restricted the kinds of research that is undertaken by industry and universities and limited the incentives to produce alternative technologies or solutions to some of the problems created by an industry. Moreover, the book demonstrates that the chief source of scrutiny of developments in different domains – pesticides, medicines, defence comes from within the university sector, both from physical and social scientists. This in itself requires that the independence of academics is maintained and that the balance of accountability shifts back from the current overemphasis on 'users' to that of assessment of research proposals by the research councils on the grounds of intellectual content and scientific merit.

Finally, I would like to acknowledge the support of the following for the production of this book. First, the ESRC for funding the seminar series. Second, Dr David Morris, Dean of Coventry Business School for supporting the production of this book. Third, Rupert Waters and Tracey Smedley for undertaking the onerous tasks of proof reading and preparing the manuscript for publication. I would also like to thank Alison Howson of Palgrave for supporting the project.

References

Abraham, J., Lawton Smith H. and Towse, A. (eds) *Regulation of the Phamacentical Industry* Basingstoke: Palgrave forthcoming.

Atkinson, M. (1999) 'Britain lags in R&D' *Guardian* (1999) 29 September 1999.

The Bett Report (1999) *Independent Review of Higher Education Pay and Conditions* London: The Stationery Office.

Blankenburg, S. (1998) 'University-industry relations, innovation and power: A theoretical framework for the study of technology transfer from the science base' ESRC Centre for Business Research WP 102 September 1998.

Branscomb, L. M. (1993) 'National Laboratories: The search for new missions and structures' Ch. 4 in L. M. Branscomb (ed.) *Empowering technology: Implementing a U.S. Strategy* Cambridge Mass: The MIT Press pp. 103–34.

Buckingham, L. (1999) 'Glaxo cranks up NHS drugs row' *Guardian* 5 October 1999, 28.

Cave, M. and Towse, A. (1997) 'Regulating Pharmaceutical Prices in the UK' paper presented at Regulatory Policy Research Centre seminar on *Regulation and Innovation in the Pharmaceutical Industry* 20–21 March Hertford College, Oxford.

Chesnais, F. (1993) 'The French National System of Innovation' Ch 6 R. Nelson, (ed.) (1993) *National Innovation Systems: A Comparative Analysis* New York, Oxford: Oxford University Press.

David. P., Guena, A. and Steinmueller, W. E. (1995) 'Additionally as a Principle of European R&D Funding' Maastricht: Merit Working Paper 2/95-012.

Dearing Report *Higher Education in the Learning Society* 23 July 1997, Hayes: NCIHE.

Department of Trade and Industry (1988) 'DTI – The Department for Enterprise' London: HMSO.

DETR (1999) *Regional Development Agencies'* Regional Strategies, www.local-regions.detr.gov.uk/rdas.

DETR (1999b) Personal Communication, 23 August 1999.

EEDA (1999) *Towards a Regional Economic Development Strategy for the East of England: A consultation draft*, Cambridge: EEDA.

Etzkowitz, H. (1994) 'Academic-industry relations: a sociological paradigm for economic development' in L. Leysdorff and P. Van den Bresselaar (eds) *Evolutionary Economics and Chaos Theory: New Directions in Technology Studies* London: Pinter.

Etzkowitz, H. and Stevens, A. J. (1995) 'Inching towards Industrial Policy: The Universities' Role in Government Initiatives to Assist Small, Innovative Companies in the US *Science Studies*, 8 (2) pp. 13–31.

European Commission (1999) Fifth Framework Programme 1998–2002: guidelines for Proposers Luxembourg: European Commission http://www.cordi.lu/fp5/src/guideline.htm.

Georghiou, L., Stein, J. A. Janes, M., Senker, J., Pifer, M., Cameron, H., Nedeva, M., Yates, J. and Boden, M. (1992) 'The Impact of European Community Policies for Research and Technological Development upon Science and Technology in the United Kingdom' Report prepared for DGXII of the Commission of the European Communities and the United Kingdom Office of Science and Technology, Brussels: EC.

Radford, T. (1999) 'Britain losing hi-tech race says Glaxo boss' *Guardian* 13 September 1999, p. 5.

Gillian, A. (1999) 'Backlash against biotechnology pushes scientist to join brain drain' *Guardian* 24 September 1999, p. 3.

Hancher, L. and Moran, M. (1989) *Capitalism, Culture, and Economic Regulation* Oxford: Clarendon Press.

Heppell, S. (1997) 'Regulation and Competition: A regulator's point of view' Paper presented at Regulatory Policy Research Centre seminar on *Regulation and Innovation in the Pharmaceutical Industry* 20–21 March Hertford College, Oxford.

Hoare, A. (1997) 'Privatisation comes to town: national policies and local responses – the Bristol case' *Regional Studies* May 1997, vol. 31, no. 3, pp. 253–65.

Kelly, H. and Hadden, M. 'Merger and joint ventures in the pharmaceutical industry' forthcoming in J. Abraham, H. Lawton Smith and A. Towse, (eds) *Regulation of the Pharmaceutical Industry* Basingstoke: Palgrave (forthcoming).

Lawton Smith, H. (1999) *Technology Transfer and Industrial Change in Europe* Basingstoke: Macmillan – now Palgrave.

Mahroum, S. (1998) 'Europe and the Challenge of the Brain Drain' The IPTS Report No. 29 November 1998 IPTS-JRC-Seville Spain, pp. 13–27.

OECD 1999 *The Science, Technology and Industry Scoreboard: Benchmarking the Knowledge-based Economies* Paris: OECD.

Observer (1999) 'Catch 22' Leader comment 3 October 1999, p. 28.

Rabinow, P. (1996) *Making PCR* Chicago: University of Chicago Press.

Roobeek, A. J. M. (1990) *Beyond the Technology Race: An Analysis of technology policy in Seven Industrial Countries* Amsterdam: Elsevier.

Rosenberg, N. (1990) 'Why do firms do basic research (with their own money)?' *Research Policy* 19 pp. 165–74.

SEEDA (1999) *Building a World Class Region: Towards an Economic Strategy for the South East of England*, Guildford: SEEDA.

Sainsbury Report (1999) *Biotechnology Clusters; Report of a team led by Lord Sainsbury, Minister for Science* August 1999 London: HM Treasury.

Save British Science (1994) *Public Investment in Research and Development* SBS 29–30 Tavistock Square, London, WC1H 9EZ.

Save British Science (1995) 'Back to square one' and 'Reduced to the ranks' Autumn 1995 Newsletter SBS 29–30 Tavistock Square, London WC1H 9EZ both page 1.

Save British Science (1999a) 'At last the CSR' Newsletter Winter 1999 SBS 29–30 Tavistock Square, London WC1H 9EZ, page 1.

Save British Science (1999b) 'Devolution and Science' Summer Newsletter 1999 SBS 29–30 Tavistock Square London WC1H 9EZ page 1.

SmithKline Beecham (1998) 'Radicalism, rationalising or rationing – what does the UK want from research in the science base and health service' *Fifth Annual SmithKline Beecham Science Policy Symposium*, Harlow: SmithKline Beecham Pharmaceuticals.

Stoneman, P. (1987) *The Economic Analysis of Technology Policy* Oxford: Clarendon Press.

Van Dierdonck, R., Debackere, K. and Engelen, B. (1990) 'University-industry relationships: How does the Belgian academic community feel about it?' *Research Policy*, pp. 551–66.

Walker, W. (1993) 'National Innovation Systems: Britain' Ch. 5 in R. Nelson, (ed.) *National Innovation Systems: A Comparative Analysis* New York, Oxford: Oxford University Press pp. 158–91.

Waters, R. and Lawton Smith, H. (1999) 'Local Economic Development and Localities in the Newly Devolved Institutional Environment: The Cases of High-Technology Industry in Oxfordshire and Cambridgeshire' Paper presented at Regional Studies Association Annual Conference on 26 November 1999.

II
The Issues

2
The Political Economy of Public Science: a Contribution to the Regulation of Science and Technology

Paul A. David

The relationship between science, technology and economic perform-ance has been a recurring subject of public discussions and policy debates throughout the past four decades, both in the economically advanced countries and newly industrialising economies. Recently, however, a greater sense of urgency has attended consideration of gov-ernmental policies affecting science and technology. With decision-making concerning major public expenditure commitments for many purposes held in the tightened grip of fiscal stringencies, resumption of the previous upward trend in the real value of government budget allo-cations for research, training and development (RTD) activities has been called into question.

Even though there has been some abatement of the pressures that developed during the late 1980s and early 1990s for fiscal retrench-ment on the part of governments, the situation as regards support for science and technology has not returned to the status quo ante. Unlike previous episodes of funding cutbacks that temporarily slowed the growth of R&D activities, the latest one appears to have marked a more permanent break in the long-term upward trend.

Although historically civilian based research absorbed a minor pro-portion of non-military public sector funding for science and technol-ogy, there is no ground for a sanguine view that its comparative fiscal insignificance automatically insulates this category of R&D expendi-tures from the adverse developments in the broader public funding picture. Indeed, whereas in former times many government agencies supported long-term basic research that was perceived as relevant to their respective missions, the budgets for such work (whether conducted by national laboratories and public institutes, or under grants to university-based researchers) have been among the first items to come under hostile scrutiny – precisely because they could be cut without jeopardising the ability of the agencies to perform their critical short-term functions. Furthermore, precisely because their findings are perceived to lie at a farther remove from predictable commercialisable results, the case for public patronage of exploratory scientific research has been seriously undercut by the new spirit of 'economic instrumentalism' that has come to characterise science and technology policy discussions.

In the first part of this study I review the economic logic of 'open science', upon which rests what I take to be the compelling general case for state patronage of the science base. From those foundations the discussion proceeds, in Part II, to critique a number of related trends that have been reshaping the political economy of public sector R&D, especially in the US, the UK and other Western European economies since the early 1980s.

I.   The logic of 'open science' and the case for state patronage

The progress of scientific and technological knowledge is a cumulative process, one that depends in the long-run on the disclosure of new findings, so that they may be speedily discarded if unreliable, or confirmed and brought into fruitful conjunction with other bodies of reliable knowledge. In this way open science promotes the rapid generation of further discoveries and inventions, as well as wider practical exploitation of additions to the stock of knowledge.

The economic case for public funding of what is commonly, if somewhat ambiguously referred to as 'basic' research, rests mainly on that insight; and upon the observation that business firms are bound to be put off in some considerable measure by the greater uncertainties surrounding investment that entails entering into fundamental, exploratory inquiries compared to commercially targeted R&D, as well as by the difficulties of forecasting when and how such outlays will generate a satisfactory rate of return.

During the past thirty years, economists have worked out cogent reasons why the price system and competitive markets should not be expected to do a good job in producing or distributing knowledge and information – certainly not by comparison with markets' performance in similarly allocating resources in the case of more conventional, tangible commodities such as fish or chips (of both the computer and the potato varieties). This conclusion rests upon the fundamental insight that ideas – especially ideas tested and reduced to codified scientific and technological information – have some important attributes found in 'public goods'. Correspondingly they may be better understood by referring to the thoroughly studied problems that would arise were one to rely upon the competitive market mechanism to provide for pure public goods, such as a smog-free environment, or defence against nuclear missile attack.

The peculiar nature of information and knowledge as commodities

Acknowledging the peculiar character of information as an economic commodity is central to the modern economic analysis of R&D. An idea is a thing of remarkable expansiveness, being capable of spreading rapidly from mind to mind without lessening its meaning and significance for those into whose possession it comes. In that quality, ideas are more akin to fire than to coal. Thomas Jefferson remarked upon this attribute, which permits the same knowledge to be jointly used by many individuals at once: 'He who receives an idea from me, receives instruction himself without lessening mine; as he who lights his taper at mine receives light without darkening me ...'. Economists, therefore, have pointed out that the potential value of an idea to any individual buyer generally would not match its value to the social multitude. The latter value, however, is not readily expressed in a willingness to pay on the part of all who would gain from the illuminating idea; once a new bit of knowledge is revealed by its discoverer(s), some benefits will instantly 'spill over' to others who are therefore able to share in its possession. Commodities that have the property of 'expansibility', permitting them to be used simultaneously for the benefit of a number of agents, are sometimes described as being 'non-rival' in use. This characteristic is a form of non-convexity, or an extreme form of decreasing marginal costs as the scale of use is increased: although the cost of the first instance of use of new knowledge may be large, in that it includes the cost of its generation, further instances of its use impose at most a negligibly small incremental cost.

It is sometimes noticed that this formulation ignores the cost of training potential users to be able to grasp the information and know what to do with it. But while it is correct to point out that there can be fixed costs of access to the information, these do not vitiate the proposition that re-use of the information will neither deplete it nor impose further costs. It may be costly to teach someone how to read the table of the elements, or the differential calculus, but any number of individuals thus instructed can go on using that knowledge without imposing further costs either on themselves or upon others.

The second property of ideas that has been noticed here is that it is difficult, indeed, costly to retain exclusive possession of them whilst putting them to use. Of course, it is possible to keep a piece of information or a new idea secret. The production of results not achievable otherwise, however, discloses something about the existence of a method for doing so. Often results obtained by methods that are not, or cannot be revealed, are felt to be less reliable, and more in the nature of magical performances than the application of reliable knowledge. Even a general explanation of the basis for achieving the observable result jeopardises the exclusivity of its possession, for the knowledge that something can be done is itself an important step toward discovering how it may be done.

Public goods and the 'appropriability problem'

The dual properties of non-rival usage and costly exclusion of others from possession define what is meant by a 'pure public good'. The term 'public good' does not imply that such commodities cannot be privately supplied, nor does it mean that government must produce it. But competitive market processes will not do an efficient job of allocating resources for the production and distribution of pure public goods, because when such markets work well they do so because the incremental costs and benefits of using a commodity are assigned to the users.

One may see the problem posed by the public goods characteristics of knowledge by asking how ideas can be traded in markets of the kind envisaged by disciples of Adam Smith, except by having aspects of their nature and significance disclosed before the transactions were consummated? Rational buyers of ideas, no less than buyers of coal, and of fish and chips, first would want to know something about what it is that they will be getting for their money. Even if the deal fell through, it is to be expected that the potential purchaser would enjoy (without paying) some benefits from what economists refer to as 'transactional spill-overs'. These occur because there may be significant commercial advantages from the acquisition of even rather general information about the nature of a discovery, or an invention – especially one that a reputable seller has thought it worthwhile to bring to the attention of people engaged in a particular line of business.

This leads to the conclusion that the findings of scientific research, being new knowledge, would be seriously undervalued were they sold directly through perfectly competitive markets. Some degree of exclusivity of possession of the economic benefits derived from ideas is therefore necessary, if the creators of new knowledge are to derive any profit from their activities under a capitalist market system. Intellectual property rights serve this end in the form of patent and copyright monopolies. But imposing restrictions on the uses to which ideas may be put also saddles society with the inefficiencies that arise when monopolies are tolerated, a point harped upon by economists ever since Adam Smith. In addition, as will be argued below (in section II) the secrecy practices that accompany serious commercially oriented research aimed at the establishment of intellectual property rights are a further source of inefficiencies.

Won't firms undertake basic research?

The specific proposition at issue here in regard to basic science funding is therefore quantitative, not qualitative. One cannot adequately answer the question 'Will there be enough?' merely by saying 'There will be some'. Economists do not claim that without public patronage (or intellectual property protection), basic research would cease entirely. Rather, their analysis holds that there will not be enough basic research – not as much as would be carried out were individual businesses (like society as a whole) able to anticipate capturing all the benefits of this form of investment. Therefore, no conflict exists between the theoretical analysis and the evidence of recent economic studies which show that R&D-intensive companies do indeed fund some exploratory research into fundamental questions. Their motives for this range from developing a capability to monitor progress at the frontiers of science, to picking up ideas there for potential lines of innovation that may be emerging from the research of others, to being better positioned to penetrate the secrets of their rivals' technological practices.

Nevertheless, it is a long-term strategy, and therefore sensitive to commercial pressures to shift research resources towards advancing existing product development, and improving existing processes – rather than searching for future technological options. Large organisations that are less asset-constrained, and of course the public sector, are better able to take on the job of monitoring what is happening on the international science and technology frontiers. Considerations of these kinds are important in addressing the issue of how to find the optimal balance for the national research effort between secrecy and disclosure of scientific and engineering information, as well in trying to adjust the mix of exploratory and applications-driven projects in the national research portfolio.

Directly valuable additions to the scientific knowledge-base

When scientists are asked to demonstrate the usefulness of research that is exploratory in character and undertaken to discover new phenomena, or explain fundamental properties of physical systems, the first line of response often is to point to discoveries and inventions generated by such research projects that turned out to be of more or less immediate economic value. Many important advances in instrumentation, and generic techniques, such as PCR and the use of restriction enzymes in 'gene-splicing' are, indeed, available for mention in this connection. These by-products of the open-ended search for basic scientific understanding also might be viewed as contributing to the 'knowledge infrastructure' required for efficient R&D that has been deliberately directed towards results that would be exploitable as commercial innovations. Occasionally such new additions to the stock of scientific knowledge are immediately commercialisable and yield major economic payoffs that, even though few and far between, they are potent enough to raise the average social rate of return on basic, academic research well above the corresponding private rate of return earned on industrial R&D investment.

The experience of the 20 century also testifies to the many contributions of practical value that trace their origins to large, government-funded research projects which were focused upon the development of new enabling technologies for public-mission agencies. Consider just a few recent examples from the enormous and diverse range that could be instanced in this connection: airline reservation systems, packet switching for high-speed telephone traffic, the Internet communication protocols, the Global Positioning System, and computer simulation methods for the visualisation of molecular structures – which has been transforming the business of designing new pharmaceutical products – and much else besides.

The sceptical economist's response to such recitations, however, is to ask whether a more directed search for the solutions to these applied problems would not have been less costly and more expedient than waiting for costly research programmes that were conducted by scientists with quite different purposes in mind to come up with these commercially useful findings. This is a telling rhetorical objection, simply because the theme of such 'spin-off' stories is their unpredictability; the argument that they are in some sense 'free' requires that the research programme to which they were incidental was worth undertaking for its own sake, so that whatever else might be yielded as by-products was a net addition to the benefits derived. Yet, the reason those examples are being cited is the existence of scepticism as to whether the knowledge that was being sought by exploratory, basic science was worth the cost of the public support it required. Perhaps this is why the many examples of this kind that scientists have brought forward seem never enough to satisfy the questioners.

The discovery and invention of commercially valuable products and processes are seen from the viewpoint of 'the new economics of science' to be among the rarer, among the predictably 'useful', results that flow from the conduct of exploratory, open science. Without denying that 'pure' research sometimes yields immediate applications around which profitable businesses spring up, it can be argued that those direct fruits of knowledge are not where the quantitatively important economic payoffs from basic science are to be found.

Much more critical over the long run than 'spin-offs' from basic science programmes are their cumulative indirect effects in raising the rate of return on private investment proprietary R&D performed by business firms. Among those indirect consequences, attention should be directed not only to 'informational spill-overs', but to a range of complementary 'externalities' that are generated for the private sector by publicly funded activities in the sphere of open science, where research and training are tightly coupled.

Complementarities between public and private R&D programmes

Resources are limited, to be sure, and in that sense research conducted in one field and in one organisational mode is being performed at the expense of other kinds of R&D. But what is missed by attending exclusively to the competition forced by budget constraints, is an appreciation of the ways in which exploratory science and academic engineering research activities support commercially-oriented and mission-directed research that generates new production technologies and products.

First among the sources of this complementary relationship, is the intellectual assistance that fundamental scientific knowledge (even that deriving from contributions made long ago) provides to applied researchers – whether in the public or in the private sector. From the expanding knowledge-base it is possible to derive time- and cost-saving guidance as to how best to proceed in searching for ways to achieve some pre-specified technical objectives. Sometimes this takes the form of reasonably reliable guidance as to where to look first, and much of the time the knowledge-base provides valuable instructions as to where it will be useless to look. How else does the venture capitalist know not to spend time talking with the inventor who has a wonderful new idea for a perpetual motion machine?

One effect this has is to raise the expected rates of return, and reduce the riskiness of investing in applied R&D. Gerald Holton, Harvard's physicist and historian of science, recently has remarked that 'if intellectual property laws required all photoelectric devices to display a label describing their origins, it would list prominently: Einstein, *Annalen der Physik* 17 (1905), pp. 132–48'. Such credits to Einstein also would have to be placed on many other practical devices, including all lasers.[1]

The central point that must be emphasised here is that, over the long-run, the fundamental knowledge and practical techniques developed in the pursuit of basic science serves to keep applied R&D as profitable an investment for the firms in many industries as it has proved to be, especially, during the past half-century. In this role, modern science continues in the tradition of the previous if sometimes imprecise maps that guided parties of exploration in earlier eras of discovery, and in that of the geological surveys that are still of such value to prospectors searching for buried mineral wealth.

Open science and research training: externalities for the private sector

That is not the end of the matter, for a second and no less important source of the complementary relationship between basic and applied research is the nexus between university research and training, on the one hand, and on the other the linkage of the profitability of corporate R&D to the quality of the young researchers that are available for employment. Seen from this angle, government funding of open exploratory science in the universities today is subsidising the R&D performed by the private business sector. Properly equipped research universities have turned out to be the sites of choice for training the most creative and most competent young scientists and engineers, as many a corporate director of research well knows. This is why graduates and postdoctoral students in those fields are sent or find their own way to university labs in the US, and still to some in the UK. It explains why businesses participate in (and sponsor) 'industrial affiliates' programmes at research universities.

It also is part of the reason for US industrial research corporations' broadly protective stance in regard to the federal budget for 'basic science' – which has escaped the most severe onslaughts by the Representatives of Congress. Acknowledgement of it has had a great deal to do with the recent announcement by the Japanese government of a dramatic reversal of its former policies, and the initiation of a vast programme of support for university-based basic and applied R&D.

Tacit knowledge and technology transfers via the circulation of researchers

A key point deserving emphasis in this connection is that a great deal of the scientific expertise available to a society at any point in time remains tacit, rather than being fully available in codified form and accessible in archival publications. It is embodied in the craft-knowledge of the researchers, about such things as the procedures for culturing specific cell lines, or building a new kind of laser that has yet to become a standard part of laboratory repertoire. This is research knowledge, much of it very 'technological' in nature – in that it pertains to how phenomena have been generated and observed in particular, localised experimental contexts – which is embodied in people. Under sufficiently strong incentives it would be possible to express more of this knowledge in forms that would make it easier to transmit, and eventually that is likely to happen. But, being possessed by individuals who have an interest in capturing some of the value of the expertise they have acquired, this tacit knowledge is transmitted typically through personal consultations, demonstrations and the actual transfer of people.

The circulation of postdoctoral students among university research laboratories, between universities and specialised research institutes, and no less importantly, the movement of newly trained researchers from the academy into industrial research organisations, is therefore an important aspect of 'technology transfer' – diffusing the latest techniques of science and engineering research. The incentive structure in the case of this mode of transfer is a very powerful one for assuring that the knowledge will be successfully translated into practice in the new location; for the individuals involved are unlikely to be rewarded if they are not able to enhance the research capabilities of the organisation into which they move.

A similarly potent incentive structure may exist also when a fundamental research project sends its personnel to work with an industrial supplier from whom critical components for an experimental apparatus are being procured. Insuring that the vendor acquires the technical competence to produce reliable equipment within the budget specifications is directly aligned with the interests of both the research project, and the business enterprise. Quite obviously, the effectiveness of this particular form of user – supplier interaction is likely to vary directly with the commercial value of the procurement contracts and the expected duration and continuity of the research programme.

For this reason, 'big science' projects or long-running public research programmes may offer particular advantages for the collaborative mode of technology transfers, just as major industrial producers – such as the large automotive companies in Japan – are seen to be able to set manufacturing standards and provide the necessary technical expertise to enable their suppliers to meet them. By contrast, the transfer of technology through the vehicle of licensing intellectual property is, in the case of process technologies, far more subject to tensions and deficiencies arising from the absence of complete alignment in the interest of the involved individuals and organisations. But, as has been seen, the latter is only one among the economic drawbacks of depending upon the use of intellectual property to transfer knowledge from non-profit research organisations to firms in the private sector.

II.   'Wealth creation' and the political economy of public science

The onset of the funding crisis of the late 1980s left in its wake a climate of political scepticism, if not outright hostility, towards the resumption of government commitments to major long-range programmes of exploratory scientific research. The underlying causes of this altered political climate are clear enough. They are to be found in the intervening transformation of the international context of national science and technology policy-making in the West. The abrupt ending of the cold war has seen the defence establishment's budgets scaled back, as well as those of civilian mission agencies of government that formerly had supported a wide array of long-term research. Furthermore, coming as they did on top of the reactions in the US and Western Europe to the intensified global market competition encountered from new industrial competitors, these developments have precipitated the first wholesale reconsideration since the late 1950s of the purposes and means of allocating public funding for scientific and technological research. A variety of long-standing practices and institutions through which governments supported the enterprise of science therefore have found themselves the subjects of unanticipated, and in many cases unwelcome critical reappraisal. Their exposure has been made more severe by the stripping away of the 'national defence' rationale that frequently and reliably had been invoked in former times.

The new economic instrumentalism and the rise of 'innovation policy'

In the ensuing scramble to protect many R&D activities from the adverse political fallout, another candidate was sought for the role of general-purpose rationale. 'International competitiveness', 'productivity-enhancing innovativeness' and even 'national economic security', already were acquiring greater potency as generic quasi-protectionist political slogans during the 1980s; it was not long before justifications for governmental support of a wide range of scientific and engineering research (and even some social and behavioural science studies) began to be re-cast by references to those even more vaguely defined national economic priorities.

Tying public funding levels to 'wealth creation'

The currently prevailing instrumentalist rationale for public subsidisation of the organised pursuit of scientific and technological knowledge has thus come to view and evaluate scientific research in the context of 'national innovation systems' that responsible governments should design, and support where necessary, in order to enhance their countries' economic performance. In a sense, this is simply a culmination of the steady drift in the political economy rhetoric, which since the 1960s has accepted economists' presentation of state funding of non-military science and technology as national investments.[2]

But, whereas that economic conceptualisation initially tended to be proposed in a rather metaphorical vein, suggesting that expenditures for civilian R&D (whether public or private) represented seed corn being planted today in the expectation of its' yielding some tangible future harvests, the idea now has taken hold in a much more literal form. The view is that government policy should be directed to 'ensuring that those investments yield an adequate return, a return ultimately reflected in enhanced competitiveness, wealth creating potential, and the quality of life'.

Numerous spokesperson for the academic science community have readily accepted the role into which this approach would cast their enterprise. In one respect this may be simply a matter of bowing to political realities. It can certainly be pointed out that to seek a deeper understanding of the natural and the made worlds is a human, and often humane cultural pursuit that has its own legitimate claim upon society's resources. Yet, the practical political issue is the size of that claim, and both the absolute and comparative scale to which the enterprise of science has grown in the world's wealthy societies makes it unavoidable that some considerations of economic instrumentalism should colour scientists' responses to the question 'What's the use of basic science?' Perhaps, too, there is an understandable disinclination to reject publicly the invitation to fulfil a designated role in responding to the currently announced set of national priorities, whether or not it seems that one has, or should try to develop, the capabilities for doing so.

Yet, the style of argument that would premiss present funding levels upon the demonstrable impact of R&D programmes upon macroeconomic performance or regional economic development,[3] is one that advocates of secure public patronage for scientific research might well take up warily. It seems very much the proverbial double-edged blade. The potential source of trouble is that by comparison with the mission of delivering 'enhanced economic performance', it is an utterly straightforward and manageable undertaking to supply the knowledge required to design and deliver advanced weapons systems, whatever the level of the scientific and engineering sophistication that would be required, and however proximate the scheduled delivery date.[4]

It takes but a moment of calm consideration to realise that processes far more costly, complex and uncertain than those involved in doing the most path-breaking kinds of science and engineering will be entailed in translating whatever new discoveries and inventions may result therefrom into perceptible improvements of national performance – in any one of those three vaguely defined dimensions, 'competitiveness', per capita real income growth, or the quality of life. Indeed, modern industrial innovation strategies acknowledge that such is the case even when the new knowledge yielded by research is of a sort that immediately suggests its potentialities for something as straightforward as profitable commercial exploitation and increased corporate net worth.

There is thus a significant political hazard in pledging the health of the scientific enterprise as hostage, pending the outcome of multifaceted dynamic processes whose management in a competitive market economy lies well beyond the powers of even the largest corporate enterprises and the most powerful government agencies, let alone of the community of scientists and engineers whose immediate sphere of competence and control lies in the planning and conduct of research. Putting this rather baldly, the designers and developers of advanced weapons systems rarely if ever are held professionally to account for the ultimate outcomes of deploying their creations under field conditions, much less for the decisions affecting whether and how such deployment occurs.

Focusing on short-run economic performance goals

Were that not worrisome enough, the logic of literal acceptance of the national investment metaphor, with science and technology policy-makers positioned to make the role of national investment fund managers responsible to the electorate, leads almost inexorably to political demands for continuous assessment, pressures for quick and symbolic results, and planning to avoid failure. Not surprisingly, an increasing number of economists have come to share the concerns expressed by many within the academic science and engineering research communities that the reigning rationale for government science and technology policies has moved too far in the direction of economic instrumentalism of a very short-sighted kind. The effort to move publicly supported R&D 'closer to the market', particularly coming at a time when the private sector itself has been curtailing long-term exploratory programmes of research of the sort formerly carried on in the central laboratories of major industrial corporations, has tended to unbalance the 'maturity structure of the overall research portfolio'.[5]

It is true that the existing knowledge-base already has identified and articulated the main principles and key implementation requirements for many if not most of the technologies that will come into economic use during the next 20–25 years. But, technologies are more interactive with one another than are the financial securities in a well diversified asset portfolio. What this means concretely is that the feasibility of commercial exploitation of a particular technology may be unexpectedly brought forward in time, and the associated gains in profits and productivities may be greatly augmented by breakthroughs in seemingly unrelated areas of exploratory research. Consequently, the short-term focusing of R&D efforts, by adversely affecting progress in areas that are potentially complementary, may well have the perverse result of delaying and curtailing realisation of the major innovation gains that were anticipated.

For individual economies and interdependent regions, the hazard this entails is that there may be a reduction in the capacity to respond in a timely fashion to unanticipated opportunities, or to adapt to competitive challenges arising from scientific and technological breakthroughs made elsewhere.

Reshaping the innovation process

Nevertheless, the plain fact of our present situation is that popular subscription to the notion that the place of public science is one that should be determined primarily with a view to enhancing the near term effectiveness of the 'national system of innovation', has combined with fiscal stringencies to promote serious reconsideration of more than simply the scale of public funding for R&D. Also under question are the objectives that would warrant continuing governmental subsidisation of research, and the appropriate forms in which the latter should be provided.

As a result, a wide array of rather fundamental questions about 'process', and relatively few about 'projects' now are on the table for discussion simultaneously: should the overall proportion of government expenditures devoted to research be determined centrally, from the top down, as part of a concerted 'national innovation strategy'; or should the nation's aggregate public research effort be allowed to emerge from the bottom up, so to speak, through the political processes of interdepartmental and interagency competition for funds to sponsor R&D support for their respective missions? In a centralised budgeting process, what principles and criteria should be applied to determine the way such funding will be allocated among fields and project areas? Can standardised methods be devised for external assessment of the performance of RTD programmes, or can judgements about the success or failure of these public investments safely be left to internal expertise and peer evaluation processes? Should one go on preserving characteristics of the supporting institutional infrastructures of an earlier era – such as the coupling of research with graduate training in university departments, or the maintenance of a separation between commercially-oriented industrial R&D conducted under proprietary restrictions, and the publicly funded work carried on by academic scientists and researchers employed in national laboratories? Or are the latter now increasingly obsolete institutional legacies, luxuries whose growing claims for public funding and styles of operation represent obstacles to effectively implementing the 'national innovation policies' which many governments now are trying to pursue?

There is much evidence to support the proposition that successful industrial innovation involves close integration between research, product design, production engineering, and marketing teams within the business organisation; and also that interactions between the producers and users of technological innovations are an important source of learning that fosters both technical improvements on the side of the vendors, and greater sophistication on the side of their customers in finding profitable ways to deploy the new technologies. It has been tempting for economists and policy-makers to generalise from this interactive process, to adopt an analogous model of the way technological change proceeds, and to elaborate a similarly interactive dynamic model of 'an innovation system' at the economy-wide level. This forms some part of the intellectual background for efforts to promote closer interaction among the variety of private and public organisations and institutions engaged in RTD activities.

What in Britain is referred to as 'wealth creation' has emerged during the past five years not only as the covering rhetorical justification, but as the explicit rationale guiding virtually all major facets of government science and technology policy. Of course, how 'wealth creation' was to be interpreted – the breadth or narrowness of the meaning of 'wealth', and the time horizon over which its growth was to be considered – and how this ill-specified goal was to be achieved, were matters not set down in principle. Rather, they have emerged through the accumulation of bits of concrete policy practice; while the selection and retention of these has been somewhat haphazard, the drive to reduce state expenditures with private funding has been a persistent and potent force behind many of the institutional changes that have been encouraged.

Dubious results of the recent reorganising of science for 'wealth creation'

Starting in the US during the 1980s, and spreading thence to British and other government circles in Europe, including the EU, there has been an emerging policy consensus that shifting academic science and engineering activities towards more market-oriented research, and forging closer university – industry collaborations offered an attractive route towards successful innovation, productivity improvement, national economic competitiveness and prosperity. This view crystalised most sharply in the position taken by the UK government's 1993 White Paper, announcing that the objective of its policy would be

> to harness strength in science and engineering to the creation of wealth in the United Kingdom by bringing it into closer and more

systematic contact with those responsible for industrial and commercial decisions.[6]

The emphasis thus placed upon increasing connections with industry, and giving greater scope for markets to guide the allocation of public as well as private R&D, subsequently was reinforced by the establishment of the 'Technology Foresight Programme'. The two-fold goal of this initiative was, first, to provide the Government with a basis for 'setting the future direction, balance and content of its own science and technology programmes', primarily by identifying future markets in which technology-based UK companies were likely to have an actual or potential competitive advantage. Only once that identification has been made was the Foresight process supposed to consider relevant technologies and the area of scientific research upon which these would rest.[7] The second major aim of Foresight was rather less dirigiste and more process-oriented; it addressed a perceived need to 'achieve a key cultural change: better communication, interaction and mutual understanding between the scientific community, industry and Government Departments'.[8]

The announced *purposes* of these policy initiatives are difficult to argue with, and because they emerged from a growing disenchantment with the previously prevailing faith that supporting science and technology was the sure route to national prosperity, they have commanded a measure of support from academic economists as corrective measures. Like many forms of 'reaction', however, policy swings in this case have shown a tendency to go too far in the opposite direction.

Disenchantments with 'Science-Push'

One of the more useful contributions that research and writing on the economics of science and technology have made during the past two decades has been to disabuse people of the ideas associated with the 'science-push' strategy of economic growth: that a tight linkage could be established between expenditures to advance fundamental scientific understanding and the translation of the latter into technological progress and productivity gains. That particular conceptualisation of the dynamics of technological progress was encapsulated in the graphical representation of a orderly sequence of stages in the process leading to innovation – the so-called 'linear model'. The descriptive deficiencies of this construction have been shown to be manifold. It presented 'science' as exogenous, seemingly isolated from market influences affecting the motivation for research and the provision of research resources. It ignored the role of technologies in shaping the aims, methods, and the productivity of research itself. It suppressed the multiplicity of feedback loops, and particularly ignored the longer-term systemic effects of research by-products in the forms of trained scientists and engineers and novel research instruments.

Science supply – push doctrine would have us focus attention and policy action exclusively upon the first link in the sequence envisaged by the linear model. Yet, it is not hard to see that this rests on an implicit assignment of 'strategic importance' that is quite arbitrary. Inasmuch as research activity requires scarce resource inputs – whether those invested from the capital and retained earnings of private firms or expended by the state out of its tax revenues – the last stage in the sequence portrayed by the linear model, in which more economic output is delivered for the given direct input of resources used in production, could just as easily be depicted as temporally antecedent to the (ensuing) round of research outlays. In other words, what we are really dealing with should at the very least be conceptualised as a recurring, circular process – strictly, a recursive dynamic system. To cut into the supposed uni-directional flow around this circle at any arbitrary linkage-point can serve to elevate one or another of the activities (fundamental exploratory research, development, commercial innovation, marketing, etc.) into the star role as 'the initiator' of the sequence.

Plainly, that is an easy rhetorical device, which can be and has been deployed effectively on behalf of the special interests identified with the activity thus selected. And, it must be said that on numerous past occasions, representatives of the 'science lobby' willingly embraced this flawed model, and oversold the case for 'better living tomorrow through investment in basic science today'. But, for economic analysts to dispose of what may be termed the vulgar science-push theory of economic prosperity, it has been sufficient simply to re-emphasise a piece of common-sense wisdom: if one is dependent upon a chain of activities, it will pay to attend to the soundness of all of its links, especially to the weakest among them, rather than looking only to the one that has been assigned the initiating position within the sequential arrangement. For that and for other compelling reasons, the 'simple linear model' has in recent years been ritually derided by economists and others as a misguided way of thinking about relationships between scientific research and the dynamics of technological change.[9]

Enchantment with 'market pull': inverting the old linear model

Instead of discarding the linear model as too simplistic, or reformulating it into a more complicated dynamic structure with counter-flows and feedback loops of the sort that have been suggested by the application of systems analysis to the sphere of science and technology, another simplistic conception appears to have dominated UK government policy during the early 1990s. The wealth creation rationale was simply used to turn the old linear model upside down, supplanting of naive 'science supply – push' thinking by the opposite, but no less simplistic formula of seeking to make the direction of scientific and technological activities respond to 'market-demand-pull', even in areas that formerly were far from the market.

The set of activities concerned with science and engineering, whose support generally is considered to be among the proper responsibilities of the State, are referred to in Britain as 'the science base'. This is a somewhat slippery concept: typically, the science base is defined only implicitly, by descriptions of what it is supposed to do, namely 'to produce highly skilled and trained men and women and to conduct research at the frontiers of knowledge ... '[10] Of course, since at any given moment in time 'the frontiers of knowledge' are enormous and varied in their extent, this formulation in itself contains no indications as to where among the continuum of specific sites those research capabilities are best situated, and how best to create them.

The term 'science base' strongly evokes the notion of 'basic science', but, unfortunately the common distinction between 'basic' and 'applied' research itself is not precise enough to provide much guidance as to what kind of research and training the 'science base' should be occupied with. The sort of research that is deemed basic from the perspective of a strategy aimed at fostering 'wealth-creating innovation' might be very closely targeted to solving a generic problem central to lines of business involved in a major sector of the country's domestic economy, such as the electronic data security needs of firms operating in its leading financial centre. This seems to call for a very 'applications-oriented' line of research, until one thinks of the direct way in which cryptographic algorithms have developed out of what most mathematicians would characterise as programmes of fundamental research in 'pure' number theory.

The upshot is that what was recommended was nothing more nor less than an effort to reconfigure the UK 'science-base' so as to make it serve more efficiently as the passive handmaiden to market-driven programmes of technological innovation. Like the logic of the old linear model, the emerging policy approach saw the causal chain of influence as flowing in one direction; but the proper direction was now to be from the market via the inducement of private innovative activity, and thence to the search for commercially exploitable inventions. Deriving from the latter would be an effort to select 'economically relevant' areas for fundamental scientific exploration.

Intellectual property protection and the urge towards secrecy

In the US and the UK, and more recently in Europe, the implementation of science and technology policies with this thrust in favour of market-orientation has led to the creation of stronger incentives for academic researchers to pursue projects leading to patentable and copyrightable results.[11] It has seen legislative and administrative rule changes made so as to permit universities and government laboratories to 'benefit' from the exploitation of intellectual property rights based upon publicly funded research, whether by exclusive licensing or by the formation of joint ventures with industry built upon intellectual property. It has encouraged university administrators to take equity positions in 'spin-off' enterprises based upon faculty research that has similarly been protected, and has not raised difficulties over the possible conflicts between the resulting financial interests of those institutions and the fulfilment of their traditional societal roles in the dissemination of knowledge through instruction, publication and the participation of faculty in public affairs.

The economic logic of extending the protection of the State to intellectual property in science and technology is that this is a better choice, from the societal standpoint, than secrecy. There are some who suggest that the problems of incomplete appropriability of benefits from research are overstated, or indeed non-existent, because industrial secrecy is sufficient to rule out the difficulties that otherwise might be caused by some firms 'free-riding' on the R&D investments of others. This comes down to two kinds of empirical questions. First, in the case of a business (or a non-profit agency seeking to derive income from its discoveries and inventions) one has to consider what costs a strategy of secrecy imposes upon the research process itself, and whether such practices can be totally effective in the face of the mobility of technical personnel and reverse engineering. Second, one must look at the matter from the societal viewpoint. On the supposition that extensive secrecy was a viable policy for firms engaged in research, what potential would be created for even greater collective wastage of R&D resources due to duplication of research, not to mention potential injury to consumers, were the developers of new products and processes actually able to maintain indefinite secrecy about their research results?

Modern economic analysis has come to view the granting of patent and copyright monopolies as a sacrifice of the short-run interests of consumers that may be justified – by the far greater gains that are expected to result (over the long run) from giving creators of new, useful knowledge more secure pecuniary incentives to reveal it rapidly to the public at large. Still, in order to pursue research profitably, it is necessary for firms to be able to control the flow of information about work that is in progress, and to build an inventory of potential future projects that it can expect to exploit, rather than seeing these walk out the door with their research personnel. Consequently, trade secrecy protections are in this respect complementary to intellectual property protection in the 'production process' for new research findings, whose benefits the firm expects to be able to appropriate.

This suggests a significant qualification of the argument made for strengthening intellectual property rights in patents, and the enforcement thereof, on the grounds that reliance upon secrecy is reduced thereby. Although the disclosure of codified information is augmented by patent systems, so is the inducement to curtail the transmission of tacit knowledge that might reduce the commercial value of the patents that have been issued.[12]

When one passes beyond these considerations the inefficiencies involved for most business companies seeking to creating new knowledge under conditions of secrecy, and contemplates what it would mean for universities to seriously pursue a strategy of protecting the intellectual property that could be derived from the research activities of their faculty and student members, it becomes difficult to suppress serious doubts about the wisdom of the whole policy.[13] Pressing university administrators to demonstrate an institutional commitment to 'wealth creation through technology transfer' in this way quite obviously creates some difficult organisational problems wherever it is thought desirable also to have university research and teaching remain, or become thoroughly integrated. But, even were one prepared to sacrifice the interests of those being taught, by assigning them to work under the restrictions of closed, 'proprietary' research projects, there would be considerably more at risk in a thorough-going attempt by universities to appropriate and manage their intellectual property.[14]

The University of Oxford, for example, claims ownership of the following:

(a) works generated by computer hardware or software owned or operated by the University;
(b) films, videos, and multi-media productions made with the aid of university facilities;
(c) patentable and non-patentable inventions;

(d) university-commissioned works (work which the University has specifically called upon the student concerned to produce, whether in return for special payment or not);

(e) computer software, firmware, and related material not within (a), (b), (c) or (d), but only if it may reasonably be considered to possess commercial potential;

(f) registered and unregistered designs and topographies.[14] The latter either is little but an amateur gesture of conformity with the new rhetoric of wealth creation, or it vitiates the core premiss of the universities' claim to patronage and political protection as an 'open knowledge community' fulfilling a unique society function as a node for dissemination of knowledge from quality-controlled, commercially disinterested sources.

The rise of 'the grantract'

Beyond the 'push to patent', in the UK recently, the logic of designing a market-driven national system of innovation has led to government directives to the research councils, instructing them to include among the criteria for grant awards the potential contributions that proposed academic research projects would make to priority areas designated by the Department of Trade and Industry's 'Technology Foresight' exercises. The effect of this is to contribute to further obliterating the former distinctions between the modes of research conduct associated with grants that allow substantial autonomy to the investigator, on the one hand, and contracts that assign substantive control to the sponsoring agency, on the other.

Now it is undeniable that the history of science and engineering offers many examples of successful technological developments initiated in response to perceived market opportunities. It is equally true that state-directed, mission-oriented scientific programmes, both civilian and military, have created a basis for large and profitable industries.[15] But to advocate either as the one most effective way in which the advance of scientific knowledge may be coupled with economic progress is both factually inaccurate and potentially misleading as a guide for public policy. More worrisome still has been the impetus that faith in the market has imparted to efforts to make public research institutions behave more like the profit-oriented corporations with whom they are meant to collaborate, and the restructuring of government research funding processes to make them less like the traditional system for awarding grants to support scientific inquiry, and more resembling a market in which R&D teams bid for fully specified contracts. Combined with the shortening of the duration of grants, and the tightened specification of research 'outputs', what is emerging is a hybrid form that might be described as 'the grantract'. The creation of a new contractual form is not in itself undesirable, but the displacement of the mode of patronage provided under grants implies an alteration of the mix, and, in the limit, an undesirable narrowing of the span of research projects that will be maintained in the national R&D portfolio.

A concluding caution

To recommend without qualification the foregoing new departures in science policy as 'best practice' measures for governments seeking long-term mechanisms for co-ordinating the research efforts and effecting technology transfers between the public and private sectors, seems very misguided indeed. It would in the end obliterate the distinctive strengths and purposes of the different kinds of research organisations, turning open science organisations that are best suited to effecting the rapid growth in the stock of knowledge into proprietary research enterprises designed to maximise the flow of 'economic rents' that can be extracted by possession of exclusive rights to exploit existing stocks of knowledge.

A well-functioning science and technology system requires getting the correct balance and maintaining active communications between these two quite different kinds of organisations, because the special capabilities of each are required to sustain the pace of innovation and economic growth over the long term. Moreover, expertise in both modes of conducting the search for scientific and technological knowledge are needed to permit society to respond adequately to a variety of environmental and other problems, challenges whose solution will call for the creation of more effective modes of international scientific and engineering collaboration.

Notes

1. See, e.g., P. Dasgupta and P. A. David, '*Information Disclosure and the Economics of Science and Technology*', in G. Feiwel (ed), *Arrow and the Ascent of Modern Economic Theory*. New York: New York University Press, 1987; P. A. David, D. C. Mowery and W. E. Steinmueller, 'A Framework for Evaluating Economics Payoffs from Basic Research', *Economics of Innovation and New Technologies*, 2(3), 1992; P. Dasgupta and P. A. David, 'Toward a New Economics of Science', *Research Policy*, 1994, 23, pp. 487–521.

2. The recent OECD Interim Report on 'Best Practices in Technology and Innovation Policy', OECD, DSTI, April 1997, both reflects and promotes the implementation of this overarching policy orientation. Earlier economic studies such as B.-A. Lundvall, (ed.), *National Systems of Innovation*, (London, 1992), and R. R. Nelson, (ed.), *National Innovation Systems* (Oxford, 1992), were influential in crystallising this emerging approach to science and technology policy. Such works by academic economists, while emphasising the goal of national economic 'competitiveness', and tending to accord little attention to the role of international co-operative efforts in science and engineering research, are careful to eschew what has been referred to as 'techno-mercantilism' – the mistaken view that one nation's increasing mastery of new technological capabilities automatically creates an economic disadvantage for some other country. See P. A. David and D. Foray, 'Accessing and Expanding the Science and Technology Knowledge Base', *STI Review* (OECD – Science, Technology and Industry), Number 16, 1996, for explicit rejection of techno-mercantilist tendencies in recent policy, and a critique of the excessive emphasis that has been placed upon generating innovations to the neglect of measures supporting fuller utilisation of the existing knowledge base.

3. See J. S. Metcalfe, 'Science policy and technology policy in a competitive economy', *International Journal of Social Economics*, 24(7/8/9), 1997: pp. 723–40. In the passage quoted (p. 723) above, Metcalfe (a former advisor to the Office of Science and Technology in the UK) goes on to say that even though its scale of expenditures is comparatively small, a country 'can legitimately expect to ensure that institutional and other arrangements are in place to make more effective use of its investments in science and technology. Indeed, to the extent that a more effective return is obtained from science and technology, this of itself provides the most powerful of arguments for increase expenditure on research and development of all kinds.'

4. It is no longer thought acceptable for leaders from the scientific community to respond in the manner of one famous individual, who when asked by a US congressional committee what his own work had contributed to defending western civilisation, replied: 'Gentlemen, its always seemed to me that the sort of research I do was one of the things that made western civilisation worth defending.' For models of the more recent style of responses, especially those offered by physicists, see, e.g., C. H. Llewellyn Smith, 'What's the use of basic science?', Office of the Director General, CERN, Geneva. Unpublished draft, 2 September 1997; J. Mulvey, 'Can academic science be valued?' Chapter 3 this volume.

5. See P. A. David, 'Difficulties in Assessing the Performance of Research and Development Programs', *Science and Technology Policy Year-book*, American Association for the Advancement of Science, (Washington DC, 1994), pp. 293–301, and other contributions to that symposium on the implications of the US Government Performance and Results Act.

6. Office of Science and Technology,: *Realising Our Potential: A Strategy for Science, Engineering and Technology*, Cm 2250 (London: HMSO), 1993, p. 4.

7. See the description in Office of Science and Technology, *Progress Through Partnership*, Report from the Steering Group of the Technology Foresight Programme, London: HMSO, 1995.

8. See OST, *Realising Our Potential*, 1993, pp. 20, and 5, respectively for the two statements of purpose quoted in connection with Foresight.

9. For a now classic critique of the 'linear model', see S. J. Kline and N. Rosenberg, 'An Overview of Innovation', in R. Landau and N. Rosenberg, (eds.), *The Positive Sum Strategy: Harnessing Technology for Economic Growth*, Washington DC: National Academy Press, 1986; further discussion appears in P. A. David, 'Knowledge, Property and the System Dynamics of Technological Change', in L. Summers and S. Shah, *Proceedings of the World Bank Annual Conference on Development Economics*, 1992 (Supplement to The World Bank Economic Review), Washington DC, 1992: pp. 215–48.

10. 'The quality of the UK science base', Office of Science and Technology, London: DTI, March 1997, p. 1.

11. Although the 1993 White Paper, *Realising our Potential*, said little about the specifics of commercialisation of public sector research results, the Office of Science and Technology (OST) in a slightly earlier paper, *Intellectual Property in the Public Sector Research Base*, argued that universities and government research institutes must adopt internal policies to ensure that, whenever possible, the commercial potential of research is identified and promoted.

12. See P. A. David and D. Foray, 'Accessing and Expanding the Science and Technology Knowledge Base', *STI Review* (OECD – Science, Technology and Industry), Number 16, 1996, for further discussion of inefficiencies that are entailed in using intellectual property protection to stimulate innovations, especially in regard to adverse effects upon the access to, and utilisation of existing knowledge that may be useful in generating future innovations. At the same time, however, it should be noted that bundling contracts for technical support services with intellectual property licenses offers a solution to problems of direct contracting for tacit knowledge that is complementary to the codified information covered by the licensing agreement. See, e.g., P. A. David, 'Rethinking technology transfers: incentives, institutions and Knowledge-based industrial development', in C. Feinstein and C. Howe, (eds.), *Chinese Technology Transfer in the 1990s: Current Experience, Historical Problems and International Perspectives*, Cheltenham, UK: E. Elgar, 1997, pp. 13–37.

13. A thoughtful and balanced examination of the issues in the UK setting is provided by the report of the National Academics Policy Advisory Group, *Intellectual Property & the Academic Community*, London: The Royal Society, 1995.

14. Not content to claim ownership of essentially all forms of intellectual property created by employed staff and others engaged under contracts for services on research projects – exempting books, articles and lectures – it has become normal for universities in the UK now to assert parallel claims even in regard to the creations made by their students. The relevant section (IV) of the *Statutes, Decrees, and Regulations of the University of Oxford*, Oxford University Press, 1997, pp. 116–117, read as follows: 'the University claims

ownership of the following forms of intellectual property; in the case of (c), (d), (e), and (f) the claims are to inventions made, and works created, by students in the course of or incidentally to their studies'

15. Marjorie Blumenthal, 'Federal Government Research Initiatives and the Foundations of the Information Technology Revolution', *American Economic Review*, (forthcoming in May 1998) compares two such cases, Project Whirlwind and the High Performance Computing Initiative.

3
Can Basic Science Be Valued?

John Mulvey

Introduction

There was a time when governments in the UK were content to leave science to the scientists. An OECD report of 1978[1] explained: 'In the UK, objectives for science and technology are not centrally defined, ... it is considered that priorities in fundamental research are best determined by the scientists themselves, ...'

In times of war, of course, the scientists and engineers had been brought out of their laboratories and mobilised to apply their knowledge and expertise to winning battles on the technological front line, feeding intensively as they did so on the 'seed-corn' of earlier basic research.

Over the last twenty or so years the possibilities for discovery and the development of new technologies have expanded enormously, and in many areas the time gap between new scientific understanding and its application has shrunk. In most advanced countries the expenditure on research and development, both publicly and privately financed, has increased substantially to take advantage of these opportunities.

The potential economic value of basic research in science and technology has become better appreciated by our politicians. And in an economic context of intensifying global competition combined with a political imperative to contain, and reduce, public expenditures, it was inevitable that governments would also wish to seek 'better value for money' in their funding of basic/strategic/long-term research; or more visible economic benefit for less money.

In the United States a new act of Congress became law in 1993. It requires every federal agency including those responsible for funding research, like the National Science Foundation (NSF), to do strategic planning, to report annually in terms of performance indicators, and to use programme evaluation. '... US research in the 1990s must be prepared to demonstrate its benefits to the nation if it is to survive let alone grow' says Susan Cozzens, Director of the NSF's Office of Policy Support,[2] adding: 'Rather than protesting, "trust me", researchers must answer the challenge "show me".' Cozzens puts her finger on a new problem facing the academic research community: the implicit 'trust' – that left to themselves scientists would advance science and technology in the most effective and beneficial way – has been withdrawn.

But – although they show little sign of realising it – the challenge for governments, responsible for delivering to the tax-payers 'better value for their money' is now very much *harder* if a *value* is to be assessed before the money is spent: the potential value of much basic research is not known, not even knowable, at the time it is done, and often not sensibly quantifiable afterwards; so what trust can be placed on prior evaluations of that which is as yet undone?

To get a measure of the task we consider a few examples of past basic[3] research, defined more in respect of its style or aim than whether it was done in a university or elsewhere.

Example 1

In 1959 at the Cavendish (physics) Laboratory in Cambridge, Perutz and Kendrew made the first identifications of protein structure, the molecules myoglobin and haemoglobin. Several years later Sir John Kendrew told an interviewer that while the work was in progress experts said they were doomed to fail, and they worked together for more than ten years with no results. The interviewer thought to correct him: "You mean no *useful* results?" "No" said Sir John, "*no results at all*", adding that Max Perutz had started work on the problem 12 years before he had joined him.

Under the current regime of 'assessment' and 'auditing' would Perutz and Kendrew have been turned off, for not delivering value for money, long before accomplishing the discovery that won a Noble Prize and started the magnificent tradition continued today in Cambridge's MRC Laboratory for Molecular Biology? Sir John, in recent conversation, said he believed such a programme of research showing no sign of getting anywhere for so many years would not survive today.

Future generations will still be counting the *value* of their work as 'fathers' of molecular biology.

Example 2

There are many examples of research given little if any value when proposed but which turn out to be of fundamental interest. Here are three:

(a) The phenomenon of superconductivity – zero electrical resistance to the passage of a current – was well understood in 1985, the Nobel Prizes had been presented and no committee would have considered it worth anyone's time looking for materials behaving as superconductors above the very low temperature of 30K. But at the IBM's Zurich Research Laboratories, Muller and Bednorz were given leave from their main research responsibilities to follow up a hunch of Muller's. They discovered a completely new class of superconducting materials retaining this property up to much higher temperatures, perhaps eventually reaching ordinary 'room temperature'. As Muller said, with some understatement, when the results were published they were met with great scepticism in the US and Europe. Their Nobel Prize arrived in 1987.

(b) James Lovelock developed a very sensitive means of detecting small quantities of molecules like the CFCs (chlorinated fluorocarbons) commonly used in devises like hairsprays and as the coolant liquid in refrigerators. Since CFCs do not occur naturally, he saw their presence could be used as a tell-tale indicator of the subsequent movement of air masses passing over densely inhabited areas. He proposed mapping CFC concentrations across the globe and asked for funding for a voyage to Australia so that he could make measurements on the way.

  The request was thrown out, one reviewer saying it was the most frivolous application he had ever seen. Lovelock eventually made his observations, finding CFCs widely distributed and leading to concern that on reaching the upper atmosphere the CFCs could destroy the ozone layer – as the British Antarctic Survey later found to be the case.

(c) Peter Mitchell, dissatisfied with contemporary ideas on the transport of chemicals across cell membranes, tried, over a period of fifteen years, to develop a new approach to the problem. Running against the tide of conventional views he experienced ridicule from colleagues and one head of department felt that what he was doing was of no use.[4] He published the 'chemiosmotic theory' of energy transfer in 1961 and later experimental work by Mitchell and others confirmed the main basis of the theory was correct. His work revolutionised the understanding of how chemical transport occurs in all types of cell – in plants, animals and bacteria – and how cells gain and utilise energy. Mitchell was awarded a Nobel Prize in 1978.

In all three cases the researchers persevered with their ideas in the face of strong scepticism based on the prevailing wisdom, and the belief of others that the outcome would be fruitless. We know their stories because they were successful, and they were proved right. Now we know how important their work was, but the concern today must be that because of such initial doubts about *value* equivalent ventures might not get a chance to be tested.

Example 3

In 1965 Penzia and Wilson, at the Bell Telephone Laboratory in the USA, were developing a sensitive radio amplifier and antenna to pick up signals from artificial satellites when they discovered a continuous, low level microwave signal, or 'noise', which appeared to come from all directions in space. Once they had excluded the possibility of less dramatic causes, such as the effect of birds nesting in the horn of their radio antenna, it was realised they had made the serendipitous discovery of what became known as '3K cosmic background radiation'. This is the still reverberating 'photon-echo' of the Big Bang, and one of the principal experimental supports of that cosmological model of the evaluation of the universe.

Does this contribution to the fundamental understanding of the universe have a *money-value*?

Example 4

One more example – the list is without end. The autumn 1995 issue of *Science and Public Affairs*[5] contained a story by Robert Hanbury Brown of his recent visit to the seaside. Hanbury Brown, Emeritus Professor of Physics in Sydney, Australia, was previously a Professor Radio Astronomy at Manchester. His name is well known in physics as two-thirds of 'Hanbury Brown and Twiss', who developed an elegant, high resolution method in optical interferometry for measuring the angular diameter of stars.

In 1936 Hanbury Brown joined a small team sent to Orford Ness by Watson Watt to test the feasibility of tracking aircraft by detecting reflected pulses of radio waves – radar. Looking back on those times after revisiting Orford Ness in 1994, Hanbury Brown draws lessons for today:

... the early work on radar depended heavily on knowledge and techniques gained from 'pure research' on the ionosphere and radio atmospherics ... their application to the urgent military necessity of detecting enemy aircraft was not, and could not, have been foreseen. The contemporary research which was obviously 'relevant' to the detection of enemy aircraft was on sound locators and would never have solved the problem.

What this early work illustrates so clearly is that the popular, often self-righteous, demand that all research should be relevant to our immediate needs is, paradoxically, one of the greatest dangers to the long term satisfaction of those needs.

Fruits of knowledge

It is simple, that by looking into the world around us, into space beyond, and into the constituents of matter and the mechanisms of life, we have developed an understanding of a huge range of natural phenomena which when applied, in mainly unforeseeable ways, has transformed, and is transforming, our whole manner of living and quality of life – sometimes too quickly for comfort.

Speaking in 1971 P. M. S. Blackett said:

Though everyone accepts that the vast wealth of the developed countries today is somehow due to science, it is by no means fully agreed as to how in detail it happened.

Now the study of 'technology transfer' has developed into a field of its own but, as the practitioners argue the merits of one model or another, we are no further forward. Nor should we expect to be. Every experience shows that the process is infinitely complex; all paths that are possible play a role including the most unlikely, and the biggest mistake we can make is to believe those who say they know how to separate 'useful' science from 'not useful' science.

It might be objected that the examples chosen are 'break-through' discoveries or otherwise remarkable; what about the great preponderance of research which is unremarkable, incremental advance – and sometimes dead-end? Here, the politicians will say, is the opportunity to apply some foresight; to choose research to maximise the return while reducing the overall cost, increasing productivity and delivering blessed value for money in double quick time.

Richard Ingrams, writing recently in the *Observer*, told a story of an accountant who became Chairman of a publishing house. Shortly after taking over he called on the Managing Director to explain a bright idea he had for increasing profitability: 'Why don't we just publish the best sellers?'

Unfortunately, in the real world one cannot have the high-value tail of the distribution without the whole distribution. While the main body of research, basic and strategic, is continuously building and rebuilding the platform of knowledge on which later major advances were based, one cannot tell when some of today's unremarkable research may be found to contain the essential seed of tomorrow's 'break-through' (the twenty years he spent studying the structure of metallic oxides led Muller to his hunch about superconductivity). And the key opening a new door is just as likely to be in the form of a new experimental technique or analytical method developed in an unrelated research field as a directly pertinent discovery. Even developments in the most esoteric domains of research can have unexpected impact in unconnected areas.

When Thomas Brock of the University of Wisconsin set off for a pleasant field trip in Yellowstone National Park to look for bugs living in or near five thermal vents, he would not have listed as potential 'customers' scientists who would one day be looking for the origins of cancer. In bacteria from the vents he found an enzyme which was stable at near boiling temperatures. Several years later it turned out to be crucial to the successful development of the polymerase chain reaction (PCRP). This allows the exact replication of specific pieces of DNA many times over. The PCR process is now the basis of multimillion-pound businesses ranging from the rapid diagnosis of disease to forensic medicine, and a vital tool in genetics research including the mechanisms by which normal cells can become cancerous.

Perhaps most important of all, academic research is the main training ground for the next generations of scientists and engineers. Who can set a *value* on the contributions they may make in the future – whether in basic or applied science?

The lesson of hindsight

If we cannot, even in hindsight, set a meaningful *value* to individual programmes of research or technological development, how can we expect to do it using foresight, which is no more than hindsight projected into the future?

The Technology Foresight exercise has great value in so far as it brings together scientists and engineers from universities, industry, government laboratories and elsewhere, to explore possible directions in science and technology, to stimulate ideas and fresh lines of thought, and to form networks of contacts which, hopefully, will be maintained.

But the government's view of 'Foresight implementation' using today's guesses as the basis for the allocation of public funds to tomorrow's research, carries great risk of long-term damage to the science base. Not truly understanding the research process, politicians and bureaucrats see Foresight 'as the "street lamp" illuminating the area of pavement where a dropped gold coin is most easily found...' but it may not be there. We need the light of original thought to shine in the dark places.

> First rate innovative science cannot be managed except by the scientists who are doing the work. If you try to manage it by pushing it around then you will waste your time.[6]

At an international conference in Washington USA, in 1995,[7] the UK government position on foresight was outlined in the following terms: there is a 'strong market focus' through the development of networks 'the results will be widely disseminated ... however, dissemination by itself is not sufficient: active implementation needs to occur ... Government ... will take account of Foresight in allocating funding for the science base through the Research Councils which support academic research ... Foresight is essentially about achieving a long-term change in the science and technology climate by increasing the contribution that the science and engineering base makes to wealth creation ... '.

It is interesting to compare this very specific, *dirigiste* use of the results of Foresight in centrally planning the programmes of academic research in the UK with the approach reported by the representatives of some other countries at the conference. Germany and Holland 'separated science or research from technology, and focussed the Foresight exercise on technology, where it is possible to be more precise about commercialisation and timescales'. In Japan the 'purpose is to increase public awareness of science and technology; the results are published nationally in newspapers etc.' any influence on programmes of academic research is indirect, and appears to be minimal.

The scientific endeavour

If individual programmes of research or projects cannot sensibly be valued in retrospect, then should we not take a holistic approach and *value* this development of a deep understanding of nature and its workings, the scientific enterprise, *for itself and as a whole*? Apart from the cultural contributions, the applications of this understanding to enhance health and create wealth more than 'pay' for the total enterprise of discovery and technical development.

The 'returns' to society from basic research should not be assigned narrowly to the particular, individual triumphs of discovery and application – depending as they do on all that has gone before – but to the endeavour as a whole.

Where few others would dare to tread, Mrs (now Lady) Thatcher was bold enough to put a lower limit on its value. In a speech to the Royal Society in 1988 she said:

> The value of the work done by Michael Faraday exceeds the total capitalisation of the London Stock Market many times over.

When attempts, rather more 'professional' than Lady Thatcher's, are made to estimate the overall return on investment in basic research the results show a high level of benefit – often much higher than that for any other form of investment.

Edwin Mansfield has made a study[8] of the dependence of technological innovation in 76 major US industries on recent academic research, done within the previous 15 years. He concluded that 10 per cent of the new products and processes commercialised during 1975 to 1985 could not have been developed when they were without the basis of academic research. His 'very tentative' but 'seemingly conservative' estimate of the 'social rate of return' from the total spent, world-wide, on academic research in the relevant period was 28 per cent.

In the late 1960s two US physicians, Comroe and Dribbs, carried out an extensive investigation to re-trace the steps of discovery and invention leading to the generation of the ten most important clinical advances of the time. The results showed[9] that of 663 'key' investigations that were crucial to one of the ten advances, 42 per cent were not, at the time they were reported, related to that clinical advance; and 62 per cent dealt with basic mechanisms of cells, tissues or organs rather than aspects of disease. For each of the ten clinical advances basic ideas, observations or discoveries had been essential.

To quote a more recent study, Francis Narin and others[10] have examined the references cited by 400,000 US Patents issued in 1987/89 and 1993/94. In brief, the authors find that US industry is far from self-sufficient in science. The great majority, 73 per cent, of the science cited comes from publicly funded research, in the US and overseas. This is largely true even for big, research oriented companies like IBM. Publicly funded research is 'a fundamental pillar' of the advance of US technology, and this science is 'quite basic, quite recent, published in highly influential journals, and authored at major universities and laboratories'.

Conclusions

Given the difficulty of assessing in any meaningful way the value to be assigned to particular programmes of basic research performed in the past, and the inevitably larger uncertainties that must exist for those not yet begun, the strong emphasis on 'wealth creation' as a criterion for public support of research, which is the central theme of the 1993 White Paper on science policy, must be a matter of justifiable concern. Working increasingly in a 'top down mode', Research Councils define research programmes guided by Foresight and solicit relevant proposals: groups with strong industrial support are favoured in the distribution of funds, and industry is being drawn increasingly into the role of supplementing poor public support. In a situation of fierce competition for seriously inadequate funds, there is, rightly or wrongly, a perception that the chance of success in an application to Research Councils – even for the so-called 'responsive mode' – will be greater for an investigation with low risk of failure and clear promise of 'relevant' results.

Of course, it would be foolish not to ensure strong support for those areas identified by Foresight as of potential importance; and they should especially attract investment in research and development within industry. But a balance must be preserved leaving scope in the research base for originality and the pursuit of objectives identified by purely scientific criteria to flourish.

The problem, strikingly revealed by comparisons with other countries, is that UK investment in civil R&D, both public and private, is far too low. Distorting the public support of research in the science and engineering research base to favour research perceived to be of more direct relevance to 'wealth creation' at the expense of support for basic research will only make matters worse in the longer term.

Agreeing that we can only talk of the 'return' on basic research in relation to the aggregate of research programmes in the long-term – not on a project by project basis – then once it has been decided how much the country wishes to spend in total on basic/academic research the most sensible thing we can do, having defined the balance of support across broad areas, is to return to 1978: leave the direction and conduct of research to the best scientists and engineers we have – and let them get on with it.

Whenever basic research is found to have made a major contribution, directly or indirectly, to 'wealth creation' the benefit to society should not be counted narrowly as a return on investment in the particular programme or research project last involved, but attributed to the whole breadth of the academic endeavour. For there is an inherent unity in science. Among the many strands of thought and of experimental method drawn together to achieve the result some will be found, if traced back to their sources, to come from surprisingly unrelated fields of research.

Basic science is invaluable.

Notes

1. *Science and Technology Policy Outlook*, OECD, 1978.
2. 'US Research Assessment: Recent Developments' Susan Cozzens, First International Conference on the Evaluation of Research, Technology and Development, Thessaloniki, Greece, April, 1995.
3. 'Basic' will be used here to specify research for which advance of knowledge was the prime objective of the scientists performing it.
4. Interviews with 70 distinguished scientists form the basis for *The Second Culture: British Science in Crisis – The Scientists Speak Out* Clive Rassum, London: Arum Press, 1993. This book provides fascinating insights into the experiences of scientists in a wide variety of research fields.
5. Published by the Royal Society and the British Association for the Advancement of Science.
6. Peter Mitchell cited in Clive Rassum, *The Second Culture* op. cit.
7. 'Setting Research Priorities: Future Scenarios for the R&D Portfolio' a conference sponsored by the US Department of Energy, Sandia National Laboratories and the US Office of Science and Technology Policy, Washington DC, 21 June 1995.
8. 'Academic research and industrial innovation' Edwin Mansfield, University of Pennsylvania, *Research Policy*, 20, 1, 1992.
9. '*The Retrospectroscope*' J. H. Comroe and R. D. Dribbs, Menloe Park, California: von Gehr Press, 1997.
10. '*The increasing Linkage between US Technology and Public Science*' Francis Narin, Kimberley S. Hamilton and Dominic Olivastro, CHI Research Inc. of published in *Research Policy*, 20, 1,1991, pp.1–12.

4
What Higher Educational System Will There Be To Regulate?

Sir Douglas Hague

Introduction

My chapter is about what kind of higher education system the UK will need in the 21st century and what that will mean for the relationship between universities and the regulatory system. In order to comment on what that will mean, I identify the key elements of change affecting the relationship between universities and their constituencies – their students, industry, the government and society at large, the barriers to the realisation of the kind of system which would be beneficial to the UK, and the challenges that both present to the regulators.

The chapter is in four sections. In the first, I examine four relentless trends which I believe will transform universities in the 21st century and which are behind all the debates about the higher educational system. In the second, I consider the challenges to the universities as a response to these and other trends. In the third, I discuss challenges to the regulators. In the last, I draw some brief conclusions.

Four trends

Economic

The first is economic. We are moving into the post-industrial society, though a substantial proportion of output will still come from manufacturing businesses. Many will be high-technology companies, whose products are knowledge-based, calling for well-educated people. For example, British Aerospace employs more graduates than any other UK business.

A sub-trend is the growth of what I call pure-knowledge businesses. Unlike knowledge-based businesses they trade in knowledge itself and are concerned, for example, with research and development, market research, consultancy, training and education.

Knowledge-based businesses will provide universities with demand for good graduates and scope for joint research projects, though some large companies are setting up what are effectively technical/business universities and are, therefore, potential competitors. The relationship of universities with pure-knowledge businesses will also contain elements of both complementarity and competition. I shall return to these issues.

Cost pressures

If the first economic trend is an important reason for the rising demand for university places in the developed world, the second brings new cost pressures. Economic development raises incomes. Because the conventional university is labour-intensive, higher education will become increasingly expensive whoever funds it. And these funders will find it hard to keep pace.

For example, in the UK since 1977, government spending on higher education has risen by 45 per cent in real terms. Since the number of students has more than doubled, funding per student in real terms has fallen by 40 per cent. Without a change in government policy, it will fall by another 6.5 per cent by 2000 (Dearing, 1997). To continue to recruit able people in competition with knowledge businesses, universities will have to be more willing to match pay in private sector organizations. Costs will have to be kept down by operating differently and especially by using more technology.

The Information and Communications Technology (ICT) revolution

The fact that there is a third trend – that the information/communications revolution is accompanying the knowledge revolution – makes this possible. The one certain prediction about the impact of ICT on universities is that it will be dramatic. The challenge for individual universities will be to work out how best they can use the developing knowledge media. At least initially, a substantial research and development effort will be necessary in order to find the best ways of using what is becoming available. And those ways will differ, perhaps, substantially, between universities. To explore possibilities, diversity of approach must be encouraged.

Those with experience in using ICT insist that, during this learning phase, all expenditure on hardware and software for teaching must be matched pound for pound by similar expenditure on R&D, to discover how to use the equipment. The learning phase may be lengthy and, again, the advice of those with experience of using ICT is that universities should begin early, even if that seems too soon.

We know a good deal now about the contribution to learning which can be made by high-quality audio and video material, whether transmitted to students through broadcasts or cassettes. And the British Open University has shown that we should never underrate the parallel contribution of well-tailored written material to learning.

We are moving into a phase where interactive computers using CD ROMs will have a big impact. These 'knowledge media' enable computer screens to provide text and graphics to explain material, reinforcing this with film clips of 'talking heads', of scientific experiments, of recent and distant events, etc. By interrogating students, well-programmed computers will discover what a student has learned from a CD and, if need be, provide further elucidation and more questions. The computer will itself be able both to assess students' performances and to reveal their patterns, preferences, strengths and weaknesses in learning. The main contribution may be in basic subjects like first-year mathematics, statistics, economics, etc. but this is not to be despised. It will release people for those tasks which only people can perform.

Virtual reality is becoming increasingly important. Already, some airlines train pilots from the very beginning on simulated flight decks, while medical students learn to operate on 'virtual' patients. The potential for improving education, and especially training, is enormous. Moreover there are potential cost savings, since students will increasingly be able to use 'virtual' scientific equipment, rather than the expensive real thing.

In the end, the Internet will have the biggest impact of all. Though in existence for 25 years the Internet has been growing exponentially only for the last four. It is likely to provide the standard way to disseminate multi-media learning material. Stanford University launched its first postgraduate degree course on the Internet in 1955. But that was only a start. Soon software like Java, which is both a computer language and itself a computer providing small 'applets' of software, will give students with PCs direct access to enormous computing power and to whole libraries of software. I therefore concur with the comment made by Sir John Daniel, based on his experience as Vice Chancellor of the UK Open University, that the coming-of-age of the Internet represents 'a defining moment in the development of technology-based university teaching and learning' (Daniel, 1996).

None of these developments will be cheap. As Mega-Universities makes clear, it will be important for universities making substantial use of ICT in teaching to find ways of achieving economies of scale. Otherwise the cost per student will be too high.

The increasing supply of graduates

The fourth trend is the increase in the amount of educated brain power in developed countries. Steadily increasing numbers of graduates mean more well-educated people outside universities relative to those within. The fact that many of them are working in pure knowledge businesses will mean more people and organisations carrying out activities very similar to those of universities. The 'metal bashers' of the 1950s and 60s could not compete with universities. Many of today's businesses could, if they chose to do so.

Of course, the universities never had a monopoly of well-trained brain power, but their own actions in training more graduates have substantially reduced what monopoly they did have, at a time when many of these graduates are actually trading in knowledge. As business people, these graduates will recognise that what they do has to be well thought-out, well-organised and delivered on time. Their messages will be practical and well-presented, using up-to-date technology. Even if they have greater academic talent, universities may not find this competition very easy to match, in the fields where it materializes. I give some UK examples later.

Because of my own experience in working with them, I point to the significance of a sub-group of pure knowledge workers – a new generation of knowledge entrepreneurs – most of whom are graduates, many aged between 25 and 35. Some are being given their heads by the firms that employ them; others are setting up their own businesses. If there is to be business competition with universities, these entrepreneurs will be among its leaders.

Challenges to universities

Partly because of these four trends, universities will have to overcome big challenges in meeting the demands of the 21st century.

Learning

Some of us have for years been astonished how few of our university colleagues spend much time studying the effectiveness of teaching. By teaching I mean judging not the presentations which teachers make, but the extent to which students 'learn how to learn' and not simply how to remember and to reproduce material from books or, even worse, from lectures.

Information technology will itself give us greater understanding of learning. The Open University's use of video conferencing, which allows 'interactive, reflective and synchronised group communication' (Daniel, 1996) is doing this. It has revealed more clearly than ever 'that many students have a very poor understanding of the course materials' (Daniel, 1996). The advent of ICT will both compel us to tackle such shortcomings and enable us to check on our success.

Team working will spread, if only because the economic and educational pressures to use ICT to provide first-class education will force universities to establish teams to develop new teaching materials and methods. The UK Open University's experience shows that this is the only way to produce high-quality material for sizeable audiences, whether that material is disseminated on paper, tape, CD or by television. Universities will have to recognise that, in many cases, the task can no longer be left to individual academics.

I hope we shall also recognise the need for much more research by cognitive scientists and other academics into the way university students learn. It is depressing that universities have in the past cared so little about individual students' learning methods and processes and, therefore, encouraging that the Dearing Report wants to put students' 'at the centre of the process of learning and teaching' (Dearing, 1997). Actually achieving this will, of course, be difficult.

There has been a good deal of research by cognitive scientists in the USA on learning in schools, whose findings have been splendidly summarised by John Bruer in his book *Schools for Thought* (Bruer, 1993). There is virtually none about universities though Diana Laurillard, in *Rethinking University Teaching* (1993), has made a good start. Far more research into teaching is now needed.

Lifelong learning

This movement to emphasise the primacy of learning is spurred on by the fact that the coming of the knowledge age is ending the notion that all the knowledge necessary for a lifelong career can be acquired in three years at around the age of 20. 'Lifelong learning' is ceasing to be a slogan and becoming a reality in the UK, as the title of the Dearing Report, 'Higher Education in a Learning Society', shows. A large new market for post-experience training is developing and it will be very demanding, though financially rewarding.

Mature students set high standards for lecturers/tutors because they have their own (not always correct) ideas of what they need to learn; and enough of them know what is current practice in their organisation to insist that what universities offer them must be more abreast of current and potential developments than is often the case. And, where appropriate, they will insist on learning through effective presentations, physical or electronic.

To ensure that there is complementarity rather than competition with appropriate outsiders, the alumni of universities, and others in business and the professions, should be encouraged to come in as partners, not simply as students. As lifelong learning develops, many 'students' will be able to contribute as well as listen so that I look forward to a substantial change in relationships, where no one is permanently either teacher or taught. Alumni and others can also make substantial contributions through lectures (which should be videoed to be presented again later), tutoring and advising; in planning courses and research; and by providing advice on commercial aspects of the university, e.g. marketing. They will bring new perspectives and, often, greater vitality.

Using information technology

As the future university learns to use information technology well and as distance learning develops, this will bring more competition between universities both outside and inside the UK. At least some UK universities will need to match organisations like the Open University (OU) in providing high-class distance learning across the world. And I agree with those who think that, with English a world language, Britain should seek to be a world leader in providing first-class learning material.

At its highest level, and for its biggest audiences, this kind of material will become a branch of 'showbiz', with some academics becoming international mini-stars, a development foreshadowed by Frank and Cook in *The Winner Takes All Society* (Frank and Cook, 1995). Both written and broadcast material will have to match the best in the world, so that universities will also have to create well-organised production teams like those of the OU, and traditional academics will have to learn how to work within them.

With unprecedented access to both information and knowledge, students will also need more guidance than ever on which sources to use and greater opportunities to discuss teaching material and related issues. Established university teachers will see this as potentially undermining their traditional role as 'gatekeepers', who give students access to their personal knowledge. But the experience of the OU shows how important the tutorial role is becoming: it should be the central role in 21st century universities. At present, the OU has 7000 tutors across the world, though most are in the UK.

At least in relatively straightforward courses, a mixture of video and CD-ROM material will begin to displace basic instruction and interchange. For example I have long argued that, in a two-year MBA programme like those at Manchester and London Business Schools, students should be required to cover the first-year material through distance learning, before they arrive. This would leave the faculty free to concentrate on the more valuable and more interesting, because it is more interactive, work with second year students. There are far too many introductory and elementary lecture courses around the world, many of which should (and I hope will) be replaced by new media.

Information/knowledge analysis and exchange

One can argue over whether universities are innovative enough in their current activities. Even if they are not, there are substantial barriers to entry which will protect at least the best of them from competitors for many years. These barriers derive especially from the reputation of established and prestigious institutions and, not least, from sheer size.

Outside the university, quite new fields are being opened up. The newest, and fastest growing, is the analysis and interpretation of information and knowledge. It is doubtful whether universities will ever play a central role with the first element – information – because they will judge information exchange (as distinct from knowledge exchange) as too low-level and unimportant to them. But that judgement should not be made casually.

In other words, information/knowledge exchange ranges over a spectrum. At one end, is the provision of simple information, on stock market or house prices for example, where businesses currently seem to have the edge through the databases they have built and through new electronic media, especially the Internet.

At the other end of the spectrum, is the exchange of complex knowledge where universities are potentially in a strong position, and should not lightly allow it to be eroded. I give one example, which may seem bizarre, but increasingly will not be. Many, perhaps most, business leaders acquire knowledge through discussion, not reading. As the knowledge age develops, periodic conversations between them and experts can become an important, even profitable, service. And, with today's technology, physical proximity will no longer matter. Before leaving this field to others, universities should look carefully at their potential role in what we may call 'distributed brain tapping'.

Such direct conversations and consultations will be paralleled by distribution of knowledge through the Internet. Here the pioneers may well be small, highly-entrepreneurial knowledge businesses, acting as knowledge brokers. They may be small, but their dynamism and inventiveness will enable them to exert a substantial influence. They will understand what their clients need, will pride themselves on knowing where expertise in given fields is to be found, and will reach and remain at the leading edge in mastering the contribution of the latest software and in understanding the Internet. Since the expertise which knowledge brokers will need to draw on in handling both knowledge and ICT is often based in universities, the latter should consider developing a role here. And perhaps they should do so in alliance with these lively new knowledge businesses.

Not all 'brain tapping' will be conducted by institutions. The Internet is its own creature and much knowledge broking is going on through individuals. 'Conferences' or 'forums' provide expert knowledge for members and enable them to pass it on to others in their networks. More important, those who get answers to questions through these conferences often receive replies from surprising sources, tapping the brains of (to them) unknown and unexpected experts. Should universities be more proactive, rather than simply watch these interchanges develop?

Research

In the 21st century research strategies will need to be revised to make the most appropriate contribution in the information/knowledge age. I hope that universities will be allowed to concentrate more on basic rather than applied research. Otherwise, there may well be too little basic research and researchers trained in it.

Businesses can then concentrate on applied research and not only in scientific and technological fields. A social science, like economics, provides example of the role businesses may play. The top 40 British economic forecasters (as ranked by the *Sunday Times*) include only two universities (LBS and Liverpool). They also include two businesses run by knowledge entrepreneurs, Bridget Rosewall at Business Strategies (and ex-Oxford University) and John Walker at Oxford Economic Forecasting (also ex-Oxford University). They find entrepreneurial success easier, more enjoyable and more lucrative outside a university-setting than inside.

More general studies of short- and medium-term term economic developments, both in the UK and elsewhere, come mainly from banks or stockbrokers in the City of London. This is partly because their publications are free to clients and to university researchers/teachers, but speed of publication is also important. These reports are well-written and authoritative, many with intellectual standards at least equal to those in universities. In this field, academic researchers seem to have largely given up already.

My experience at the ESRC emphasised two other points. First, established peer groups, including journal editors, have too much influence in approving research proposals and assessing results. We all know that many of today's paradigms will be overturned, and we need to speed the process. We therefore need to find ways to encourage sceptical researchers who challenge such paradigms – to help, not hinder, the critics of established thinking. The information/knowledge age is no time to allow peer groups to cut themselves off from currently heretical ideas, from which new paradigms often come.

I say this more urgently because I was alarmed, in July 1997, by the enthusiasm with which the 50 senior academics and administrators from 15 countries, who attended the Hong Kong Conference (See Acknowledgement) supported the imposition of 'standards' on material on the Internet. Of course there is a case for ensuring that both teaching and research material is of good quality, but we should not step beyond that to censorship of both. It is this kind of censorship which peer groups too often try to impose on research.

Second, there is too little emphasis on 'scholarship', using them to mean interpreting whole fields of other peoples' research rather than researching on one's own. Bruer's book, quoted above, is an excellent example of this. The value of 'scholarship' is inadequately recognised in most universities, while 'original' research (even if not very original) has too high a status. The Dearing Report acknowledges that the control procedures of bodies like the HEFCE have given too much prominence to research, which has led to 'the downgrading and devaluing of teaching' (Dearing, 1997).

I tried to encourage 'scholarship' at the ESRC but found it extremely difficult, because it diverts academics from 'real' research. Yet what is the point of producing half-a-dozen books through research costing, up to £20 million, if no one is then prepared to make overall sense of them. It is unrealistic to assume that many individuals will take on such huge tasks, on their own initiative, but the resulting lack of interest in 'scholarship' is one of the worst results of the hyper-specialisation which universities throughout the world have bred.

Simultaneously, technology is generating a knowledge overload. 'Scholarship' will be crucial if that overload is not to waste research findings. If 'voluntary' scholarship is so unpopular in universities, perhaps the role of providing it should be passed to commercial knowledge brokers. This is one field where academics would apparently prefer competitors to take over.

Business competition

Corporate universities

I see little likelihood of businesses replicating or replacing complete universities in the foreseeable future, but the amount of university-like activity in businesses is growing, though it is still very fragmented (see Hague, 1996).

Of course, the development of knowledge business depends significantly on the quality of the graduates universities produce. I have therefore been predicting that, beyond a certain point, failure by universities to provide the types and standards of teaching and research training which business requires would lead them to put pressure on universities to raise standards. Alternatively, it would cause them to establish their own 'corporate universities'. This is now happening. In the USA, where the term 'corporate university' was coined, there are now said to be over one hundred, and the UK is following on. The stimulus is a wish to provide skills which the corporation requires and/or a shared ethos/culture among employees. 'Current academic curricula simply are not meeting their needs' (Meister, 1996).

Even so, there is interest in working with universities. In the USA, employees are keen for 'corporate universities' to form partnerships with academic institutions, so that employees can obtain qualifications from 'an accredited academic institution'. But it is claimed that businesses seeking to do this are often then 'frustrated with the reception they get from academia .... Universities and corporations speak two different languages, there is inevitably a period of awkwardness, of trying to understand each other' (Meister, 1996). But I believe partnerships are what will be needed.

The UK is at an earlier stage. British Aerospace – the country's largest employee of graduates – has recently threatened to establish its own university, because of a shortage of good engineering graduates

(*Financial Times*, 1997a). In 1995, British Telecom established a virtual university for its employees with 'classes, lectures and tutorials and experiments all presented and prepared by many universities and organisations around the world selected because they are regarded as the best of the best' (Gell and Cochrane, 1996).

In total, some six businesses in the UK are currently (September 1997) establishing corporate universities, but there will be many more. And there will also be more joint ventures. One between Warwick University and Rover/BMW, provides technical and/or management training. Another by Microsoft aims to establish a European basic research laboratory in England, through a joint project with Cambridge University – an important development. The laboratory will work on aspects of computer science and Microsoft will spend £50 million over five years (*Financial Times*, 1997b).

The rich mixture of change in prospect therefore brings both opportunities and threats to universities. To the extent that they fail to grasp the opportunities, the threats will be greater. And some opportunities may require alliances with businesses and 'corporate universities' rather than independent initiatives.

One could easily be patronising because so much of the training in 'corporate universities' is currently at a relatively low level. It is 'Further' rather than 'Higher' Education. But that is where these organisations have to begin. And at least some corporate universities are progressive. Unipart University in the UK, established by an international business making and distributing automobile parts, and it led most conventional universities in recognising the need to put much more emphasis on enabling 'students' to learn how to learn.

Databases

There is clearly going to be a huge business contribution to the development of databases, CD ROMs, video and television programmes, etc. in ways I have already described and links between large and small companies will develop. For example, Pearson/Longman have acquired Henley Distance Learning, which is a spin off from Henley Management College. But the evidence is that alliances between very small and very large businesses are likely to be seen by the latter as ways of buying expertise, with the small partner absorbed or discarded once the necessary lessons have been learned. This does, however, mean that large companies will soon have mastered the skills needed to use ICT to provide material for good lower-level education. They will then move onto provide university-level material. Their potential muscle, which is both enormous and international, will make them very strong competitors for universities in this field.

A commercial university?

If one goes on to ask the question how long it will be before any business establishes a complete university for outside students rather than employees, my guess is that it will take a long time. What does seem certain is that to be able to do this a company would have to have a very strong intellectual base and great competence in both computing and communications. So perhaps the first venture in this field will be IBM University, or Hewlett Packard College.

Challenges to regulators

The basic issue

No one has put the biggest general issue facing UK universities better than Michael Dixon of the *Financial Times*. The conventional argument for increasing the proportion of young people being given an academic training is that this will stop Britain's relative economic decline, or even reverse it. Yet, as Michael Dixon has pointed out, this was 'glossed over by the Committee of Inquiry headed by the late Lord Robbins which in 1963 recommended the first post-war expansion of higher education. No one seriously challenged the belief that more young people educated to what universities considered to be a higher level would somehow make the nation more productive as well as civilised' (*Financial Times*, 1993). Despite its massive size, the Dearing Report does little to resolve the issue. This resolution must begin from a recognition that there are three conflicting cultures in universities, something which is rarely discussed.

There is, first, an *academic* culture concentrating on producing future teachers and researchers. Closely linked to this is a *discipline* culture, seeking to enable students to acquire knowledge for its own sake across the whole range of subjects, but in the hope that both this specialist knowledge and the general skills of thinking and learning acquired from a university education will help in later careers.

The academic and discipline cultures are very similar, perhaps because the academic culture overlaps, and indeed exerts too much influence on, the discipline culture. Both cultures derive from the ethos of pre-war universities which catered largely for an elite, put great emphasis on producing a self-perpetuating cadre of 'scholars' and provided little explicit training for a career. The *professional* culture associated with career training, for example in engineering, business studies or law, has been distinctly frowned on by the first two cultures, which dominated most of the 53 universities in the UK before 1992. Now that the current total of 120 universities and colleges include the former polytechnics assimilated in 1992, the 'professional' culture has a bigger overall weight, because it is more important in former polytechnics. But that culture still lacks kudos in too many universities.

Beyond this, I see it as a misfortune that the wholly laudable concept of the polytechnic, which concentrates on instilling the knowledge and developing the skills which would 'make the nation more productive', has been overwhelmed by the desire of those working in them to pursue the status associated with a 'university'. It may be possible to develop a university that gives adequate respect to all three cultures, but I doubt it. Whether, or how, we resolve Michael Dixon's question, we shall need more first-rate 'professional schools'.

But we also need clearer recognition of the issues involved and an abandonment of the fudge in official thinking which Michael Dixon has identified. Some universities – or substantial parts of them – should determine to become the cross-disciplinary polytechnics of the 21st century. I do not believe that, as a nation, we can afford to avoid this issue any longer.

Economies of scale

This issue of economics of scale will arise in many areas, not least because of the need to make higher education less labour-intensive and therefore capable of paying higher salaries. I highlight two issues.

First, some of the most crucial decisions will have to focus on the best way to finance the production of high-quality educational videos and CD ROMs. These decisions will affect not just British higher education but that of the whole world and knowledge businesses will play an important role alongside universities. It is, for example, estimated that there are already some 10 000 CDs providing reference and learning material. Most of these, together with the much smaller number of educational CD ROMs, have been produced by businesses, not by universities or governments. Most are still primitive, but one can see the potential they will have for education as they develop. Over the next couple of decades, therefore, large amounts of good, high-technology teaching material will be produced – some by universities, some by businesses and some in partnerships between universities or between businesses and universities.

The second big issue over economies of scale relates to universities themselves. To keep down unit costs, the average size of universities will have to increase. Eleven universities in the world now have over 100 000 students. The UK in 1963 had only some 200 000 university students in total. Today, the OU alone has 150 000; hence its 7000 tutors (see Daniel, 1996). With around one million students in over 100 universities and colleges, there is clearly scope for an increase in size, and one that must surely be accompanied by a reduction in the number of institutions. Perhaps it will be a substantial one. Are the regulators worrying sufficiently about that?

Working for pluralism

Given any analysis, one has to ask how (or if?) Britain can develop a higher education system which is resilient enough to create the universities fully appropriate to the 21st century. They must be able to compete and collaborate effectively with knowledge businesses and to do so while technology makes competition between universities and between them and businesses increasingly international. In the 21st century universities must be innovative and flexible, and it is hard to see what direct role regulators can play in developing such a system of higher education.

I say this because the big funders – the DFEE, the HEFCE and the Research Councils – do not recognise that what is going on in the knowledge society is a typical example of the diffusion of innovation, and that universities must be part of this. Even less do they understand how to orchestrate a diffusion process effectively. This remark is less critical than it may sound. The basic ethos of a civil service is to inculcate non-innovatory thinking and practice, since the task of all but the most-senior civil servants is to devise conventional rules and apply them strictly. The problem is that, because of the culture which they have absorbed, those at the top in Whitehall find it difficult to respond to the need to open up, even to dismantle, centralised systems so that innovation can take place.

This applies to universities as much as any other sector. Radical innovation cannot be managed from the centre. Experimentation is needed to create a diversity of institutions and that means pluralism. In the UK, perhaps ten – even twenty – of the current 120 universities and colleges should be encouraged (and funded) to experiment, to develop and run the university of the 21st century. (And perhaps a group of knowledge entrepreneurs from outside universities should be asked to put in their own bid.) These bids should show how they would create a vision of such a university and put it into effect; to set objectives for genuinely innovative teaching and research by drawing on research in cognitive science; to use the emerging ICTs imaginatively; to encourage specialisation, even in less-prestigious fields like teaching and scholarship to open themselves up to more outside influences, including those of knowledge businesses; and, to find more effective ways of disseminating their messages and so influencing the outside world.

The results of such experimentation should be captured by a parallel, high-quality research programme and be made widely (and quickly) known in imaginative ways to other universities, which should be encouraged to adopt the lessons and models which appear to them most appropriate. This sounds messy and dangerous, but that is what innovative processes are.

No regulator can carry out this role well. Too few of them, and too few of their top teams, are good enough lateral thinkers or futurologists to stay ahead of a rapidly challenging world. Even those who work inside a university will find it difficult to know the right course for their own university to take. Indeed, there may be no one 'right' course. So long as there is a regulatory system, the proposal in my two previous paragraphs is the basis for a solution. But, in the end, it will not be enough. The best pluralistic system is a market system, not a regulated one.

I have therefore gone on, in the past, to argue that we should reduce the role of HEFCE to one of providing grants for students (see Hague, 1991). Students would then pay their own fees, which would provide most of the university income, though some students might receive grants to help them to pay those fees. Students would choose which university to attend, and would have both a bigger opportunity and a bigger incentive, to influence what it provided. Universities would have to explain carefully what they were offering to students and why, and would then be free to design and redesign what they did without regulatory supervision. But the freedom to do that would be accompanied by the freedom to go out of business. When the first university fails we should not regret it. Human capital must circulate if the knowledge society is to thrive (Dearing, 1997).

As I finally revise this chapter, the Dearing Report takes the argument of a long way in my direction. As well as proposing that in future modest fees should be paid by all students as argued above, Dearing proposes that Britain should move 'in a planned way' towards 'a target of distributing at least 60 per cent of total public funding to institutions according to student choice by 2003' (Dearing, 1997). What is not yet clear, and what is essential, is that universities which can attract more students under this system must be allowed to expand in order to take them, even if that means that others languish and fail.

We do not know yet how the government will react to Dearing's proposal or, if it accepts it, what its timetable for reaching the 60 per cent target will be. In any case, because all this will take time, I press my proposal for experimentation to create 21st century universities.

There is a final important point. If we do move towards a 'market' system, it will be essential to give as much information as possible about the current offerings and plans, strengths and weaknesses, of universities to their potential clients – 'clients' not 'students' because of the importance of lifelong learning. The 'market' would then work better, giving the ultimate degree of pluralism in decision making (Hague, 1991).

The Dearing Report recognises this but believes that it is for 'representative bodies' of students, universities etc. to identify 'better information' for students and disseminate it quickly (Dearing Report, 1997). For those who accept my arguments this typically cosy, centralised process will not be enough. Markets need pluralism of information as well as of operation. For example, the university 'market' would need independent, clear sighted and hard-hitting 'Good University' guides. Unless supplemented by such information for potential students, the process Dearing envisages will not enable market pressures to transform the university system to meet the opportunities and pressures I have outlined.

Concluding remarks

Despite these doubts, I had never expected to end this study so optimistically. If money is going to 'follow the student' I can turn round my initial question. We can ask not what education system there will be to regulate. We can ask whether any regulatory system for higher education will remain by, say, 2010. That is a tremendous advance.

Acknowledgement

This chapter draws on papers presented to a private seminar of the Committee of Vice Chancellors and Principals in London in February, 1996; to a Forum of World Leaders in Higher Education at the City University of Hong Kong in July 1997 and to a Conference of the

Swedish National Agency for Higher Education in Sweden in September, 1997. All of these are unpublished.

References

Bruer, J. T. (1994) *Schools for Thought: A Science of Learning in the Classroom*, Massachusetts Institute of Technology, MIT Press.

Daniel, J. S. (1996) *Mega-Universities and the Knowledge Industries*, London: Kegan Paul.

Dearing, R. (1997) *Higher Education in the Learning Society: Report of a National Committee of Enquiry*, London: HMSO.

Financial Times (1997a) 11 March.

Financial Times (1997b) 18 June.

Financial Times (1993) 17 March.

Frank, R. H. and Cook, P. J. (1995) *The Winner Takes All Society: why the few at the top get so much more than the rest of us*, New York: Penguin.

Gell, M. and Cochrane, P. (1996) 'Learning and Education in an Information Society' in W. H. Dutton (ed.) *Information and Communications Technologies: Visions and Realities*, Oxford: Oxford University Press.

Hague (1991) 'Beyond Universities', Hobart Paper 115, *Institute of Economic Affairs*, p. 75.

Hague, D. (1996) 'The Firm as a University' DEMOS Quarterly Issue 8.96, p. 22.

Laurillard, D. (1993) *Rethinking University Teaching: A Framework for the Effective Use of Educational Technology*, London and New York: Routledge 1993.

Meister, J. (1996) 'Corporate Universities', *Computer Careers*, 15 July.

5

Can Managed Public Science Enhance Wealth and Quality of Life? A Process Industries' View

Richard C. Darton

Introduction

The UK government spends about £3.1 billion on civil research every year (HMSO, 1995). This is a large sum of money, and the taxpayers – and on their behalf the government – are entitled to ask whether this is money well spent. To ask this question presumes that there must be an objective for the expenditure, against which the benefits of research can be measured. In the past, the objectives of government-funded research may have been many, diffuse and not explicitly formulated. Spenders of government cash are sometimes advantaged by lack of objectives – it makes it much easier to continue the expenditure! However, in the *Realising our Potential* White Paper of 1993, these objectives were clearly stated: government expenditure on the science and engineering base was to enhance the nation's wealth creating potential, and/or to improve the quality of life of its citizens (HMSO, 1993). We can loosely call these the *health* and *wealth* criteria. (In this convenient shorthand we understand that 'health' also includes environmental health, and those intangible aspects of human existence that contribute to a good quality of life.)

In this study we look at public policy towards science and engineering R&D and the consequence of a more structured approach, from the perspective of one particular industrial sector, the process industries.

R&D position of the process industries

The process industries have a dominant position in the funding of industrial R&D in this country. The top five UK spenders on R&D all have an essential process element in their business (Glaxo-Wellcome, SmithKline Beecham, Unilever, Zeneca, Shell). The R&D spend by these five companies together (£2994 million) was 40 per cent of the total spend by UK companies on R&D in 1994 (Company Reporting Limited, 1995). Only a little further down the list we encounter companies like ICI, BP and many others whose R&D spend is large, and which are important international players in the process industry. In no other industrialised nation do the process industries play this role. For example, in Japan the top five R&D spenders are electronics and IT companies; in the USA the top five are General Motors, Ford, IBM, AT&T and Hewlett Packard. Germany does have the pharmaceutical/fine chemicals companies Hoechst and Bayer at position three and four, but the top spenders are Siemens and Daimler Benz. Only perhaps in Switzerland, where the ABB engineering group is followed by Hoffmann La Roche, Ciba-Geigy, Sandoz and Nestle, do the process industries approach the same dominance.

The process industries are a crucial part of the UK's economic strength. In 1992 the chemicals and pharmaceuticals sector contributed a positive £3.5 billion to the balance of trade, the largest of any sector, and 50 per cent larger than the next positive contributor (aerospace). The sector is, by nature, international, very highly competitive, and highly reliant on technology. It may therefore be instructive to examine how the sector views R&D. Of course, within such a large group of businesses there will be a wide variety of views, but a particularly well-informed view was put forward in the 1993 Danckwerts lecture, by Dr H. L. Beckers, an adviser to the European Commission and the Dutch government on research policy, and previously a director of Shell Research. Some quotations will illustrate the position:

> Firstly the simple objective of industrial R&D is to put the company in a position to be technically capable of being better than its competitors in providing services and products. To put it more bluntly, to be able to kill its competitors. It is as simple as that.
>
> Therefore judging an industrial research project on its quality and originality alone, as is often done by academic experts for, as an example, EC or government funding is utterly wrong.
>
> Naturally, companies will not be inclined to set up research cooperations with their competitors. It is done only when it fits the company strategy ... .
>
> ... government officials, used to the culture of their academic advisors, rightly consider research co-operation and personnel

exchange between the various research institutes or universities to be a natural and good thing to do. But they often wrongly think that that must be true in industry too.

Unfortunately, in many discussions on industrial innovation within the triangular circles of governments, universities and industries, the attention is often focused much more on R&D ... than on how to handle the technological capabilities of the company. It is often forgotten that there is a lot of technology available in the world and that the problem of companies, and not only smaller ones, is really how to get hold of and deal with the existing technologies (Beckers, 1993).

Thus, in the commercial sector, R&D policy is as much a part of company strategy as marketing or manufacturing policy, with very clear objectives of competitive edge and profitability. The objectives, and the methods, of industrial R&D are completely different to those in universities and the non-profit sector.

Recent changes and pronouncements may seem to have weakened this basic difference between commercial and publicly funded research. Many companies have responded to intense commercial pressure by downsizing their in-house technical effort, and have announced plans to rely more on contractors, consultants, universities and others, for technical support, and even new technology. They have shed researching areas outside their core businesses, or where small gains only can be expected. Thus between 1993 and 1994, seven of the nine oil majors reduced their R&D expenditure, in total by an average of 10 per cent (and BP by a massive 48 per cent). However, within this policy it will be found that companies that have a competitive edge in the technology of a business that is important to them, will still do all they can to maintain and increase it. R&D may be more carefully targeted, but it is still intensely competitive and a part of overall company strategy.

The foresight process

In the 'Forward Look' survey of government-funded R&D, the distinct roles of government and industry are clearly stated:

Government funds basic research which is conducted without a specific end in view ....

R&D which aims to secure specific commercial advantages should be funded by industry and commerce....

but can one detect a slight hesitation in the justification of more commercial direction of the government's funding role? Here it is:

> However public funding may be justified in circumstances where investments in commercial R&D offer a good economic return to the nation but not to an individual firm and in order to ensure that the United Kingdom is competing on a level global playing field. (HMSO, 1995)

There is no mention in Beckers' lecture that industry is looking, or should look, to publicly financed research for the technological breakthroughs that will support and enhance business profitability. The emphasis is rather on universities as a source of skilled manpower for industry to use. This represents perhaps the most detached view. The 'Foresight' process has encouraged the expectation that university research will deliver new technology to industry. Although not all industrialists share this expectation, most will echo the words of Sir William Barlow, President of the Royal Academy of Engineering, commenting on the direction of government funding towards the *health and wealth* objectives: 'In my view, the assessment of policy will benefit greatly from those who understand the global markets the research should address' (Barlow, 1993). In other words, industrial priorities, should at the very least, influence decisions on government civil R&D expenditure.

The process industries welcomed the Foresight process, and from its first reports identified the following key themes:

- the importance of government funding to maintain the basic science and engineering infrastructure,
- the need to encourage more multidisciplinary R&D,
- the benefits of engineering and quantitative concepts in developing business processes,
- the importance of the process/product interface,
- the importance of the links between education and research, including the education of the public. (IChemE, 1995)

However, Foresight has been subtitled 'Progress through Partnership', and this partnership between organisations that have fundamentally different objectives, as discussed above, is important. The idea that Foresight will allow industry to set its own goals for academic research seems dangerous for several reasons, not least that it will create expectations that cannot be delivered. The idea does have currency though.

This statement appeared in a recent collaborative research proposal from industry: 'It is exciting because, for the first time, we the technology users and suppliers, will be in a position to influence and direct the way that academic research and development is conducted ....

Collaborative research

There are a number of reasons why a company should want, on occasion, to collaborate in joint, publishable, research with a university. Here are some:

(a) Early access. Results will be accessible considerably before they are seen by non-participating competitors. This can be a significant benefit to a company that has, in any case, been closely monitoring the work in progress.
(b) Staff training. The company's own staff has close contact with researchers at the cutting edge, keeping them abreast of new developments.
(c) Facilitating recruitment. Excellent contacts within the academic community are a great help at spotting and attracting new staff.
(d) Cost sharing. Government agencies and sometimes commercial competitors share the bill, which is thus much cheaper than in-house effort.

Of course there are benefits to the university too, so there are many examples of mutually beneficial collaborations, some lasting very many years. Given the encouragement of a programme like Foresight, through which facilitating funds are being supplied, many more will spring up.

Larger companies in the UK process sector enjoy excellent relations with academia, having supported teaching programmes and underwritten professional and training activities for staff. The process sector is the largest industrial employer of PhDs in the UK. However it does not have a strong tradition of direct support of university research, or at least, not in proportion to its size and profitability. It is hard to say why this should be so. A very strong in-house R&D capability has perhaps reduce the need for outside effort. Possibly the absence of government as a purchaser in this sector (compare aerospace, defence electronics) has led to a more competitive and self-reliant R&D culture.

Whatever the reason, there has been an effect on that part of the university sector which looks particularly to the process industries for support: departments of chemical and process engineering, of which there are 23 accredited in the UK, some of them very small. Various Foresight panels called for multidisciplinary research in areas like catalysis, new materials, biotechnology, environmental matters, but there is a real concern that the academic research base is too small to meet all these demands, and take the necessary initiatives. One of the benefits of Foresight is the light it has shed on the relative strengths and weaknesses of elements in the science and engineering base. In this particular case it may result in steps by funding agencies to strengthen the UK's academic process engineering capability. Currently EPSRC's process engineering programme takes about four per cent of its total programme expenditure (HMSO, 1995).

An alternative system?

Another perspective is obtained from asking the question: if we were to start anew spending £3.1 billion on research each year with the objectives of enhancing wealth and improving quality of life, how would we organise this expenditure? What would a purpose-built system for publicly financed research look like? This seems a rather sweeping and extreme question, but in fact, if governments, acting for society, consistently and over a long period, pursue the same *health and wealth* criteria, then we will slowly evolve a new science and engineering base that is geared to deliver to these objectives.

One feature of the new system would, I guess, be a much smaller role for the individual university professor or lecturer who is also a principal investigator with a research grant. Attempts to manage this widely dispersed and heterogeneous group of researchers towards set goals will certainly lead to considerable difficulties, since the system has not been designed for such management. Three year grants are the norm, and the trend is towards even shorter term funding. Much research is therefore carried out by students or assistants on a steep learning curve, with no job security. What company would tolerate an average turnover of research staff of 30 per cent? Or what company would spread its R&D effort over more than 100 institutions in a country the size of the UK? Or what company would be able to divorce decisions on programme funding, from the management problems that swings in such funding bring with them?

From the academic side it is already difficult to balance the parallel demands of teaching, research and administration. It seems likely that there would be increased specialisation (in the biological sense), with some academic staff concentrating on teaching, and some on research. Of course, this already happens, but it would become the rule, driven by the needs of both funding bodies and universities to concentrate resources to maximum effect. We would see most research done in 'research units', 'research centres' and 'research institutes', many of which would have a tenuous link with universities, or no link at all. Such centres would deliver specific research programmes, probably to a mixture of government and industry clients, both at home and abroad.

The advantages of developing this professional and full-time research activity are certainly many. Such centres would deliver research in an effective way, geared to the *health and wealth* criteria, with no distractions of student counselling, examinations, lectures, etc. They would be able to offer professional, and moderately secure careers to research staff. By providing centres of excellence they would have the advantage of economy of scale, and an enhanced ability to compete internationally for funds, and people.

However, there may also be disadvantages. We would lose the enthusiasm and iconoclasm that young researchers bring to their research when working in a university environment, that is almost impossible to recreate in a commercial setting. We would also miss the link between teaching and research, where the discipline of teaching continually forces the researcher to re-examine the principles of his subject, and undergraduates are exposed to the excitements of new technology developing around them.

Finally, perhaps there is the warning of previous example. Very many such institutes exist around the world, and without denigrating the excellent science and engineering they produce, it is clear that they do have intrinsic problems. Institutes that are heavily reliant on government funds must spend effort on tracking the policy and spending decisions, and trying to influence them. Such institutes lack a 'home', and can experience severe problems when funds dry up. Heavy commercial involvement can also result in avoidance of innovation, as the industrial partners look nervously at the loss of competitive edge that joint programmes can involve. There are several examples of this problem in the research institutes funded by the process industries.

The international dimension

Companies in the process sector are mostly highly international in character, able to choose the locations of their activities independently of national borders. Decisions about the location of R&D activities are complex, but at least one factor is the availability of highly skilled manpower. The number of countries able to offer advanced science and engineering skills is growing, especially in regions like SE Asia which also offer high rates of market growth to attract company interest. In this competition to provide the best science and engineering infrastructure, we are highly dependent on government policy on research, and on education.

UK government funding agencies have not always been happy with supporting activities, such as joint research programmes, in which the industrial partner, because of its multinational character, might be perceived as 'foreign'. This can be a problem in the process sector, where so many of the major players fall into this category. After all, company X may have major R&D and manufacturing facilities in the UK, but for the particular project of interest the collaborating industrial engineer may be located in Germany, or the USA. Should the UK public purse then support a joint R&D project, most of which will be located in the UK, but the results of which will be used globally? Such R&D does not fall squarely into the remit from 'Forward Look 1995', quoted above, for government funding. And yet, if such projects are not supported, in the longer term the UK's research base suffers, as the work is done elsewhere.

Understandably the European Community R&D support programmes have been more tolerant of 'foreign' involvement, having indeed an international base to support, and an international outlook. The problem here has been, in the view of trade organisations like CIA and CEFIC, that the process industries have received far less than their 'fair share' of community supported R&D, compared with, say, aerospace or information technology. This is a serious criticism, as the process industries are hugely important to the Community. The EU is the world's largest manufacturing area for chemicals, with a turnover in 1993 of $350 billion (Chemical Industries Association, 1995). The European manufacturing sector is showing a relentless shift away from cheaply produced bulk products towards those with higher added value. This is a technology-intensive process, in which the European area had an initial competitive advantage which could easily be lost through failing to invest in the science and engineering base underpinning the technology shift.

Conclusions

More openness about the direction and funding of government financed research has given industry a welcome chance to influence spending priorities. Partnerships between industry and academia are now receiving more encouragement. Nevertheless, because of competitive pressures, the process industries do not look to academia for breakthroughs in technology, rather for a strengthening of the general infrastructure and the supply of skilled manpower. These are essential to maintain the UK as a leading player in the international process sector. Consistent pursuit of the *health* and *wealth* criteria for government funding will reveal the difficulties of trying to manage academic research towards specific goals, and lead to change in the system to facilitate achievement of these goals. The consequences of such changes for the whole system, need to be carefully considered.

Acknowledgement

I am grateful to the colleagues at Shell, at Oxford and within the Institution of Chemical Engineers, who have helped to form my views on these subjects. Nevertheless, these remain my own personal views, and are not those of any organisation.

References

Barlow, W. (1993) *National Prosperity: the role of the Engineer* Presidential Address. Royal Academy of Engineering.
Beckers, H. L. (1993) 'Industrial R&D and competition. Seventh P. V. Danckwerts memorial lecture' *Chem Eng Sci* 48(8) 1359.
Chemical Industries Association (1995) *Chemical Industry Research Priorities.*
Company Reporting Limited (1995) *The 1995 UK R&D Scoreboard.*
HMSO (1993) *Realising our Potential* White Paper Cm2250.
HMSO (1995) *Forward Look 1995.*
IChemE (1995) *Technology Foresight. Process through partnership* vols 1–15, London: Office of Science and Technology, HMSO.

III

The International Context

6

The Evolution of European Science and Technology Policy and its Links to the Cohesion Agenda

David R. Charles

Introduction

There have been considerable shifts in EC/EU[1] approaches to policy supporting science and technology since its real emergence in the early 1980s, with a complex and non-trivial relationship with the cohesion argument. As with other spatial policies, technology policies often appear to operate to the detriment of objectives to enhance social and economic cohesion, but in recent years there has been action within the EU to re-direct at least part of technology policy to better address the needs of the less favoured countries and regions (LFRs). There remain considerable tensions however, especially between the need to achieve cohesion and the perceived needs of industrial competitiveness at the EU scale.

Initial EC approaches to science and technology policy were seen as addressing the need for the Community to support centrally certain areas of science where national governments could not meet the scale requirements, and where the results of the research could meet another objective of the EC, e.g. nuclear power meeting energy policy objectives. This policy was broadly enlarged in the early to mid 1980s on three fronts: to support strategic technologies where the EC was being left behind (e.g. IT), to work in areas where a common public interest could be identified (e.g. environment), and to encourage international co-operation and mobility within the science community. The latter began to address certain issues of cohesion, but the prime concern was still support for scientific excellence on a pan-European basis.

In the late 1980s partly arising from the third enlargement (Spain and Portugal) and the need to raise research and technological development (RTD) in the LFRs some of these developments were strengthened. In the strategic technologies there was a shift in emphasis towards the application area rather than the foundation innovations, although the continued crisis in the competitiveness of the major EC IT firms has led to some vacillation over the best means for providing support. The scope of the Framework Programme in areas such as the environment and health was broadened considerably, with new fields of competence being introduced. Finally, in the interests of cohesion, the mobility and training element has been considerably expanded. In parallel with these developments of the Framework Programme however has been the growth of a large number of complementary policies in technology transfer, in the dissemination of research results, and in supporting RTD activities at the regional level. There remains a question as to how the anti-cohesion aspects of the Framework Programme might be moderated or counterbalanced by these other activities, although the member states in the European South retain ambitions in gaining more direct benefits from the main research programmes.

This chapter reviews these trends in the RTD policy of the Community (now Union) through to the late 1990s, and the parallel response from the Structural Funds which are used to support the less favoured regions, and which have begun to take on an RTD dimension. The conflicts between these two key policy agenda within Europe are brought out and discussed, before a final section outlining the future shape of the technology policy arena, in the light of current plans, through into the new century.

Evolution of European technology policy – the importance of the excellence criterion

Until the mid 1980s the evolution and development of EC technology policy was strongly oriented to the raising of European capacity for high quality and large scale R&D. As such a fundamental criterion in the support of particular developments and projects was that of scientific excellence. The enshrinement of the excellence criterion was thus to become a major problem on enlargement of the Community and the consideration of cohesion issues.

Origins in the treaties

At the outset there was only very limited provision for the support for science in the treaties establishing the European Communities, with no mention at all within the Treaty of Rome which established the European Economic Community. However, Jean Monnet had foreseen a European Technological Community within his Action Committee for a United States of Europe, although it was to be many years before such a foundation for action was laid in the revisions to the treaties (Sharp, 1991).

There was some provision for RTD though in the European Coal and Steel Community (ECSC) Treaty in 1955, in the very specific form of coal and steel research. This was further extended with the signing of the Euratom Treaty in 1957 (Stubbs and Saviotti, 1994), which committed the Community to the establishment of the Joint Research Centre (JRC) as a major in-house research facility, initially to develop new techniques for nuclear fission energy generation, although this remit was significantly extended in the 1970s to focus on nuclear safety and on alternative energy sources. The role of the Joint Nuclear Research Centre as it was then known was a practical concern to design nuclear reactors, although such commercial objectives were met with failure. As a result the experience of the JRC tarnished the perceptions of such international collaborations, but also as a long term research facility set the foundations for a policy of pre-competitive research at the European scale.

Bilateral arrangements during the 1960s

The 1960s were a period of strong national technology and industrial policies and consequently there was little attempt to develop the EEC competence in research. The Treaty of Rome required a unanimous decision of the Council of Ministers to exceed those powers specified, leaving technology policy out in the cold. The industrial affairs brief of DG III was only introduced in 1967, and at that subject to debate between interventionist and liberal stances (Sharp, 1991). Instead collaborative technology policy was pursued at a bilateral level between countries.

During the 1960s, although a time of great expansion in natural science and technology policy, and especially in public financing, international collaboration was also growing in the more expensive fields of technology, such as aerospace. Such one-off bilateral collaborations between state-backed companies set the scene for the emergence of new intergovernmental alliances, the most significant of which was in the field of space exploration where a series of European consortia were assembled (ELDO, ESRO, ESA). Another key step was the formation of COST (European Co-operation in the field of Scientific and Technical Research) in 1971, as a committee of government officials that sought to stimulate collaboration, and included all OECD members in Europe rather than just EC members. COST stimulated a number of collaboration programmes with relatively small additional funds for exchanges and meetings to share the results of research and avoid excessive duplication of effort.

Collaboration was not limited to the sharing of the costs and risks of expensive research however, and it was recognised that there was a need for collaboration in the structuring markets and regulation to encourage European innovation. The need to apply for a patent for each country in Europe in order to protect intellectual property posed significant costs and barriers on European companies relative to those operating in large single markets such as the USA. To reduce these costs and simplify procedures it was proposed that a single European patent could be issued by a central European Patent Office (EPO), which would be defensible in all signatory countries, and agreed by a European Patent Convention in 1973. The EPO was established in 1977 with a membership drawn from the European Community, but outside of its institutional structures and with the inclusion of non-EC members (Stubbs and Saviotti, 1994).

Despite the emergence of a European Community policy in the early 1980s, such bilateral and multilateral agreements have continued, notably with the EUREKA programme. Launched in 1985, following the initiative of the French government, EUREKA is a framework within which groups of European countries can grant aid companies to collaborate in relatively near market development projects.[2] As such EUREKA does not require any pooling of sovereignty in funding or decision-making, but it provides a mechanism for bilateral and multi-lateral collaboration (Petersen, 1991, 1993).

Emergence of a 'common policy'

From 1967, with the first meeting of the Council of Science Ministers, the Community looked to expand the scope of support for RTD, beginning with studies on transport, oceanography, metallurgy, the environment, IT and telecommunications. Whilst these plans were hampered by wider issues such as the first enlargement (to include the UK, Ireland and Denmark), and failings in the development of industrial policy, the main emphasis of debate over Community technology policy at this time was the response to the growing power of US technology, and especially IBM. There was also an emerging disenchantment with the national dirigiste policies of the 1960s, the national champions or 'winners' picked for public support had mainly under-performed, protected from excessive foreign competition by non-tariff trade barriers, and feather-bedded against internal competition by virtue of policy. Policy interests therefore shifted away from direct intervention in market structures to a more supply-side policy on framework conditions for all firms, including support for generic technologies across a wider community of firms (Stubbs and Saviotti, 1994).

The last throws of the old policy emerged in a Council of Ministers Resolution in 1974 to initiate a medium term programme on data-processing which was to underpin proposals to merge the computing interests of Siemens, Olivetti and CII-Bull in a European champion. The failure of Unidata, as the venture was to have been named, led to a reduction in the scope of the support, and a postponement of significant new funds until the early 1980s. However, there were a number of other institutional developments that set the scene for a full blown EC science and technology policy.

In 1974 the Council had decided to progressively develop a 'common policy in the field of science and technology' with the combination of a co-ordination of national policies plus the development of a new set of research programmes of EC interest. Underpinning this was the establishment of three expert committees (CREST, CODEST and IRDAC)[3] which would advise on the fields to be supported.

Implementation of the Council's intentions proved difficult due to the lack of obvious funds, but in 1977 the Commission produced a set of guidelines which suggested support for four main themes of research for 1977–80 (CEC, 1977)

- Securing the long-term supply of resources – notably raw materials, energy, agriculture and water
- Promote internationally competitive economic development
- Improvement of living and working conditions
- Protection of the environment and nature

In addition, a number of criteria for support were specified. First, Community intervention was justified where there was a possibility for international level rationalisation and increased efficiency through action at the EC level. This was anticipated particularly in those areas where there were high costs or a need for large scale of research, such that individual member states would find it difficult to meet the costs.

Secondly, there had to be a need for transnational action, so that the Community was only funding research that would not be capable of being undertaken at national level: in other words they were not infringing on subsidiarity. Another prime criterion for support was that the Community faced intense international competition, and therefore research would underpin the economic success of member states. This was linked to the need to spread development costs within many industries where rising costs and the fragmented nature of the EC market penalised European firms compared with US firms with a large domestic market. Related to this also was the need to develop common standards, and the EC has sponsored a number of programmes to develop common standards as a means of underpinning the emergence of new markets. Finally there was a need for programmes to meet common national requirements, rather than just the needs of one member state, but also to address threats such as environmental problems that affected several states and where collaboration was required. Arising from these criteria a number of small programmes did emerge, although more importantly the criteria set the conditions for a more fundamental rethink of the European dimension to technology policy.

The external trade threat and the IT industry

The main motivation for a revival of a determined effort to support industrial technology came with the declining competitiveness of the European IT sector at the onset of the 1980s and a perceived widening of the technology gap between European and US/Japan. As a result the large member states were also seeking to launch major national industrial R&D programmes such as the Alvey Programme in the UK, and the Plan Calcul in France. These, and the success of the Japanese collaborative programmes on IT in the late 1970s, prompted the response in Europe, with Etienne D'Avignon, Commissioner for Industry, bringing together a round table of the major European companies in 1979, to discuss a European response.

The IT Round Table[4] were unsympathetic to ideas of further state-led restructuring, but supported the idea of collaborative research, a view also shared in a separate informal group of large firms arguing for the end to nationally based systems of subsidies, trade barriers and R&D programmes in favour of a more collaborative approach.

Here though was the critical policy conflict. EC Competition policy makes no differentiation between collaboration for the purposes of direct market supply, and common ownership as a result of merger. So collaboration between major firms could not be allowed in cases where merger between those firms would not be permitted because of their market dominance. Yet in order to launch a collaborative research programme involving the Community's biggest firms such partnerships were desirable. The way around this conflict was the limitation of collaboration to the permitted activity of pre-competitive research i.e. that research which does not immediately lead to marketable products, and where all parties can go on to develop competing products in the marketplace. This point was crucial in that a restriction was placed on the programmes which was designed to enable the participation of the larger firms, whilst placing entry barriers to smaller firms in that they had to be willing and able to part-fund pre-competitive research for which there was no immediate payback. Using this manoeuvre the European Strategic Programme for Research and Development in Information Technology (ESPRIT) was proposed in 1980.

Launch of ESPRIT

The revised ESPRIT proposal was finally presented for approval in 1982, and the Council of Ministers gave the go-ahead for a pilot programme of 11.5 million ECU. This first tranche of 38 projects, culled from 200 proposals, commenced in late 1983 and consisted of a combination of large firms, SMEs, universities and public research centres, but with 70 per cent of resources going to the Club of Twelve large firms. The perceived success of this pilot programme overcame the reservations of member states and was swiftly followed by the approval of 750 million ECU for a main phase ESPRIT I programme for 1984–88 (with prior commitment to a second five year programme), and a huge response to the initial calls for proposals. This main phase focused on microelectronics, advanced information processing, software technology, computer-integrated manufacturing and office systems and involved 227 projects with 240 companies and 180 universities and research institutes.

Parallel programmes

ESPRIT was quickly followed by a host of other specific programmes in what Stubbs and Saviotti (1994) term a tribe of acronyms (RACE, BRITE, BRIDGE, BAP, ECLAIR, FLAIR, AIM etc.).[5] Each of these programmes followed the same basic model of pre-competitive research involving collaborations between firms, universities and other institutes, in at least two member states. These other programmes were all smaller than ESPRIT and often more heterogeneous participants: many involved a range of types of firms along a supply chain, including small customer firms from traditional sectors. However the basic principles of scientific or technological excellence remained sacrosanct.

The R&D programmes were soon to be joined by a set of supporting actions such as the training based programmes COMETT and ERASMUS, which were intended to promote the international mobility of students as well as strengthening the internationalisation of training. And throughout these developments there was continuing support for the JRC in Energy.

With the legislative pressure introduced by the demand to introduce such a number of parallel programmes the Commission sought agreement for the idea of a Framework Programme in which overall approval of a set of action could be obtained, building on concepts of Research Action Programmes for specific themes or areas of technology as was already in existence. In 1983 this was accepted in principle by Council, and the First Framework Programme was approved as a set of outline objectives although the budget for each individual action programme was being debated individually throughout 1984.

Orientation

The formula that was developed was aimed at addressing a certain range of problems by the use of a specific type of programme, with an eye to the question of subsidiarity. Thus the programme was to support only pre-competitive collaborative research, drawing together firms, public research organisations and higher education. This limitation of EC involvement to pre-competitive research enabled DGs XII and XIII to avoid direct conflict with competition policy on state aids, although the question of how firms use the EC research funds remains an area of debate.

Furthermore, excellence was seen as a prime concern, and led to the major conflict with the regional policies, in that it was the leading firms and universities in the core countries of the community that were able to best justify their participation in this measure. Although not explicit, and often disputed, the programmes have had the effect therefore of providing most support to the larger firms, to some extent tacitly acknowledging the existence of a set of EC champions in place of the former national champions.

Although usually neglected in reviews of EC RTD actions, the pre-normative role of much of the technological research is also extremely important. By pre-normative, what is implied is that the Commission is using its RTD funds to support firms that are engaged in carrying out research into new forms of industrial standards, such as open systems interconnection (OSI) standards for the IT industry, or telecommunication standards for ISDN or broadband transmission, or even standards for television broadcasting. The intended output of this work is therefore of a wider application to a whole industry of potential users, although participants in the pre-normative research project may gain an advantage, and can impress their internal standards on the wider industry.

The Commission uses pre-normative research as an element of industrial policy, (see CEC 1990, 1991) in that by arguing in favour of the early development of public and open standards, rather than allowing the development of proprietary standards, it is defending European industry from the potential threat of lock-out positions. What would be undesirable would be if major non-European firms were able to gain a dominant position in the European market as a consequence of a proprietary standard, which European competitors could only use in return for high royalty payments. The success of this policy has been noted in areas like mobile telephony where European firms have succeeded commercially on the basis of a large harmonised market for GSM phones, whilst in the USA the market has been riven by fragmented propriety standards.

Thus it is clear that the direction of EC technology policies when extended to industrial applications have been primarily intended to enhance the competitiveness of the larger firms with existing technological resources. Whilst smaller firms and those in the LFRs have been able to participate in the programmes, their involvement has often been a token effort, and in some case has added legitimacy to the development of industry standards based on the orientation of the dominant European firms.

RTD policy and the single European Act of 1987

The Single European Act (SEA) of 1987 provided a considerable step forward in a number of different policy areas of the Community, reinforcing many adopted practices and policy areas, and extending the competence of Community institutions in order to facilitate the development of a Single European Market. A key difference from the original Treaty of Rome was the introduction of a new section on Research and Technological Development (Title VI) in which it was stated that:

> The Community's aim shall be to strengthen the scientific and technological base of Europe's industry and to encourage it to become more competitive at international level.

In order to do this, it shall encourage undertakings including small and medium-sized undertakings, research centres and universities in their research and technological developments; it shall support their efforts to exploit the Community's internal market potential to the full, in particular through the opening up of national public contracts, the definition of common standards and the removal of legal and fiscal barriers to that co-operation.

In the achievement of these aims, special account shall be taken of the connection between the common research and technological development effort, the establishment of the internal market and the implementation of common policies, particularly as regards competition and trade (Article 130f).

The SEA specified a number of means by which a common RTD policy was to be implemented formalising the modalities established in the various programmes that had been running in previous years. One specific action to streamline decision-making was the introduction of the concept of a Framework Programme as a multi-annual agreed framework for priorities and budgets, within which individual technology programmes could be negotiated and reshaped on the basis of qualified majority rather than unanimity. The Framework Programme structure brought a number of advantages, in addition to the procedural benefits of qualified majority voting. It provided a platform for debate on the orientation and priorities within the EC's RTD programmes, and made more visible the degree of concentration of funding on particular programmes. It also allowed the operation of programmes that involved only some member states, and the flexible inclusion of non-members. Consequently programme negotiation has become a two stage process, with a drawn-out setting of priorities and lines of action for each Framework Programme, now extending over several years, and almost being a continuous negotiation between political and expert interests. In contrast the individual programmes are shaped by a more restricted technical community without the same level of political involvement, and hence with greater flexibility if at the cost of a degree of path dependence. Consequently there has been both an increasing sophistication of prioritisation of technology areas, as can be seen by the evolution of programme areas over time, plus a framework whereby member states could negotiate the inclusion or scale of specific technology fields of national interest. Thus direct trades can be made for the inclusion of marine technology or aerospace at an outline level separately from the later negotiations over the detailed structure of action programmes.

Another major development of the SEA is the recognition that support for science and technology goes beyond industrial competitiveness, thus opening the way for a more cohesion friendly policy. Indeed the Commission argued in its proposals for the Second Framework Programme that the Single Act had:

> legitimized, as it were, the Community dimension of technological cooperation by linking it closely with the other objectives geared to the attainment of a genuine European economic area, i.e., mass market without frontiers, economic and social cohesion. European Monetary System and social policy. (CEC, 1986)

Comparison of the first four framework programmes

In the account above we have noted the expansion of Community involvement in RTD from origins in energy and an initial high commitment to IT in the early 1980s. With the development of subsequent Framework Programmes there has been a gradual expansion of the scope of support in terms of areas of technology or theme and also the kinds of actions supported. There has also been a steady increase in budgetary allocations.

The growth in the budget over the period has been quite dramatic, both in absolute figures and as a proportion of the Community budget. Using 1992 prices, the Community budget for R&D has climbed over a decade from less than 1 billion ECUs per annum to near 3 billion, with the biggest boost coming in 1992 with the overlap between the second and third Framework Programmes (Table 6.1). The step increases in the budget at various points indicates the effect of the Framework Programme approach in that each programme provides a budget to be allocated during the life of that programme, but this is typically done through a series of calls for proposals, such that many projects only start as a programme reaches its end and consequently run over into the time period for the following programme. As a proportion of total

Table 6.1: Community expenditure on RTD 1985 to 1997

Year	Community Budget Appropriations for RTD (Million ECU, 1992 Prices)	Community RTD Expenditure as a percentage of total Community Expenditure
1985	991.9	2.43
1986	1 139.5	2.24
1987	1 186	2.75
1988	1 373.9	2.75
1989	1 636.4	3.72
1990	1 978.2	4.06
1991	1 988.9	3.18
1992	2 863.2	3.28
1993	2 651.4	3.49
1994	2 665.4	4.20
1995	2 890.8	3.84
1996	2 958.9	3.78
1997	n.a.	3.81

Source: DG XII-AS4, Data: European Commission Services, (European Commission, 1997).

Community expenditure, growth in RTD expenditure has been less dramatic, peaking at 4.2 per cent in 1994. This must be seen against the background of a dominant share of Community expenditure for the Common Agricultural Policy, and significant increases in Structural Funds also over the same period.

Thematically, the main changes can be seen in Tables 6.2 to 6.5, and are summarised below:

Energy research was highly significant in the first FP with 47 per cent of the budget but has subsequently decreased in importance to only 16 per cent of the third and 18 per cent of the fourth FP. In spite of the decline in percentage of funding there has been a doubling in spend over the period in current prices, with a marked increase in non-nuclear energy.

IT research has been a dominant element throughout the period rising to 42 per cent of the budget of the second FP and declining to 28 per cent in the fourth FP. As with energy, the growth of other areas has led to this relative decline, but the absolute investment has continued to grow with a change in orientation towards applications rather than basic technologies.

Industrial technologies have grown steadily in importance over the period with a number of mechanisms to enhance and encourage SME participation, and to develop applications of technology that are relevant to traditional sectors.

Table 6.2: First Framework Programme 1984 to 1987

	Million ECUs	
1. **Promoting agricultural competitivity**	130	
Agriculture		115
Fisheries		15
2. **Promoting industrial competitivity**	1 060	
Removing and reducing barriers		30
New techniques and products for the traditional industries		350
New technologies (ESPRIT, biotechnologies, telecommunications)		680
3. **Improving the management of raw materials**	80	
4. **Improving the management of energy resources**	1 770	
Nuclear fission		460
Controlled thermonuclear fusion		480
Renewable energy sources		310
Rational use of energy		520
5. **Stepping up development aid**	150	
6. **Improving living and working conditions**	385	
Improving safety and protecting health		190
Protecting the environment		195
7. **Improving the effectiveness of the Community's scientific and technical potential**	85	
8. **Horizontal actions**	90	
Total	**3 750**	

Source: CEC, 1994

Life sciences have also grown steadily over the period, from a minimal position at the outset to 13 per cent in the fourth FP.

Environmental research has remained constant in relative terms, growing at the same rate as the programme as a whole.

A number of new fields have emerged in the fourth FP, notably transport and socio-economic research (European Commission, 1997).

In parallel with such thematic changes have been the introduction of new activities such as the dissemination of the results of research

Table 6.3: Second Framework Programme 1987 to 1991

	Million ECUs	
Quality of life	375	
Health		80
Radiation protection		34
Environment		261
Towards a large market and an information and communication society	2 275	
IT		1 600
Telecommunications		550
New services of common interest including transport		125
Modernization of industrial sectors	845	
Science and technology for manufacturing industry		400
Science and technology of advanced materials		220
Raw materials and recycling		45
Technical standards, measurement, reference materials		180
Exploitation and optimum use of biological resources	280	
Biotechnology		120
Agro-industrial technologies		105
Agricultural competitiveness and resource management		55
Energy	1 173	
Fission; nuclear safety		440
Controlled thermonuclear fusion		611
Non-nuclear energy and rational use of energy		122
Science and technology for development	80	
Marine resources and exploitation of the sea bed	80	
Improvement of European science and technology co-operation	288	
Stimulation, enhancement and use of human resources		180
Forecasting, assessment and other back-up measures		30
Dissemination and utilisation of science and technology results		23
		55
Total	5 396	

Source: CEC, 1994

and technology transfer, and changes in the modalities through which the programmes operate. Such changes are discussed in the next section which considers the effect of the cohesion agenda on RTD policies.

Table 6.4: Third Framework Programme 1990 to 1994

		Millions of ECUs
I.	**Enabling Technologies**	
1.	*Information and communications technologies* 2 491	
	Information technologies	1 517
	Communication technologies	548
	Development of telematics	426
2.	*Industrial and material technologies* 997	
	Industrial and materials	840
	Measurement and testing	157
II.	**Management of Natural Resources**	
3.	*Environment* 581	
	Environment	464
	Marine Sciences	117
4.	*Life sciences and technologies* 831	
	Biotechnology	184
	Agriculture and agro-industry	373
	Biomedical and health	149
	Life sciences for the Third World	125
5.	*Energy* 1 052	
	Non-nuclear	259
	Fission safety	231
	Controlled fusion	562
III.	**Optimisation of Intellectual Resources**	
6.	*Human capital and mobility* 581	
Total		**6 600**

Source: CEC, 1994

Inserting cohesion into technology policy

As the Framework Programme has grown, and especially since the adhesion of Spain and Portugal to the Community with ambitions for an expansion of their RTD base, so greater pressure has been placed on the RTD programmes to spread the resources more widely. This has been paralleled by a growing concern over the results of the programmes, and specifically the extent to which funds are well spent in high risk, high cost projects involving the largest firms. Consequently, the late 1980s saw an expansion of the Framework Programme, with a reorientation of projects, new areas of science being brought in, and a

Table 6.5: Fourth Framework Programme 1994 to 1997

	Millions of ECUs	
First activity (RTD and demonstration programmes)	10 686	
Information and communication technologies		3405
Telematics		843
Communication technologies		630
Information technologies		1932
Industrial technologies	1 995	
Industrial and materials technologies		1707
Measurements and testing		288
Environment	1 080	
Environment and climate		852
Marine sciences and technologies		228
Life sciences and technologies	1 572	
Biotechnology		552
Biomedicine and health		336
Agriculture and fisheries		684
Energy	2 256	
Non-nuclear energy		1002
Nuclear fission safety		414
Controlled thermonuclear fusion		840
Transport	240	
Targeted socio-economic research	138	
Second activity (co-operation with third countries and international organisations)	540	
Third activity (dissemination and optimisation of results)	33	
Fourth activity (stimulation of the training and mobility of esearchers)	744	
Total	12 300	

Source: European Commission DC, XII

greater concern for the distribution of funds both to less favoured countries and to smaller firms.

The need for the Framework Programmes to address issues of cohesion emerged in the background documentation for the first and second Frameworks. However although the first Framework was to create and sustain the conditions for 'joint growth', the second specifically states the objective of strengthening economic and social cohesion. The activities intended to offset the effects of improved competitiveness and assist in strengthening cohesion were the health, environment and researcher mobility schemes, and emphasis was placed on all of the Community benefiting from the research rather than being able to participate in its formation.

The third Framework programme was much clearer on the meaning of cohesion, as a political commitment to reduce disparities between regions and to enable the LFRs to compete at the level of excellence. Nevertheless the selection of programme activities still focused on the need of the Community to respond to international competitive pressures, and by implication on the problems of the major technology based firms. Cohesion was therefore more a statement of faith rather than of real intention. Indeed it can be argued that the actions of the Community in supporting existing excellence continued to act against cohesion, only to be balanced by a trickle down effect based on the mobility of researchers back to their home regions from a period of learning in the core, or else by the wider dissemination of the results of EC research. The emphasis therefore is on the transferability of knowledge and information, but without a conceptual model of how this is to occur. There is also an assumption that the LFRs will benefit from the harmonisation of technology rather than there being any recognition that their technological needs may be different, or that they may pursue alternative development paths.

One important element in the move towards the interests of the less favoured regions has been the shift to application programmes. As a response to the criticism that the main beneficiaries of the RTD programmes have been the corporate research centres of the large firms in the core regions, new applications programmes have been developed seeking to create products based on the enabling technologies (such as ICTs) but oriented to needs that are more diffuse (Shoults, 1991). Examples include medical informatics (AIM), road informatics (DRIVE), and telecoms applications for rural areas (ORA). In these projects a much greater significance is placed on collaboration with users in the LFRs, to develop products that address social needs as well as enhance industrial competitiveness. In particular ORA has stressed the need to develop technologies that are sympathetic to the problems of the rural LFRs rather than to impose standardised solutions drawn from the core regions.

The growing concern for the regional, or at least national, distribution of EC RTD funding has also been demonstrated via a number of attempts to examine the allocation of resources. A study which sought to identify the need for the STRIDE regional technology programme for the Community was one of the first of these, and included an analysis of the patterns of EC R&D funding by region (NBST, 1987). This has been followed by a number of one-off reports, and work to develop indicators on the distribution of RTD funding. More recently Eurostat has been developing regional RTD indicators to be used by DG XVI and XXII in assessing regional RTD disparities including the effects of the EC's own programmes.

Another aspect of the programmes causing continued concern is the rate of SME participation. Clearly this overlaps with the problem of regional participation to the extent that most of the LFRs lack the large firms with big R&D centres that are the major participants, and therefore LFR participants tend to be the smaller firms. The issue of whether small firms can really benefit from participation is also frequently raised, and there are some small scale initiatives (such as CRAFT) that have been developed to address that problem, allowing consortia of SMEs to participate as one member of a project for example, and awarding small grants to SMEs to work up projects.

By the beginning of the 1990s, after several studies into the relation between RTD policy, and aspects of cohesion, the Commission established an evaluation panel under its SPEAR evaluation programme to assess the effects of the Framework Programme on European cohesion. This study found that participation in EC programmes was of considerable benefit for firms and researchers in the LFRs, through the access to leading edge research, cultural changes in LFR research and the breaking down of established bureaucratic barriers. However industrial participation from the LFRs was noted to be weak, especially for SMEs, and recommendations were made concerning the relevance of the programmes. further support for dissemination and utilisation and awareness raising. The report was in favour of maintaining the current split between the roles of the structural funds and the RTD programmes, but there was a need for greater coordination, and complementary initiatives should seek to support eventual participation by the LFRs and overall growth in RTD performance in those regions Caraca, 1991).

Alongside the reorientation of the Framework Programme towards applications of the technologies, there has been an emergence and rapid expansion of support for the diffusion and dissemination of the results of time research, and indeed a general support for technology transfer. The primary action in technology transfer has been SPRINT which has *inter alia* established a considerable number of networks linking together individual technology transfer organisations and contract research centres to encourage inter-state exchange of technology. Inevitably to ensure member state coverage, many of these participants are based in the cohesion countries, or even in the LFRs of the more affluent member states. More important however has been the orientation of SPRINT towards SMEs and more traditional industrial sectors, such as clothing and mechanical engineering (see European Commission, 1996a for a review of actions). There is a general orientation in many of these programmes towards the international level, partly arising from a subsidiary question. Mostly the Commission attempts to work with existing institutions in the member states such as regional technology initiatives.

A parallel programme VALUE provided a closer link to the main Framework Programme activities by supporting the dissemination of the results of EC funded research. This activity is still developing under the new label of the Innovation Programme, but a recent innovation is the introduction of a network of Relay Centres to disseminate information on EC programmes and results via local offices in the member states.

These pilot actions are now being earned forward under the Innovation Programme against the background of an Innovation Action Plan developed after extensive consultation. The Action Plan focuses on the need to develop the underlying framework conditions for innovation at the level of culture and institutions, but so far has been addressed with relatively little funding. The major funding as will be explored below comes from the Structural Funds.

Many of the problems of the relationship between the Community's science and technology policy and cohesion arise from the range of objectives that the programmes are required to address. The nature of the Community is such that there are conflicts between the desired thematic impacts of the policy, combined with conflicts between the member states in terms of how those impacts are shared out. The whole is a delicate balancing act, with trade-offs between cohesion oriented developments and the industrial ambitions of the large countries.

One problem however is that there is a varied interpretation of what is meant by applying technology to enhance cohesion. Many of the low RTD countries see the EC programmes as a means of developing a stronger RTD capacity. This may include a simple replication of research conducted elsewhere, rather than the development of a unique and regionally specialised facility. By contrast some low RTD LFRs, which may be located in countries that have a higher economic and RTD performance, focus instead on the potential of EC funding for economic development. The key to resolving such problems in terms of the provision of funds, and the retention of subsidiarity in the setting of objectives for regions, is the Structural Funds and how they are being redirected into areas of research and innovation support.

The response of community regional policy

The structural funds

In seeking to address the developmental problems of the less favoured regions of Europe, and stimulate economic and social cohesion, the principal approach of the EC has been to use financial support through the Structural Funds,[6] rather than seeking to bend policy tools developed to address other purposes. Thus, as with RTD policy, financial support for infrastructure, training and business development is used to offset the negative consequences of other Community policies on the LFRs, as well as overcome the historic consequences of uneven development in Europe (Amin, Charles and Howells, 1992). Such support, introduced following the first enlargement for the UK and Ireland, but intensified with the accession of relatively poor Mediterranean countries such Greece, has gone through a similar developmental path as the RTD funds, moving away from basic infrastructure and a Keynesian public works emphasis, towards a supply-side innovation and business development focus and an emphasis on competitiveness. In doing so there has been a movement towards greater integration and mutual reinforcement of RTD and cohesion policies, although as will be argued, some tensions still remain.

Reform of the structural funds and RTD

The earliest signs of these kinds of changes can be seen in the 1984 reform of the Structural Funds, specifically in the shift away from simple infrastructure objectives to a more industrially oriented regional policy. As part of this a key change was the increasing proportion of the Fund (up to 20 per cent) to be used for financing programmes that reflected CEC objectives. Thus, earlier experimental non-quota activities were replaced by a series of multi-annual programmes related to regions dependent on sectors facing structural crises. A further innovation, along similar lines, were Community Programmes (later termed Community Initiatives) that aimed to exploit 'indigenous potential' for development in LFRs.

A significant aspect of the 1984 reform was the move to a more integrated approach to regional development. The CEC had been developing, on a very small scale, this approach since the end of the 1970s. The 1984 reform, however, included a formal adoption of this approach that aimed for a co-ordinated and coherent intervention of the three structural funds. The aim of the new programmes, through an integrated package of measures was to build a new capacity for growth in the regions, typically through the formation of new small and medium enterprises.

The next reform of the Structural Funds in 1988 (CEC, 1988) consolidated the role of the CEC in the development regional policy objectives. On the one hand, the accession of Spain and Portugal had further accentuated regional disparities. On the other hand, the process of integration, signalled in the signing of the Single European Act, compelled a new concern with 'cohesion' and 'convergence'. Indeed article 130d of the SEA required the CEC to bring forward proposals to reform the Funds. However, while the SEA provided the impetus, the reforms can best be seen as the further development of trends established in earlier periods. Underpinning the reform was a stated desire to develop the integrated approach to regional and sectoral problems, to develop a partnership with national and regional governments and to further emphasise the development of Community initiatives to deal with Community problems.

Community initiatives – linking regional policy to other policies including RTD

Whilst the majority of EC Structural Funds support continues to be provided to member states and regions as a subsidy for an agreed programme of local initiatives, the growth of the Community Initiatives since the 1988 reforms provided a route by which broader cohesion concerns could be addressed.

The Community Initiatives were introduced under the regulation revising the Structural Funds to enable the Commission 'to propose to member states that they submit applications for assistance in respect of measures of significant interest to the Community', but which might lie outside of the normal activities contained within regional development plans. These measures addressed problems which were 'associated with the implementation of other Community policies, the application of Community policies at regional level and problems common to certain categories of regions'.[7] Specific mention is made of the problems which frustrate the ability of citizens to 'break into the virtuous circle of rising prosperity offered by the Internal Market'.

There are four specific aspects whereby the Community Initiatives (CIs) differ from the mainstream funds under the Community Support Frameworks (CSFs).

- CIs can encompass measures that can transcend national borders, providing a framework for transnational cooperation.

- They provide a means by which Community funding can be used to support Community interests and priorities rather than simply follow national policy.

- They provide flexibility through the ability of the Commission to quickly introduce new targeted initiatives to address emerging problems of industrial restructuring.

- They contribute to innovation in regional policy in terms of new forms of regional policy and administrative approach, which may later be included in the mainstream CSF.

Specifically then, Community Initiatives are intended to link together the objectives of cohesion and those of other common policies, and in this technology support featured strongly at first. Examples of this are STAR and Telematique that combine regional policy with telecommunications policies, STRIDE that supports RTD in the regions, VALOREN that assists indigenous energy strategies, and the sectoral initiatives (RECHAR, RETEX, RENAVAL etc.) that aim to offset the regionally concentrated employment loss in key sectors adversely affected as a consequence of Community actions.

Within the 1990–94 round of Community Initiatives, three were of particular relevance to issues of technology policy and cohesion. STRIDE supported RTD and technology transfer initiatives in the regions, including projects aimed at improving LFR participation in the EU Framework Programme. Telematique supported the application of advanced telecommunications and IT services within the LFRs to enhance the performance of SMEs and the public sector. And finally, Prisma groups together three measures that were aimed at improving the competitiveness of LFR SMEs in the Single Market: testing facilities and support for technical standards and quality management; services to improve the awareness of SMEs of public procurement contracts elsewhere in Europe; and support to industrial sectors affected by the removal of the Article 115[8] measures as part of the SEM programme.

STRIDE is the most central to our discussion and is examined further below.

The STRIDE programme

Some of the regional fund money has been used in the past to support technology initiatives at the local level, although largely on an ad hoc basis. An exception to this was the Business and Innovation Centre (BIC) movement in the mid 1980s. At that time a number of countries were interested in developing BICs as an extension of the managed workspace concept, providing additional support for individuals and small firms with innovative projects. DG XVI supported the formation of an international network of these organisations and laid down a standard format, which was then applied to those seeking non-quota or ECSC funding from the Commission (Goddard *et al.*, 1987). Other individual initiatives were supported, but in the late 1980s there was a parallel development of a Community Initiative on technology, STRIDE, and the insertion of technology initiatives as a major action in the new CSFs.

The Directorate General for Regional Policy (DG XVI), although primarily involved in funding infrastructure through the 1970s, began to take an interest in programmatic approaches to regional policy as early as 1979, commissioning a Community-wide study on indigenous potential. This, and subsequent studies on new information technologies (IT), IT production and individual national studies of technological development in regions contributed to a growing awareness by DG XVI of the role of technology in regional inequalities throughout the early 1980s. This was reinforced by the uptake of technology based programme funding from within the non-quota funds, and also the submission of technology-based infrastructure projects to the main ERDF. The Commission has estimated that between 1980 and 1989 some 190 million ECU were spent through the ERDF on research centres and technical schools in the LFRs.

Arising from this heightened awareness, DG XVI commissioned a study in 1986–87 into the status of research and technological development activity within the less favoured regions of Europe, and its potential for aiding the development of these regions (Goddard *et al.*, 1988; NBST, 1988). This study was to set the foundations for a new Community Programme on R&D in the regions, following on earlier programmes such as STAR and a programme for the use of indigenous energy sources (VALOREN).

One of the principal issues that the new Community Initiative was to address was the creation of synergy between R&D and regional objectives, recognising that with low potential for R&D, the more peripheral regions, and indeed countries, could not participate in EC funded R&D programmes. Thus the EC was seen by less favoured member states as an important additional source of R&D funding, and access to technology, but the scientific quality criteria imposed by the EC often block this potential. Only by providing assistance for R&D development in these regions on the grounds of benefits to cohesion (hence regional development) could such intervention be justified.

The problem in this debate however was that the EC research programmes could not be seen to show undue favour to the LFRs if this dilutes the excellence of research, as this would create problems over the creation of a two tier system of high quality research being rejected in the core countries to fund lower quality research in the periphery. However, by focusing on internationally excellent research, the EC risked isolating researchers in the periphery from the needs and capabilities of their local infrastructure. In short, a cathedrals in the desert situation could be fostered, but to what benefit? What alternative policies could be instituted to aid diffusion of technology as well as its generation?

Progress was inevitably delayed by the major revisions to the Structural Funds, although this delay also followed changes in other aspects of both regional and technology policy, to the benefit of the co-ordination of these two aims. On the regional policy side this involved the raised status of R&D infrastructure proposals within the new negotiated programmes, particularly in Objective 1 regions, thus alleviating the need for a strong infrastructure element to STRIDE. On the technology front, there had been a broadening of research programmes, with a greater emphasis on applications appropriate to the more traditional industries prevalent to LFRs (agriculture, engineering, materials) and some attention placed in developing applications specifically to address the problems of certain LFRs. Also diffusion policies had been strengthened via the SPRINT and VALUE programmes for example, which, although oriented to the national level, addressed some of the development problems seen in the poorer countries.

The STRIDE programme was formally launched in July 1990. The programme was mainly aimed at strengthening the R&D capacity of the regions 'whose development is lagging behind', the euphemism for the poorest or Objective 1 regions. Consequently the major proportions of funding went to these areas, although the 'industrial decline'

(Objective 2) regions were also eligible for a more restricted list of measures of a smaller budgetary requirement. The budget was just over 400 million ECU drawn from the ERDF and ESF for the period 1990 to 1995.

Within Objective 1 regions STRIDE was able to assist investment in basic R&D infrastructure through regional technological assessments and new investments in capital and project running costs to start up R&D activities. Further, the link for R&D in such regions into the main research and technological infrastructure and networks by assisting R&D centres to prepare for and participate in EC-funded research programmes will be encouraged. This latter aim therefore overcame the problem of participation in international networks, whereby quality criteria cannot be relaxed, but additional support is required to ensure LFR participants can be involved on equal terms.

A third form of support available both to Objective 1 and 2 regions related to links and networks between research centres and industry. This covered a wide range of consortia and technology transfer mechanisms building upon existing EC mechanisms such as the COMETT University–Enterprise Training Partnerships (UETPs), SPRINT networks and VALUE initiatives.

In terms of implementation, however, the characteristics of the programmes in each of the member states varied tremendously according to the priorities and capabilities of the member state governments and agencies within those states, although it has been observed that a high proportion of resources were devoted to investment in basic RTD infrastructure, such as new research centres. This, coupled with smaller scale programmes to encourage Framework Programme participation did however lead to a large number of new organisations including SMEs entering into Framework Programme projects. Subsequently RTD measures have been mainstreamed into the Structural Funds, and comprise around 5 per cent of expenditure in the current period (Table 6.6). The effect of this has been very significant in many LFRs, considerably expanding public support for innovation, although the long lead times for economic impact mean that the effects will not be fully known for some time yet.

An identified weakness of Structural Funds support for RTD has been the low capacity in the regions for strategic planning and the alleged poor fit of RTD investments with regional needs. Having been identified within DG XVI, resources were made available through the 'article 10' funds for policy experimentation to establish a scheme for Regional Innovation Strategies. These projects along with a parallel

Table 6.6: RTD support within the Community Support Frameworks of Objective 1 regions for 1994–99

Country	Overall allocation of funds under the CSFs (mECU)	RTD allocation within the CSFs (mECU)	Percentage of RTD allocation in CSFs
Belgium	730	97.3	13.3
Germany	13 640	*613.2	*4.5
Greece	13 980	662.8	4.7
Spain	26 300	1 007.6	3.8
France	2 190	**80.0	**3.6
Ireland	5 620	362.4	6.5
Italy	14 860	969.5	6.5
Netherlands	150	22.9	15.3
Portugal	13 980	576.0	4.1
UK	2 360	137.9	5.8
Total Objective 1 areas	93 810	4 529.6	4.8

Note: * provisional figure   ** estimate
Source: European Commission DC, XVI

scheme RITTS from DG XIII developed a methodology for assessing regional supply and demand for innovation support as a foundation for strategy building and subsequent programme funding. Innovation support continues to grow within the mainstream Structural Funds programme and may be expected to take a greater proportion of funding again in the next programming period.

Reinforcing cohesion and competitiveness through RTD and innovation

In 1998 the Commission released a communication on cohesion and RTD policy (CEC, 1998). This sought to bring together the ideas of cohesion, competitiveness and RTD in a common framework for the first time, and stressed the importance of innovation as a means of addressing the structural weaknesses of the LFRs. The effects of the long process of enfolding cohesion issues into the RTD programme were finally becoming visible, and the criteria for the new Framework Programme were even more oriented to employment and economic development, with an emphasis on exploitation, on themes that fit with LFR needs, and with special programme elements to address the cohesion issue. The basic question of the level of RTD investment in the LFRs had been addressed through the Structural Funds, and was now being seen in the growth of R&D as a proportion of GDP in the cohesion countries, Portugal, Greece, Ireland and Spain. All four saw an increase in R&D of between 50 per cent and 100 per cent as a share of GDP between 1985 and the mid 1990s, and so the issue switched more to the question of absorption.

What then does the future hold for the EU RTD programmes? It is clear that the development argument has been won, and RTD is being emphasised in negotiations with new applicant countries from Central and Eastern Europe, but new problems and tensions are emerging. In the LFRs a much greater emphasis on international projects is inevitable as a result of participation in the Framework Programme, and such participation is relatively more likely in these regions due to the low national spend. There may be further moves within the ERDF programmes to encourage greater international linkages also to promote interregional learning and transfer of experiences. Possible new forms of European-wide dependency may be emerging as SMEs and research organisations in the LFRs become linked into multinationals in the core regions. National systems of innovation may be eroding in favour of regionalised systems and international networks. The key to sustainable development in the LFRs depends on their ability to embed the benefits of the additional resources into local production systems. The EU is now providing the tools, but success is not guaranteed.

Acknowledgement

This chapter was based on research funded through a variety of sources, including projects under the Economic and Social Research Council's programmes on 'The European Context of UK Science Policy' (contract L323253009) and the 'Single European Market' (contract W 113251001) and various consultancy contracts for the European Commission.

Notes

1. During the study I will switch between European Community (EC) and European Union (EU). Strictly speaking it would be incorrect to use EU before the Act of European Union (also known as the Maastricht Treaty) in 1991, and so I will use EC when describing events before that time. For greater clarification I will also use CEC for the Commission of the European Communities to differentiate this specific Community institution.
2. Countries can select which areas of technology they wish to fund, they only fund their own national partners, and they can each follow their own rules on eligibility and funding mechanisms.

3. CREST is the Scientific and Technical Research Committee and comprises representatives of the ministerial and scientific services of the member states, CODEST is the Committee for the European Development of Science and Technology and comprises representatives of the scientific community. IRDAC is the Advisory Committee on Industrial Research and Development and comprises representatives of major European companies.
4. The IT Rountable consisted of the heads of ICI, GEC, Plessery, AEG, Nixdorf, Siemens, Thomson, Bull, CGE, Olivetti, STET and Philips.
5. R&D in Advanced Communications Technologies for Europe, Basic Research in Industrial Technologies for Europe, Biotechnological Research for Innovation, Development and Growth in Europe, Biotechnology Action Programme, European Collaborative Linkage of Agriculture and Industry through Research, Food Linked Agro-Industrial Research, Advanced Informatics for Medicine.
6. The Structural Funds refers to a collection of funds including the European Regional Development Fund, the European Social Fund, the European Agricultural Guidance and Guarantee Fund, and more recently the Cohesion Fund. Most of what follows specifically refers to initiatives under the ERDF, although some of the programmes discussed have ESF funding also.
7. Green Paper on the Future of Community Initiatives, CEC 1994.
8. Article 115 provided exemption from aspects of the treaty for certain vulnerable industrial sectors in the less favoured regions. These include highly traditional sectors such as clothing, footwear etc. Under the revised Treaty, these exemptions were to be lifted exposing these industries to international competition.

References

Amin, A., Charles, D. R. and Howells, J. (1992) 'Corporate restructuring and cohesion in the new Europe', *Regional Studies*, 26, 319–32.

Caraca, J. M. G. (1991) *Evaluation of the Effects of the EC Framework Programme for Research and Technological Development on Economic and Social Cohesion in the Community*, Commission of the European Communities, Brussels.

Charles, D. R. and Howells, J. (1992) *Technology Transfer in Europe: Public and Private Networks*, London: Belhaven.

Charles, D. R. and Howells, J. (1993) 'European Technology and Regional Policies Implications for the Periphery of the UK' in Harrison R. T. and Hart, M. (eds) *Spatial Policy in a Divided Nation*, London: Jessica Kingsley Press.

Charles, D. R., Hayward, S. And Thomas, D. (1995) 'Science parks and regional technology strategies: European experiences', *Industry and Higher Education*, 9, 332–9.

Commission of the European Communities (1977) 'Common policy for science and technology', *Bulletin of the European Communities*, supplement March.

Commission of the European Communities (1985) 'Community Research and Technology Policy: Developments up to 1984', OOPEC, Luxembourg.

Commission of the European Communities (1986) *Proposal for a Council Regulation Concerning the Framework Programme of Community Activities in the Filed of Research and Technological development (1987 to 1991)*, COM (86) 430 final, CEC, Brussels.

Commission of the European Communities (1990) *Industrial Policy in an Open and Competitive Environment*, COM (90) 556 final, CEC, Brussels.

Commission of the European Communities (1991), 'European Industrial Policy for the 1990s', *Bulletin of the European Communities* (Supplement 3/9) CEC, Luxembourg.

Commission of the European Communities (1992) 'Research after Maastricht: An assessment, a strategy', *Bulletin of the European Communities*, Supplement 2/92, OOPEC, Luxembourg.

Commission of the European Communities (1993) 'Cohesion and RTD Policy – Synergies Between Research and Technological Development policy and Economic and Social Cohesion policy', Communication from the Commission to the Council and the European Parliament, COM (93) 203 final, CEC, Brussels.

Commission of the European Communities (1994) 'Competitiveness and Cohesion: Trends in the Regions', Fifth Periodic Report on the Social and Economic Situation and Development of the Regions in the Community, CEC, Luxembourg.

Commission of the European Communities (1994) *The Future of Community Initiatives under the Structural Funds*, COM (94) 46 final/2, CEC Brussels.

Commission of the European Communities (1994) 'First European Report on S&T Indicators', 1994, OOPEC, Luxembourg.

Commission of the European Communities (1994) 'The Implementation of the Reform of the Structural Funds 1992', Fourth Annual Report, OOPEC, Luxembourg.

Commission of the European Communities (1998) 'Reinforcing Cohesion and Competitiveness through Research, Technological Development aid Innovation', Communication from the Commission, COM (98) 275 final, CEC, Brussels.

Commission of the European Communities (1995) *Research and Regional Development*, OOPEC, Luxembourg.

Commission of the European Communities (1996) 'Inventing Tomorrow: Europe's Research at the Service of its People: Preliminary Guide-lines for the Fifth Framework Programme', OOPEC, Luxembourg.

Commission of the European Communities (1996a) 'Final Evaluation of SPRINT', Report presented to the Commission, OOPEC, Luxembourg.

Commission of the European Communities (1997) 'Practical Guide to Regional Innovative Actions (RIS, RITTS)', OOPEC, Luxembourg.

Commission of the European Communities (1997a) 'Second European Report on S&T Indicators, 1997', *Nuclear Science and Technology series*, OOPEC, Luxembourg.

Goddard, J. B., Charles, D. R., Howells, J. and Thwaites, A. T. (1987) 'Research and Technological Development in the Less Favoured Regions of the Community', Report to the Commission of the European Communities, DG XVI Regional Policy.

Howells, J. and Charles, D. R. (1988), 'Research and technical development in the less favoured regions of the European Community', in K. Dyson, (ed.) *Local Authorities and New Technologies: The European Dimension*, Beckenham: Croom Helm.

Howells, J. and Charles, D. R. (1989), 'Research and technological development and regional policy: a European perspective', in Gibbs, D. (ed.) *Government Policy and Industrial Change*, Beckenham: Routledge.

Laredo, P. (1995) 'Structural effects of EC RT&D programmes', *Scientometrics*, 34, 473–487.

National Board for Science and Technology (1987) 'Science and Technology for Regional Innovation and Development in Europe', Report to the Commission of the European Communities, DG XVI Regional Policy.

Peterson, J. (1991) 'Technology policy in Europe: explaining the Framework Programme and Eureka in theory and practice', *Journal of Common Market Studies*, XXIX, 269–90.

Peterson, J. (1993) 'Assessing the performance of European collaborative R&D policy: the case of Eureka', Research Policy, 22, 243–64.

Pike, A. and Charles, D. R. (1995) 'The impact of international collaboration on University industry links', Industry and Higher Education, 9, 264–76.

Sharp, M. (1991) 'The single market and European technology policies, in Freeman', C. *et al.*, '*Europe and the New Technologies*, London: Pinter.

Shoults, T. (1991) 'Policies, Viewpoints and debates on RTD and Social and Economic Cohesion in the Community Institutions, Prospective dossier No 1 Science Technology and Social and Economic cohesion in the Community', Vol. 15, FAST Occasional papers No 239, CEC, Brussels.

Stubbs, P. and Saviotti, P. (1994) 'Science and Technology Policy' in M. J. Artis and N. Lee (eds) *The Economics of the European Union: Policy and Analysis*, Oxford: Oxford University Press.

7

The Creation of Harmonised Patent Protection in Europe

Gerald Paterson

Introduction

The idea underlying every patent system is to encourage technical research and development by granting an inventor a monopoly for a limited period of time, usually twenty years, in return for a full written disclosure of how to work the invention, which is then published. Consequently also, inventors are encouraged to make their inventions public, instead of working their inventions secretly, and the availability of such information provides a basis for further research and development. The monopoly which is granted is a legal right to prevent others from using the invention as defined in the patent without the permission of the patent proprietor, during the period of time when the patent is in force. The inventive technology may then be exploited under the protection of the patent either exclusively by the inventor or his employer, or by way of assignment or licence, in combination with associated know-how when appropriate. The future development of the inventive technology may be regulated in accordance with the chosen method of exploitation.

The expense and uncertainty and consequent commercial risk involved in much research and development work is of course such that it would not be commercially viable without the potential reward of patent protection.

All patent systems have certain characteristics in common. Thus for an invention to be patentable, the following requirements must be satisfied:

(i) it must be new;
(ii) it must involve an inventive step compared to what was previously known;

(iii) the patent must contain a sufficient description of the invention to enable the skilled public to carry it out and reproduce it after publication;

(iv) the invention must be of a kind which constitutes patentable subject-matter. As a generality this means that the subject of the invention must be technical rather than abstract in nature; but beyond this, certain categories of subject-matter may be excluded from patentability for reasons of policy, as will be discussed further below.

The need for harmonisation

Until relatively recently, individual countries have each operated their own national patent systems in accordance with their own national patent laws and legal systems. Each national patent law in Europe had many individual peculiarities and characteristics, both procedurally and as regards the determination of what was patentable. As one important example, for reasons of national policy a number of countries did not grant patents for chemical or pharmaceutical products.

It has become increasingly recognised, however, that a geographically fragmented patent system makes little sense, not only because of the duplication of examination and associated procedural work with ultimate extra expense, but also because, as trade in technical products and services increasingly crosses national frontiers, it makes no sense to have different levels of legal patent protection in geographically adjacent countries, or indeed within any countries which participate in such trade.

Since about 1960, the main western European countries have been working together to create a single integrated European patent system. A major part of such a system has been in operation for twenty years and has provided useful benefits in relation to the regulation of European technical research. The European system is increasingly recognised as a model for other industrial trading areas, such as Asia.

The harmonisation of European patent laws

(1) Establishment of a written European patent law

The first stage in the creation of a European patent system was achieved during the 1970s by the creation of the framework of a new European written patent law which is set out in two treaties, the

European Patent Convention (EPC) and the Community Patent Convention (CPC).

(a) The European Patent Convention (EPC) came into force for six countries in 1977 and currently covers nineteen European countries. It created the first half of what is intended to become a unitary, integrated system, by providing centralised procedures before the European Patent Office (EPO) which is based in Munich, for the grant of European patents, and for post-grant opposition to such patents by third parties within nine months from grant. When granted by the EPO, a European patent has the legal effect of a number of individual national patents in the countries which are chosen by the applicant. The enforcement of such a patent takes place in individual national courts, and its validity may also be challenged in such courts – possibly with different results in different countries.

The EPC also sets out standardised provisions for the four previously mentioned patentability requirements – novelty, inventive step, sufficient description and patentable subject-matter, and these provisions are important from the regulatory point of view.

As regards the requirement for patentable subject-matter, the EPC contains a number of specific provisions, the most important of which are as follows:

   (i) 'Computer programs as such' are not patentable.
  (ii) Chemical and pharmaceutical products are patentable (subject to the right of any individual country to exclude such products from patentability during the first 15 years of the EPC's operation i.e. until 1992).
 (iii) 'Methods of medical treatment' are not patentable.
  (iv) 'Plant and animal varieties' are not patentable.

A further important provision is that:
   (v) Inventions whose 'publication or exploitation would be contrary to public order or morality' are not patentable.

Provision (i) is important to the electronics industry. Provisions (ii) and (iii) are obviously of great importance to the chemical and pharmaceutical industries, and provisions (iv) and (v) have become of crucial importance to biotechnology research, as applied in agriculture and the pharmaceutical industry, as will be discussed further below.

(b) The Community Patent Convention (CPC) was intended to come into force at about the same time as the EPC, but primarily for political reasons it has not yet been ratified by a sufficient number of countries to bring it into force. It contains the legal framework for the second half of the European patent system, concerning enforcement of European patents, and provides for an appeal system from national countries to a 'Common Appeal Court' which would constitute the highest patent court in Europe, and which would therefore ensure judicial harmonisation of European patent law: that is, a consistent interpretation both within the European Patent Office and in all national courts of the written patent laws set out in the EPC and the CPC.

There is an important formal distinction between the EPC and the CPC. As its name implies, the CPC is a treaty between the member states of the European Community (as it then was), or European Union (EU). In contrast, the EPC originally included several member states which were not members of the EU, and still includes one such state (Switzerland). Since the CPC is not yet in force, the EPC is not yet directly linked to the European Union, and the European Patent Office is not an EU institution. Nevertheless, almost all European countries are members of both the EU and the EPC, so that the creation of a harmonised European patent system is a common European aim.

(2) Harmonisation by judicial interpretation of the written European patent law

This constitutes the second stage in the creation of a harmonised European patent system, and is of great practical importance. As will be apparent, since the EPC and the EPO have been functioning for twenty years but the CPC is not yet in force, only one half of the overall system has so far been in operation. Since the Common Appeal Court is not yet in existence, the standardised written provisions of the EPC are applied both within the European Patent Office and in individual national courts in parallel. A harmonised interpretation and consistent application of such provisions to individual European patent applications and patents can therefore only be achieved by a mutual respect between the judges in the European Patent Office and those in all the individual national courts of the nineteen member countries of the EPC, when they issue their decisions and judgements in individual cases.

Perhaps surprisingly, such a harmonised interpretation of European patent law has already been achieved to a considerable extent.

Obviously, patents have to be granted before they can be the subject of enforcement proceedings in national courts. Inevitably, therefore, the standardised patentability requirements of the EPC have first been the subject of interpretation in the context of many individual cases within the European Patent Office, during the past fifteen years or so.

The European Patent Office has its own internal appeal system, with its highest 'courts' constituted by a number of Boards of Appeal, and an Enlarged Board of Appeal which constitutes the highest legal authority within the EPO. These courts have issued numerous judgments setting out by way of case law how the written European patent law should be interpreted and applied to individual cases before the EPO.

Such precedent case law is not legally binding either within the EPO or in national courts, but has almost always been followed voluntarily by national courts concerned with similar patent disputes. The achievement of a common practical application of the EPC has been greatly helped by the attitude of many individual national judges, as reflected for example by what was stated in a recent judgement of the House of Lords in an important patent case:

> The United Kingdom courts ... must have regard to the decisions of the European Patent Office (EPO) on the construction of the EPC. These decisions are not strictly binding upon the courts in the UK but they are of great persuasive authority: first, because they are decisions of expert courts (the Boards of Appeal and Enlarged Board of Appeal of the EPO) involved daily in the administration of the EPC and secondly, because it would be highly undesirable for the provisions of the EPC to be construed differently in the EPO from the way they are interpreted in the national courts of a Contracting State.

Nevertheless, it would seem to be clearly desirable that European patent protection is regulated not only by common legislative provisions, but also by a common European patent appeal court to which appeals on points of law would lie both from the judicial levels of the EPO, and from judgments of national courts. Such a European patent appeal court would regulate the practical interpretation of the legislative provisions, and thus ensure that patent protection in Europe is judicially harmonised.

The practical application of European patent law to biotechnology

It is interesting to examine how the new European patent law has been applied to a most important and relatively new technical field, namely biotechnology, or genetic engineering. The initial development of this technology began in 1973 (that is, after the patentability requirements of the EPC had already been agreed), with the discovery in America that it is possible to insert genetic material from one species of living matter into another species. The possibility of selective breeding within one species of living matter has been well-known for centuries. Modern genetic engineering can transfer genetic information contained in genes between different species.

Enormous benefits to mankind are foreseeable from the current and future development of this technology, especially in medicine and agriculture. But such development work has to be supported by high financial investment, which would not be forthcoming without the ultimate potential availability of appropriate patent protection for the results of such research and development. To give some idea of the current scale of investment in biotechnology in the United Kingdom, the shares in the four largest companies working in this field are together valued at more than £2 billion (making the British biotechnology industry second in size to that in America), yet product marketing is only at a very early stage. Such a level of investment is based on the hope of successful products and consequential profit levels such as have already been achieved by American companies, with the help of appropriate patent protection there.

The basic tool in biotechnology is the gene, which is an ordered sequence of chemical substances, and the ordered sequence defines specific genetic information. In general terms, genetic products and processes have become the subject of European patents by the application of the same legal rules which have traditionally been applied to chemical and pharmaceutical products and processes. However, one highly controversial kind of invention has emerged from biotechnological research, where the inventive subject-matter relates to living matter.

Under earlier national patent laws, any kind of living matter was considered unpatentable on ethical and religious grounds, but since living material never was the subject of industrially applicable inventions, the issue had little or no practical relevance anyway.

The present position under the EPC

Since the EPC was written before biotechnology began, problems inevitably arise in the application of an older law to such a major new technology.

Under the EPC, the patentability of genetically modified material has been a very sensitive issue for many years. There are numerous patent applications relating to the genetic engineering of living material pending before the EPO, and some patents have already been granted for such subject-matter. Such granted patents have been routinely opposed by organisations such as Greenpeace, representing the 'Green movement', primarily on the legal ground already referred to, namely that the genetic engineering of living matter is not patentable because its publication or exploitation is contrary to morality. Objections have also been raised on the separate ground that genetically modified living material is not patentable because it constitutes a 'plant or animal variety'. Such an objection to the patentability of genetically modified plants has been successful in one appeal case.

These important issues are currently under continuing consideration during proceedings before the EPO, including the Boards of Appeal, and questions of law have been referred to the Enlarged Board of Appeal for an authoritative interpretation of the relevant provisions. Nevertheless, the current position in relation to the patentability of biotechnological inventions under the EPC is one of considerable legal uncertainty. Furthermore, the procedural mechanism for providing greater legal certainty, by way of appeal in appropriate cases to the Boards of Appeal and the Enlarged Board of Appeal and the eventual issue of a reasoned decision, is relatively slow.

The position in the USA

In contrast to the European position under the EPC, American patent law is relatively more generous and more certain in relation to the patentability of living material and of biotechnological inventions generally (as well as in relation to the patentability of methods of medical treatment). In contrast to the EPC, United States patent law does not exclude from patentability either 'methods of medical treatment', or 'plant and animal varieties', or 'inventions the publication or exploitation of which would be contrary to public order or morality'. Furthermore, in a landmark judgment of the Supreme Court issued in 1980 (Diamond v. Chakrabarty), the court held that a genetically engineered bacterium was patentable, on the now famous and often quoted basis that under United States patent law, 'anything under the sun made by the hand of man' is patentable subject-matter. This judgment led to a very generous approach to the patentability of biotechnological inventions within the United States Patent Office, which in turn is considered to have been of considerable benefit to the American biotechnological and pharmaceutical industries. The level of investment in research and development in these industries, (based upon an expectation of patent protection and consequent high rewards), the extent of patent protection and the number of successful products, all show a consistent positive and accelerating trend.

The position in the European Union

In an effort to improve the legal certainty surrounding biotechnological patentability in Europe, in 1988 the European Commission published a proposed 'Directive on the Legal Protection of Biotechnological Inventions', whose aim was to clarify and to regulate what was patentable within Europe and what was not, and thus indirectly to encourage biotechnological research and development in Europe.[1]

While some of its provisions merely essentially repeated corresponding provisions in the EPC, the Directive also attempted to interpret the legal provisions of the EPC, for example by giving indications as to what would and would not be considered contrary to public policy and morality.

After about six years of discussion and amendment, this directive was eventually rejected in March 1995 by the European Parliament, primarily because of the controversial nature of the ethical problems which patenting in this area of technology raises, and a lack of sufficient consensus as to the correct legislative wording to be adopted in relation to such problems. This rejection was a considerable disappointment for those working in the European biotechnology industry.

Since then, a new draft Directive with modified contents was proposed by the European Commission in December 1995, and has recently (July 1997) been passed by the European Parliament. When this Directive is issued by the European Union, its contents will be binding upon the member states of the European Union, and will thus affect the interpretation of the law concerning biotechnological patentability in the courts of such states. Its contents will not directly affect the interpretation of the EPC within the European Patent Office, since as previously explained the EPO is not part of the European Union.[2] Nevertheless, such a Directive will inevitably provide a strong indirect influence on the extent of patent protection available from the EPO in relation to biotechnological inventions.

Conclusion

While the value of appropriate patent protection as a means for positively regulating European research and development in biotechnology (as in all other technology) is generally recognised, the legal mechanisms for such regulation involve making a delicate balance between conflicting interests, both in the choice of legislative wording, and in the manner in which such wording is interpreted by the judicial organs of the European Patent Office and by national courts.

Notes

1. The Directive was adopted by the Council of the EU in July 1998, and brought into force in Member States by July 2000.
2. The EPO amended the Rules of the EPC to include a number of provisions directly corresponding to those of the EU Directive: these Rules entered into force in September 1999.

8

How Has Tax Affected the Changing Cost of R&D? Evidence from Eight Countries

Nicholas Bloom, Lucy Chennells, Rachel Griffith and John Van Reenen

Summary

This chapter describes the evolution of the tax treatment of investment in R&D in Australia, Canada, France, Great Britain, Germany, Italy, Japan and the USA between 1979 and 1994. Estimates of the cost of R&D are provided and the methodology used is contrasted with other ones used in the literature. Four findings are highlighted. First, there appear to be substantial differences in the cost of R&D across countries at any given point in time. Second, there has been a general trend towards more generous tax treatment of R&D, although some countries have moved much more rapidly than others. Third, there is an increasing diversity in the cost of R&D between countries. Finally, in order to illustrate the substantial within-country heterogeneity that can arise from differences in design and implementation, several stylised tax systems are applied to a sample of firm level data and the resulting distribution of tax rates is presented.

Introduction

Throughout the industrialised world there has been a general growth in the proportion of GDP allocated to privately funded research and development (R&D) expenditure (see Figure 8.1). Although there are varying opinions about the causes of this phenomenon and the reasons why some countries have experienced faster growth than others, it is commonly agreed that industrial production and global competition are increasingly based on the introduction of new technologies.[1] In parallel with this empirical development, theorists of economic growth have formalised Schumpeter's notion that investment in intangible assets (such as R&D and human capital) is the crucial factor in generating faster rates of output growth.[2] R&D is likely to be underprovided in market economies for a variety of reasons. Most famously, R&D generates new information and information is a partially nonrival good. In the absence of a perfectly functioning patent system, this will lead to socially sub-optimal levels of R&D. Imperfections in other markets, which provide complementary assets to R&D, will reinforce this problem. For example, low levels of training or poor access to financial markets will tend to depress R&D investment.[3]

Given these empirical and theoretical developments it is not surprising that policy makers have become concerned with the impact of the tax system on the economy's innovative capacity. In particular many countries have turned to explicit fiscal incentives to encourage R&D investment. The current wisdom on the impact of these fiscal incentives, based primarily on single country studies, usually the United States, is that the effects could be substantial. This study takes an international approach examining eight major industrialised countries (Australia, Canada, France, Germany, Italy, Japan, the UK and the USA). We extend previous cross-country studies by examining the evolution of the effects of the tax systems in these countries over a sixteen year period (1979–1994).

The cost of capital methodology used in this study is an extension of the methodology developed most notably in King and Fullerton (1984) to R&D expenditures. It is a useful way of summarising the influence of different parts of a complex tax system in a single, quantitative measure. Comparing the cost of R&D across countries gives us some information about the extent to which different countries subsidise or penalise R&D investments relative to a no-tax regime. This enables valid cross-country comparisons to be made.

The effects of tax on the cost of R&D are illustrated in two ways in this study. First, we calculate the cost of R&D for a representative firm which receives the full amount of credit. This measure does not, however, reflect the heterogeneous way that a tax system can affect firms. To illustrate this, stylised versions of the main features of four of the tax systems are applied to a sample of firm-level data and firm-specific effective marginal credit rates are calculated. The representative firm generally corresponds to the mode of this distribution of credit rates.

The structure of this study is as follows. Section 2 outlines the approach taken to measuring the cost of R&D; section 3 briefly summarises previous studies. Section 4 describes the general trends in tax systems and the tax treatment of R&D over the 1980s and 1990s. In Section 5 the distribution of firm level rates are presented and some concluding comments are offered in Section 6. To pre-empt our conclusions, the key findings are that: (i) there is substantial variation in the cost of R&D between countries; (ii) there exists a general downward trend in these costs, (iii) variation in the cost of R&D increased over the period; (iv) differences in the design and implementation of R&D tax credits means that there is also large within country variation in their impact.

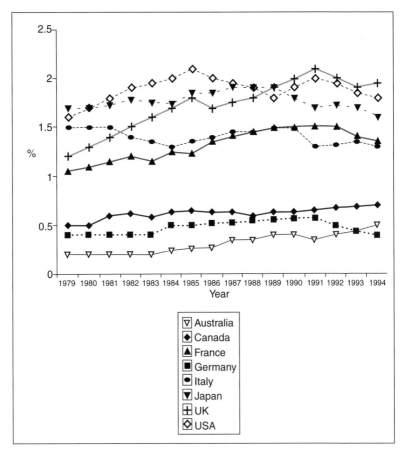

Source: author's calculation Figures 8.1–8.5.

Figure 8.1   Business expenditure on R&D as proportion of GDP

Previous work

Previous empirical work that has measured the impact of tax on the cost of R&D has largely examined the evolution of the US R&D tax credit. This was introduced in the Economic Recovery Tax Act of 1981 and subsequently reformed several times. One of the most studied features of this tax credit is the way in which incremental spending is defined and the impact that this has on the effective value of the credit. For most of the life of the credit, incremental R&D has been defined as spending above the average of spending in the previous three years. A pioneering study by Eisner, Albert and Sullivan (1984) evaluated the impact of the tax credit using a measure of the marginal effective tax credit (METC). They highlighted the fact that the net present value of the credit was substantially less than the statutory rate. The METC measures discounted the present value of the credit on an extra unit of R&D – that is, it accounts for the future stream of marginal benefits that will accrue from the credit. Although the statutory rate of the credit was 25 per cent, they found the METC to be very low – on average zero for 1980 and 4 per cent for 1981 – and negative for around one-fifth of firms. A negative METC can arise when a firm is considering an increase in its R&D spending that will leave it below the base in its current year, but expects to be above the base in subsequent years. No tax credits will accrue from the increase in R&D in the current year, but the increased base will reduce the size of the credit in subsequent years. This surprising feature of the tax credit arose for three main reasons: the incremental nature of the credit; the company-specific moving-average definition of the base; and the fact that many firms (ranging between 14 per cent and 43 per cent) could not claim the credit due to tax exhaustion.

In a study using firm level tax return data Altshuler (1988) examined the impact of the US tax credit, taking into account the dynamics of the firm's tax position. Her main finding was, for companies with no tax liability, the necessity of carrying forward non-indexed credits and the discounting of future returns dramatically reduced the incentives provided by R&D credits. A large number of firms were in this position: in 1981 nearly three-quarters, although this had dropped to just over one-half by 1984. Hall (1993) extended Eisner *et al.* (1984) by calculating a measure of the after tax price of R&D, O_t, which included a value of the depreciation allowances, as well as tax credits. Her estimates showed the considerable heterogeneity of the METC facing her sample of about 1000 firms, both at a point in time and over time. She concluded that one of the significant advantages of moving to a fixed based scheme in the 1990s was the reduction in this variation in the tax price facing different US firms.[4]

There are several studies which have made international comparisons. Leydon and Link (1993) provide some descriptions of different tax systems and Hall (1995) offers a more comprehensive evaluation, although neither give estimates of the cost of R&D. Warda (1994) examined 11 countries (and regions within the USA and Canada) using a slightly different measure, the B-index, to measure and rank the relative cost of R&D. The B-index is the present value of before-tax income necessary to cover the cost of an initial R&D investment and to pay the applicable income taxes so that an R&D project becomes profitable for the firm that undertakes it. Griffith, Sandler and Van Reenen (1995) present calculations of the cost of R&D for the G7 countries. None of these studies examine trends or changes over time. All of the international comparisons make the common point that tax systems have large effects on the implied costs of R&D, at least at a point in time.

Measuring the cost of R&D

This section briefly lays out the methodology used to calculate the cost of R&D. This methodology follows most closely King and Fullerton (1984) and Keen (1991). The idea is to derive a single quantitative measure to summarise the effects of a complex set of tax regulations on the cost of investing in R&D. We present the cost of R&D, which is the pre-tax real rate of return on the marginal investment project required to earn a minimum rate of return after tax (gross of economic depreciation). It will be a function of the general tax system, economic variables and the treatment of R&D expenditure in particular. To focus purely on the tax effects, economic variables such as inflation and interest rates are held constant across countries and over time.

Consider a profit maximising firm with a net present value of its net income stream given by:

$$(1-p)v_t = y\Delta_t + V_{t+1} \tag{1}$$

where p is the shareholder's discount rate and D is dividends paid to the shareholder (gross of any imputation credit at the shareholder level). We consider a tax exempt shareholder so that the shareholder's discount rate is equal to the nominal interest rate $p = i$ and the 'tax discrimination' parameter is given by $y = 1/(1 - c)$ where c is the imputation rate.

The dividend stream to the shareholder is equal to income minus investment. The tax system will affect this income stream in a number of ways. The net revenue will be taxed at the statutory tax rate r^r, the firm may be given depreciation allowances worth ϕr^r on current investment and on the tax written-down value of past allowances, and the firm may also receive a tax credit on current investment worth Tc. Equating the sources and uses of the fund, the dividend stream is given by:

$$\Delta_t = \Pi\left(G_{t-1}\right)\left(1 - r^r\right) - R_t\left(1 - \phi r^r\right) + T^c + \phi r^r G_{t-1}^T \tag{2}$$

where Π is the net income function, $Gt = (1 - \delta)(1 + \pi) G_{t-1} + R_t$ is the firm's stock of R&D, r^r is the statutory tax rate on retained earnings, R_t is investment in R&D, δ is the economic depreciation rate, ϕ is the tax depreciation rate, T^c is the effective credit rate and G_{t-1}^T is the tax written down R&D stock at the end of the period t – 1 and π is the rate of inflation.

The net present discounted value of depreciation allowances and tax credits is given by

$$A = \phi r^r\left[1 + \frac{(1-\phi)}{(1+p)} + \frac{(1-\phi)^2}{(1+p)^2} + \ldots\right] + T^c = \frac{\phi r^r(1+p)}{\phi + p} + T^c \tag{3}$$

where the value of the tax credit T^c is given by

$$T^c = \left(1 - dr^r\right)r^c\left[1 - inc\frac{1}{k}\left(\sum_{i=1}^{k}(1+p)^{-k}\right)\right] \tag{4}$$

where d = 1 if the tax credit is included in taxable income, r^c is the statutory credit rate, inc = 1 if the credit is given on incremental R&D investment, and is the number of years over which the base for determining the incremental amount of R&D is computed. As some credits apply to incremental expenditure, the following definitions of base are considered: (i) last year's expenditure (k = 1), (ii) the previous largest expenditure, (iii) a fixed year in the past, (iv) an average of the last two years' expenditures (k = 2), (v) an average of the last three years' expenditures (k = 3). All of these can be in real or nominal terms. We assume that the last year's expenditure is also the largest previous expenditure, so that (i) and (ii) are identical, and assume that (iii) has no impact on the net present value of the credit.

We consider a one period perturbation to the firms stock of R&D, such that $dG_t = d\bar{G} + 1$ and $dG_{t+s} = d\bar{G} \forall s \neq 0$, is the rate growth of the firm's R&D stock. In the next section we assume that where $d\bar{G}$ is constant and at a level such that the firm is eligible for any tax credit on incremental R&D. In Section 4, where we look at heterogeneity across firms, we relax this assumption and use the firm level data to estimate dG for each firm in each period.

This one period perturbation is achieved by letting R&D investment rise by one extra unit in period t and decline by one unit, less depreciation plus inflation in period t + 1, i.e. $dR_t = 1$, and $dR_{t+1} = -(1 - \delta)$ $(1 + \pi)$. The after tax return from this investment includes a financial return plus compensation for depreciation. Inflation is included because this compensation is delayed by one period. This is given by $d\Pi = (p + \delta)(1 + \pi)$.

The cost of R&D can be obtained by setting the level of rents (given by differentiating 1 equal to zero and solving for the financial rate of return, p

$$p = \frac{(1-A)}{(1-\tau)(1+\pi)}\big[p + \delta(1+\pi) - \pi\big]\delta \tag{5}$$

The next section shows how this measure of the cost of R&D has changed over time in eight countries. First let us consider several criticisms made of this and equivalent measures. First, the exact definition of qualifing R&D differs across countries. In the USA, for example, that part of R&D designated for enhancing foreign sales is treated differently from R&D aimed at the domestic market.[5] See Hines (1994) for a detailed analysis of these rules. In this study we assume that all R&D qualifies for any credit or depreciation allowance so do not reflect differences in qualifying rules across countries. Second, the value of the credit depends on whether or not the credit is capped. In some countries there are absolute caps while in others the caps are proportional. It is assumed in Section 3 that the investment expenditure falls between any maximum caps or minimum expenditure thresholds. In Section 4 this is relaxed. Third, in calculating the cost of R&D we have assumed that firms are expecting their R&D to grow in all years. If firms were planning to hold their R&D investment constant or even cut it, the cost of R&D would differ due to the definitions of the base, as is illustrated in the figures presented in Section 4. A final difficulty relates to the role of expectations. We are assuming that firms expect the current conditions to last indefinitely. Firms may anticipate a tax change (indeed, it may be preannounced), or they may anticipate a revision of the definition of the base in the future.

Trends in the cost of R&D

Reforms of systems of taxing corporate income over the past decade have tended towards lowering statutory rates and broadening the tax base. What has happened to the tax treatment of R&D over that time period? This section documents some of the main changes in the tax treatment of R&D in the eight countries over the period 1979 to 1994. More details about the tax systems in each country are given in Appendix A. It is worth noting that the cost of R&D figures reported in this section are calculated assuming that the R&D investment qualifies for any credit, that the amount of credit is not constrained by any capping rules and that the firm has sufficient tax liability against which to offset the credit. In the next section we investigate how the various credits affect firms in different positions. The figures presented in this section can be thought of as the mode, i.e. the most common value of the effective credit rate.

The following assumptions are made concerning the type of investment to be analysed. We consider a domestic investment, financed from retained earnings, in the manufacturing sector and divided into three types of asset for use in R&D – current expenditure, buildings, and plant and machinery. An important assumption in the modelling strategy used here is that current expenditure on R&D is treated as an investment – that is, its full value is not realised immediately but accrues over several years. Current expenditure on R&D is assumed to depreciate at 30 per cent a year, buildings at 3.61 per cent and plant and machinery at 12.64 per cent.[6]

Figure 8.2 shows how the tax treatment of R&D has changed over time. This graph shows the tax wedge of a typical R&D investment in Australia, Canada, France and the USA. These are the four countries that had the most generous treatment of R&D. The tax wedge is the difference between the cost of R&D, that is the minimum rate of return required pre-tax to make the profit break even after tax, and the real interest rate, which is assumed to be constant at 10 per cent.

The wedge is weighted across assets (90 per cent current expenditure, 3.6 per cent buildings, and 6.4 per cent plant and machinery).[7] Inflation and interest rates are held constant across time and across countries in order to emphasise the differences in tax systems. Taking any year in isolation, it is clear that large differences exist between countries. These have been highlighted in previous studies. Overall, there is a downward trend.

It appears that Canada has the most generous treatment of R&D, except during three years in the mid 1980s when Australia gave a larger subsidy. Furthermore, in all of these countries the tax treatment of R&D has become *more* generous since the early 1980s, although there has been considerable turbulence. The relative position of countries

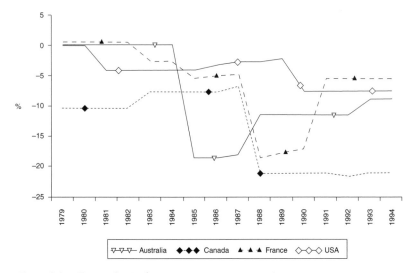

Figure 8.2   Tax wedge in four most generous countries

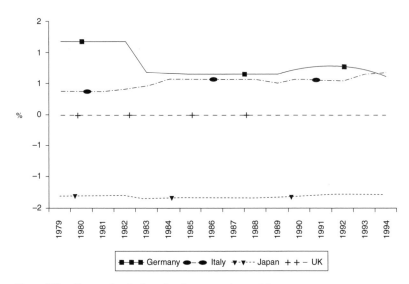

Figure 8.3   Tax wedge in four least generous countries

has moved around and there are substantial changes in the tax wedge on R&D due to changes in tax policies. The mid to late 1980s was a period of particular change. This turbulence illustrates the difficulty for firms considering long term investment plans, that there may be considerable uncertainty about the permanence of fiscal incentives.[8]

The reasons for the periods of large change in the cost of R&D vary across countries. In Australia, the large drop in 1985 was due to the introduction of a 150 per cent 'superdeductibility' for R&D. The subsequent increase was due to the lowering of Australia's statutory rate of corporation tax. The generosity of the Canadian system is driven by the fact that the credit rate is relatively high on the incremental amount of R&D (50 per cent). The fall in the cost of R&D in 1988 was precipitated by the introduction of a second credit Thein Ontario (the province which we model here). In France, the introduction of the credit in 1983 had much less effect than the redefinition of the base (from a moving to fixed base and than back again) which occurred between 1987–1990. Similarly in the USA, the base redefinition in 1990 had a greater effect than the introduction of the credit in 1981. These points illustrate that the statutory credit rate is not of overriding importance to the cost of R&D. The design and implementation of the schemes (such as the definition of the base) and the effects of other parts of the tax system (such as the statutory tax rate) are at least of equal importance in explaining the trends over time.

Figure 8.3 shows the tax wedge in the four less generous countries. In these countries the tax systems are broadly neutral to R&D (i.e. the tax wedge is close to zero). There have not been many changes in the tax treatment of R&D in these countries over this period. Japan occupies an intermediate position, however, as the only country in this group which has an R&D tax credit although the UK does also give an allowance for R&D capital expenditure.[9]

Another striking feature of Figure 8.2 is the fact that the range of the tax wedges at the end of the period is greater than at the start. In 1979 the mean effective marginal tax wedge on the typical R&D investment was –0.5 with a standard deviation of 1.6. By 1994 the mean had fallen to –3.7 and the standard deviation increased to 4.8.

How sensitive are the estimates of the cost of R&D to the assumptions underlying the calculations? The results are not sensitive to changes in the appropriate rate of depreciation for R&D capital – a variable for which there are few reliable estimates. For example, when the rate is changed from 30 per cent to 15 per cent the main features of Figure 8.2 remain the same.

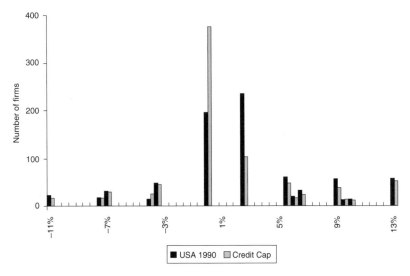

Figure 8.4   Marginal effective credit rate

Recall that in Figures 8.2 and 8.3 we have been considering a typical R&D investment, which is 90 per cent current expenditure. Current expenditure of any sort is fully deductible in all countries, which means that only subsidies through tax credits and superdeductibility affect the tax wedge for this asset. However, expenditure on plant and machinery and buildings are not fully deductible, therefore, depreciation allowances have a significant impact on the tax wedge for these assets. The different rankings of the tax wedge on these assets mirror those found with investment in physical capital – current expenditure is treated most favourably, plant and machinery next and buildings the least favourably.

The tax wedge varies significantly with the type of financing for investment in R&D, as it does with investment in physical capital. However, survey evidence strongly confirms that R&D is overwhelmingly financed from internal earnings.[10]

Heterogeneity due to design and implementation

The tax wedges presented in the previous section do not reflect the substantial heterogeneity in the marginal tax rates that different firms face. For example, the impact of the various capping rules are not incorporated into the tax wedge. In order to illustrate the differential way in which these credits will affect firms, we have applied several stylised tax credits to a sample of R&D performing firms.

The representative firm we used in our analysis in the previous section was assumed to increase its level of R&D year on year and to have sufficient tax liability to be able to claim any tax credit in full. The assumption of positive R&D growth is important for the analysis of incremental tax credit systems. Firms whose R&D expenditure does not grow at a constant rate but fluctuates over the cycle can experience both negative and positive effective tax credit rates. The assumption that the firm has sufficient tax liability to claim the credit in full is also important, since a non-refundable credit is worthless when firms are tax exhausted. New or high growth firms may experience prolonged periods where they are investing highly in R&D but not yet earning profits or paying taxes.

To examine these issues in more detail we use a sample of USA manufacturing firms drawn from the 1985–1994 Compustat files. This sample includes 813 publicly traded manufacturing firms which account for about 75 per cent of R&D performed and paid for by industry (see Table 8.1). The results presented use 1990 as a representative year.[11] We use USA firm data to model a variety of stylised tax systems based on those in operation in other countries. This allows us to focus on differences due to design and implementation, rather than those which arise from the sample of firms they are applied to. We use data from the USA due to the large sample size, the strength and consistency of its R&D reporting requirements, and to assist comparison with other studies of R&D tax credits which are predominantly based on USA data.

We begin by examining a stylised version of the US 1990 system. We take this to be our base case for comparison, and change specific elements of the tax system one at a time, which allows us to examine the specific impact of these changes in isolation. Thus, when we examine the effect of applying a French-style total cap on R&D tax credit payments, we apply that rule to the base system to

Table 8.1: Descriptive statistics on firm sample

Year	No. firms	Total R&D ($billion)	Total sales ($billion)	R&D nominal %	Growth rates real %	% firms paying tax
1988	813	51.5	1 625	10.1	6.2	86
1989	813	57.1	1 747	7.0	2.7	83
1990	813	61.1	1 895	6.2	2.6	80
1991	813	64.9	1 873	7.2	4.6	78

Source: authors' calculations using Datastream.

allow us to focus on the impact of this capping rule. When a moving average incremental base is used, as in the standard system, we need to model firms' expectations about the future path of their R&D expenditure. For this purpose we assume perfect foresight for three years on the part of firms. Thus, the marginal credit rate for each firm is calculated assuming that the firms' expected future R&D expenditure is their actual expenditure in those years. In fact, as far as modelling the tax credit is concerned, the results do not require firms to be completely accurate in their predictions but simply to be able to predict whether their future R&D will rise above or fall below the base. Given the high adjustment costs of R&D and its long term planning schedule, the assumption that firms can predict whether future R&D expenditure levels will be rising or falling does not seem too restrictive. We assume that firms use a 10 per cent nominal discount rate between periods and that tax credits cannot be carried backwards or forwards between periods.

As pointed out above, using a common data set and a standard tax credit system allows us to examine the impact of different individual rules in isolation. We tabulate the results for five tax credit systems chosen to reflect some of the most interesting aspects of the actual systems in Table 8.2. The five systems reported are:

1. The Base Case (US 1990): this system is used as the base tax regime, and replicates the main features of the actual tax system in the USA in 1990. The main features are: a 34 per cent rate of corporation tax; a 20 per cent tax credit rate on incremental R&D; a three year moving average base, above which any expenditure is deemed incremental R&D; and the R&D tax credit is taxable. This last feature means that the after tax value of the 20 per cent credit is actually 13.2 per cent (with the statutory corporation tax rate of 34 per cent).

2. Credit Cap ($1 million): as in the Base Case but with the total tax credit paid to any firm in any one year capped at $1 million. This reflects features of the French tax credit system, which has had a cap on the total amount of the R&D tax credit which could be claimed in any year (see Appendix A.2). About 25 per cent of firms in our sample would be affected by a cap set at this level.

3. Fixed Base Case (1987): as in the Base Case but with the base above which any R&D is considered incremental defined by each firm's nominal R&D expenditure in 1987. This reflects features of the French tax credit during 1988–1990, which used a fixed base of nominal R&D expenditure in 1987 to calculate incremental R&D.

4. Fixed Base Case (1989 real): as in the Base Case but with incremental R&D defined above a fixed base of real R&D expenditure in 1989. This reflects the fact that from 1991 onwards, the French tax credit indexed the R&D base for inflation (although the actual base used at the time was a moving average).
5. All R&D: as in the Base Case but with all R&D expenditure eligible for the tax credit. This reflects the Canadian system and a feature of the Australian special depreciation allowance which effectively applied to all R&D (since the qualifying base of A$10 000 would, in the USA, include more than 99 per cent of all USA business R&D expenditure). The Australian scheme actually operated as a depreciation allowance, but this could equivalently be implemented as a tax credit applied to all R&D.

All data in Table 8.2 relate to the sample of USA firms in 1990. The first six *rows* describe the distribution of the marginal effective tax credit (METC), given in equation 4. For example, an average R&D weighted METC figure of 4.3 per cent (the first figure in the first row) indicates that the USA 1990 tax credit effectively reduced the average cost of R&D by 4.3 per cent. The seventh row contains the revenue cost, in millions of 1990 US dollars, whilst the following three rows report statistics on the concentration of the credit across firms and the coverage of the credit. The final row presents a guide to the relative cost effectiveness of each credit in raising the marginal effective tax credit and so stimulating additional R&D expenditure.[12] Note that in order to estimate the absolute cost effectiveness of each tax credit system we would need to estimate the level of new R&D stimulated by the credit. This would require an estimation of R&D prices elasticities, which are discussed and estimated using this data in Bloom, Griffith and Van Reenen (1998).

From the results displayed in Table 8.2, it is clear that a prominent feature of all of the systems is the large variation in the effective tax credit rates, as evidenced by the standard deviation. The first two systems, with moving average bases, generate large negative effective tax credits, so that for some firms in some years the tax credit system actually discourages R&D expenditure. This arises because of a combination of the moving average marginal base, the fact that R&D expenditure is cyclical, and the fact that some companies have zero or negative tax payments. Under a moving average base, increasing current R&D expenditure raises the base used to measure incremental R&D in the future. Firms which are currently unable to claim a tax credit on their additional R&D expenditure (because they are below the base or tax exhausted) can face a negative tax credit if they expect to

Table 8.2: Calculations of five potential R&D tax credit variants

	Standard US 1990 %	Credit Cap $1 million %	Fixed Base 1987 %	Fixed Base 1989 real %	All R&D no base %
Marginal Effective Tax Credit Average (R&D weighted	4.3	0.31	11.2	12.9	10.5
unweighted average	2.5	1.5	11.1	11.7	9.6
mode	2.26	0	13.2	13.2	13.2
minimum	–10.9	–10.9	0	0	0
maximum	13.2	13.2	13.2	13.2	13.2
standard deviation	5.2	5.11	4.9	4.2	5.9
Revenue Cost $million[13]	1.244	245	1.875	437	6.708
% going to top 5% of firms	69	17	70	71	69
% firms eligible for credit	72	72	74	60	96
% firms receiving full credit	59	60	59	50	70
$m cost per % of METC	289	790	167	34	639

Source: author's calculations.

Notes: 1. Firms are eligible for a tax credit if their R&D expenditure is above the base.
   2. Firms receive a full credit if they are eligible and have sufficient tax liability to claim it.

claim in the next three years. In reverse, firms which are currently claiming a tax credit but do not expect to be able to do so in future years will face an effective credit rate well above the average rate. In general, the scheme operates to encourage a wider range of R&D expenditures, since the highest effective tax credits apply to firms which are temporarily above the base, while large negative effective rates apply to firms which are temporarily below the base.[14] This system will also encourage more lumpy R&D expenditure. Firms could maximise their credit receipts by lumping all R&D expenditure into expenditure bouts which take place only every fourth year (since their three year moving average base would always be zero). The Credit Cap system uses a moving average base so displays a similar distribution of METC rates, except there is a larger number of firms at zero. This reflects high R&D-spending firms which consistently face the credit cap, and so have an effective tax credit of zero on any increase in R&D. Figure 8.4 displays this wide distribution of actual marginal effective credit rates under the US 1990 tax credit system, and the Credit Cap system.

The fixed base systems do not display this distribution of effective credit rates because the fixed base prevents any feedback from current R&D to future levels of the base. Under a fixed base system, firms either face an effective credit rate of 13.2 per cent if they are above the base and paying sufficient tax, or 0 per cent otherwise. For both fixed base systems, about 85 per cent of firms face the full credit rate of 13.2 per cent (which is equivalent to about 75 per cent when they are weighted by expenditures on R&D). As a result, the average marginal effective credit rates are far higher than those found under a system with a moving average base. Two fixed base systems are presented to highlight the importance of the choice of base year and indexation for inflation. As the base year moves further back in time, the revenue cost of the credit system increases without any compensatory increase in the marginal tax credit, especially if the base is not indexed. We present a 1987 nominal base and a 1989 real base as relatively polar cases which generate similar marginal effective tax incentives, but dramatically different revenue costs. This suggests that an ideal base would be a recent year, indexed for inflation, so that only the additional dollars of R&D expenditure are eligible.[15] This is why the 1989 indexed base represents the most cost effective policy tool for raising the average marginal effective tax credit rate, as shown by the last column. However, since R&D expenditure tends to increases over time, any fixed base will include a progressively higher share of R&D over time. In order to prevent revenue costs from increasing, governments would need to redefine the base frequently. This would unfortunately reintroduce the potential for large negative effective credit rates in years in which the rebasing took place. These calculations do not take into account the need for rebasing over time, and so should be considered as an example of a one-off and temporary fixed base tax credit.

The All R&D system considered in column 5 has some similar properties to the fixed base systems, since there is no feedback from current

R&D expenditure to the future base (it is in fact equivalent to a system where the base is fixed at zero). The distributions of marginal effective tax rates across firms for the All R&D system closely replicates those for the Fixed Base system (column 4). The main distinction between the All R&D and Fixed Base systems is the revenue cost. The All R&D system makes no attempt to distinguish between the additional R&D, and that R&D which would have been carried out anyway. It is by targeting additional, or incremental, R&D that tax credit systems have their impact. Introducing a high base which falls just below the level of additional R&D significantly reduces the revenue cost of the tax credit without reducing its efficacy. The all R&D system subsidises both existing and additional R&D, making it the most expensive system considered.

These five systems also have implications for the distribution of tax credits across firm sizes. Figure 8.5 splits the firms into ten deciles by R&D expenditure and plots the weighted average marginal effective tax credit for each decile. The USA 1990 system clearly favours large firms over small firms. One reason for this is that larger R&D-performing firms will tend, on average, to be above their base level of R&D, whilst smaller R&D-performing firms will, on average, tend to be below their base level. In addition, larger firms tend to pay tax more frequently, i.e. they are tax exhausted less often than smaller firms. This pattern is repeated under the Credit Cap system up to about the 7th decile, after which the cap begins to bite sufficiently to drive the effective marginal credit back towards zero. The fixed base systems mildly favour large firms, again because they tend not to be tax exhausted as often as smaller firms.

A final point to note is that these tax exhaustion problems are not evenly distributed across all industry classes, so that different tax credits have implications for the industrial structure of R&D. Thus, whilst 11 per cent of all firms were unable to claim the full credit due to insufficient tax payments, about 50 per cent of biotech firms and 40 per cent of plastics and elastomer firms could not claim their full credits. In contrast, no petroleum, aerospace equipment, or telephone equipment firms were tax exhausted.

Summary and conclusions

Despite the widespread concern that policy makers and economists have expressed about the amount of innovative activity undertaken, quantitative assessments of technology policies across countries are rare. In this study we consider the effects of tax systems on the cost of R&D in eight countries over 16 years. An important feature of many of the main industrialised countries is the generous treatment of R&D

compared to other forms of investment. Previous studies have only considered the time series profile of one country or international comparisons at one point of time. The numbers presented here reveal several interesting patterns. First, as other studies have found there is considerable variation in the cost of R&D between countries at any point of time, even holding inflation, depreciation and interest rates constant across countries. Second, there is a discernible trend towards more generous tax treatment of R&D in half the countries in our sample. Third, there is a lot of within country variation in the impact of a tax credit – they will vary across firms depending on the precise way in which the credit is designed and implemented. The impact of an incremental tax credit is significantly affected by the way the base is calculated. The benefits of tax credits are often highly concentrated among a few firms.

Why do we see this diversity in the taxation of intangible assets? One reason might be a diversity of opinion on what the optimal tax treatment of intangibles is. Some countries believe a strong R&D base is a way of improving competitiveness. Evidence of international spillovers has led others to argue that a large domestic R&D base is no longer necessary for economic growth and therefore there is no reason for governments to provide substantial subsidies for R&D. Thus policy -makers differ in their opinions over what the appropriate role for the state should be in encouraging R&D, and this is reflected in different national tax policies.

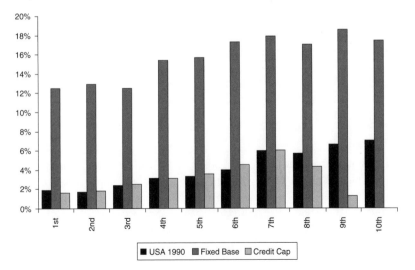

Figure 8.5   METC by R&D decile

Appendix: Tax data

This appendix details the tax treatment of expenditure on R&D in eight OECD countries. The tables under each country section give the statutory tax rate on retentions and the net present value of depreciation allowances and tax credits on the three R&D assets considered. The figures show the tax wedge on investment in each of the three assets.

The statutory tax rates shown below are on retained earnings and are based on the rates in force as a result of any change in that calendar year. For example, if the tax rate falls from 35 per cent to 33 per cent on the 31 March 1993, the rate for 1993 is given as 33 per cent. If two changes occurred in one year then only the final change is recorded. The statutory tax rate includes surcharges or other special taxes that are levied on corporate income at the national level. Where a tax on corporate income is levied at a local level, for example by states or provinces, we have tried to construct an average of these rates to indicate the average additional tax at the local level. This has not always been possible and in several cases the local tax rate is set at the 1991 rate in every year due to lack of information. Where there are local credits on R&D expenditure we have generally taken the most generous. Local taxes only include local corporate income taxes. In general they do not include taxes on property. In many countries local taxes are deductible from the national tax and this is taken into account. See Table A.1, for statutory tax rates.

Most countries allow a wide range of depreciation methods and rates. We have, in general, used the most favourable method and rates that are commonly allowed on the various classes of asset. The two most commonly used methods are straight -line (SL) and declining balance (DB) depreciation. In addition, many countries give extra first year allowances or provide accelerated depreciation allowances in the first few years. In general, plant and machinery is depreciated using the DB or a combination of DB and SL methods, while buildings are depreciated using SL.

Australia

Australia introduced a special 150 per cent depreciation allowance for qualifying R&D in 1985: 150 per cent of current expenditure can be written-off in the first year, plant over three years, and buildings over 40 years. This dramatically reduced the tax wedge on current expenditure and plant and machinery R&D (as shown in Figure 8.2), providing a large subsidy for R&D expenditures. This special depreciation allowance did not affect the tax wedge on buildings used for R&D as much, since a rapid

Table A.1: Statutory tax rates

Year	Australia	Canada	France	Germany	Italy	Japan	UK	USA
1979	50	30.0	50.0	56.0	36.3	52.7	52	46
1980	50	31.8	50.0	56.0	36.3	52.7	52	46
1981	50	31.8	50.0	56.0	36.3	52.7	52	46
1982	50	31.8	50.0	56.0	38.0	52.7	52	46
1983	50	30.9	50.0	56.0	41.3	52.7	50	46
1984	50	30.0	50.0	56.0	46.4	52.7	45	46
1985	50	31.8	50.0	56.0	46.4	52.7	40	46
1986	50	31.8	45.0	56.0	46.4	56.2	35	46
1987	50	29.1	45.0	56.0	46.4	56.2	35	34
1988	39	26.8	42.0	56.0	46.4	56.2	35	34
1989	39	25.8	39.0	56.0	46.4	54.8	35	34
1990	39	24.8	37.0	50.0	46.4	52.7	34	34
1991	39	23.8	34.0	51.9	47.8	54.8	33	34
1992	39	23.8	34.0	51.9	47.8	54.8	33	34
1993	33	22.8	33.3	50.0	52.2	54.8	33	35
1994	33	21.8	33.3	45.0	53.2	53.9	33	35

Source: Chennells and Griffith, 1997

three year depreciation provision was already in existence. Qualifying R&D included expenditure on innovation or projects that involved technical risk, and was carried out in Australia for the benefit of Australians. Australia is unusual in that it has a minimum threshold of A$50 000 to receive the full 150 per cent, with a sliding scale between A$20 000 and A$50 000, and no additional allowance for expenditure below A$20 000. The fall in the overall tax subsidy in 1988 reflects the cut in the statutory tax rate on retentions from 50 per cent to 39 per cent, which reduced the value of the additional R&D depreciation allowance.

Canada

Canada allows full deduction on current expenditure, expenditure on plant and machinery for R&D purposes throughout the period and for R&D buildings from 1979 to 1987. A national Scientific Research Credit of 50 per cent on incremental expenditure above the average of the previous three years was also provided during 1979 to 1982. This was replaced by the national Investment Tax Credit (ITC) of 20 per cent of total R&D expenditure, which fully reduces the cost of the asset for deduction purposes. We have modelled the provincial credits available in Ontario as they are some of the most generous. This includes a 25 per cent superallowance on all expenditure that qualifies for the national credit, minus the amount given for the national credit. This superallowance is designed to offset the fact that the national credit reduces deductible costs by its value, and lower deductions would normally lead to a higher tax payment. In addition, Ontario gives a 35.7 per cent credit on incremental expenditure. Incremental expenditure is defined as additional spending about the average of the past three years expenditure.

France

In 1983 a 25 per cent tax credit was introduced on the real increase in qualifying R&D expenditure over last year, with a FF3 million per year cap. This led to a small fall in the tax wedge (as shown in Figure 8.2). The credit rate was increased to 50 per cent in 1985 and the cap raised to FF5 million, leading to a further fall in the marginal tax wedge. In 1988 firms were given two alternative choices. The first was a 50 per cent credit on the increase over the previous year's expenditure, up to a maximum of FF5 million (increased to FF10 million in certain cases). Alternatively, for the years 1988, 1989 and 1990 they could receive a 30 per cent credit on the increase over their 1987 expenditure, up to a maximum of FF3 million. This latter option is worth more to firms expecting to increase their R&D spending and is what we model. Although the headline rate of credit fell (from 50 per cent to 30 per cent), the value of the effective subsidy to R&D increased sharply because the base used to calculate the increase in R&D expenditure was fixed at the 1987 level. This eliminates the impact of current R&D spending on the calculation of the future base. In 1991 the credit returned to 50 per cent on the increase in real expenditure, but the base was extended to the most recent two years and the cap raised to FF40 million. This reduced the effective value of the subsidy due, since the base reverted to a moving average. From 1983 to 1986 expenditure on buildings used for scientific research was given an accelerated depreciation allowance of 50 per cent straight line.

Germany

There are currently no special tax allowances for R&D. Between 1983 and 1989 industrial buildings and plant and machinery enjoyed limited accelerated depreciation provisions. A building that was at least two-thirds used for R&D purposes could be depreciated at up to 15 per cent of the cost over five years, or 10 per cent if only one-third used for R&D. Plant and machinery used exclusively for R&D, could receive an additional 8 per cent allowance of up to 40 per cent of the initial cost over five years. These accelerated depreciation provisions dramatically reduced the marginal tax wedge on plant and machinery and building

R&D expenditure. However, since current R&D accounts for 90 per cent of total R&D expenditure, this has not had a large effect on the total R&D tax wedge (see Figure 8.3). The reduction in the statutory tax rate on retentions from 56 per cent to 45 per cent has reduced the net present value of the deductibility of current expenditure by a far greater amount.

Italy

No special tax depreciation provisions or credits are given on R&D expenditure. Italy's statutory tax rate has risen from 36.3 per cent in 1979 to 53.2 per cent in 1994 and thus increased the marginal effective tax wedge on R&D plant and machinery and R&D building expenditure. However, the immediate expensing of current R&D expenditure (which accounts for 90 per cent of total R&D expenditure) leaves the total marginal tax wedge relatively unaffected (see Figure 8.3).

Japan

Japanese firms can claim a 20 per cent credit on R&D spending exceeding the largest previous annual R&D expenditure. The credit is limited to 10 per cent of tax due before the credit. Buildings and plant and machinery used for R&D activity are also eligible for accelerated depreciation allowances. Several additional special credits are also available, although we do not model them here.[16] While the statutory tax rate reported here remains remarkably stable over this period, its composition has changed over time.

The UK

Capital expenditure on equipment and buildings used for R&D in the UK qualifies for a 100 per cent first year allowance under the Scientific Research Allowance. Current expenditure receives no special treatment.

The USA

Since 1954 all R&D expenditure has been fully deductible. The Economic Recovery Tax Act of 1981 introduced a tax credit on incremental R&D expenditure which has remained in place, although there have been many subsequent changes to its design, and the credit has never been made a permanent feature of the tax system. The rules governing the operation of the USA tax credit are complex and are only sketched out here. A detailed explanation can be found in Hines (1994) and Hall (1995). In particular, we do not consider the foreign allocation rules as we consider only purely domestic firms. The statutory rate of the credit was 25 per cent between 1981 and 1985 and has been 20 per cent since then. From 1981 until 1990 incremental expenditure was defined as spending above the average of the last three years expenditure. In 1990 the definition of the base changed to the three year ratio of R&D over sales (up to a maximum of 16 per cent) times sales. In addition, the rules governing the deductibility of the credit have change. Before 1988 corporation tax was not levied on the R&D tax credit itself. In 1988 50 per cent of the credit was made taxable income and from 1989 onwards 100 per cent was made taxable income.

Acknowledgements

The authors would like to thank Stephen Bond, Michael P. Devereux and Bronwyn Hall for helpful comments. This work was funded by the ESRC Centre for Microeconomic Analysis of Fiscal Policy at the Institute for Fiscal Studies.

Notes

1. See, for example, Van Reenen (1997).
2. See, *inter alia*, Aghion and Howitt (1992), Grossman and Helpman (1991).
3. For evidence of failures in the market for skills see Booth and Snower (1996); for evidence of failure in credit markets for R&D see Himmelburg and Peterson (1995).
4. Other important studies include Hines (1994) who adapted Hall's method for multinational firms taking into account the impact of foreign tax surpluses. He also found large responses to the tax-induced fall in the cost of R&D capital. Also, Mansfield (1986) adapted the Eisner approach for Sweden and Canada.
5. See Hines (1994) for a detailed analysis of these rules.
6. The depreciation rates for buildings and plant and machinery are taken from OECD (1991). In most empirical work, the depreciation rate used for current expenditure of R&D lies between 15 per cent–30 per cent: see the survey in Mairesse and Sassenou (1991).
7. Figures taken from OECD (1991) and UK Economic Trends (1996).
8. Hall (1993) emphasises that companies may have been reluctant to commit themselves to large changes in their R&D programmes in the early years of the US credit due to worries about its longevity.
9. Note that Japan gives a range of additional tax credits for specific types of R&D. For example, small and medium sized firms can elect to receive 6 per cent of total expenditures as a credit (limited to 15 per cent of the firm's tax bill). Additional R&D tax credits are also available for: (i) investment in promotion of basic technology – 7 per cent of total expenditure; (ii) R&D carried out in cooperation with government – 6 per cent of total expenditure.

10. See the evidence cited by Mayer (1992).
11. The panel that is analysed here is restricted to R&D performing firms with complete data for 1990–94. In order to model a three year moving average base and expectations over future R&D tax status we need three years of data prior to, and three years of data following, the particular year being analysed. This restricts us to examining results from the central part of our data period. ie: 1988–91. When there are marked differences in the results from looking at other sample years, for example because of the effects of the business cycle, this is also reported.
12. Note that in order to estimate the absolute cost effectiveness of each tax credit system we would need to estimate the level of new R&D stimulated by the credit. This would require an estimation of R&D prices elasticities, which are discussed and estimated using this data in Bloom, Griffith and Van Reenen (1998).
13. This is based on the assumption that firms do not change their behaviour in response to the credit and that the accounting definition of R&D equals the definition of eligibility for the tax credit (see Hall 1993).
14. This system will also encourage more lumpy R&D expenditure. Firms could maximise their credit receipts by lumping all R&D expenditure into expenditure bouts which take place only every fourth year (since their three year moving average base would always be zero).
15. In our example we index by inflation but other choices, such as indexing by aggregate nominal R&D growth, for example, could also be chosen depending on the required trade-off between credit coverage and revenue cost.
16. These include a 6 per cent credit for small and medium sized firms, a 7 per cent credit for investment to promote basic technology and a 6 per cent credit on R&D carried out in cooperation with government.

References

Aghion, P. and Howitt, P. (1992) 'A Model of Growth through Creative Destruction', *Econometrica* 60, 323–51.

Altshuler, R. (1988), 'A Dynamic Analysis of the Research and Experimentation Credit', *National Tax Journal*, vol. 41, pp. 453–66.

Bloom, N., Griffith, R. and Van Reenen, J. (1998) 'Do R&D tax credits work? evidence from an international panel of countries 1979–1994', London: Institute for Fiscal Studies.

Booth, A. and Snower, D. (1996) *Acquiring Skills*, Cambridge: Cambridge University Press, W89/9.

Chennells, L. and Griffith, R. (1997) *Taxing profits in a changing world*, London: Institute for Fiscal Studies.

Devereux, M., and Pearson M. (1995), 'European Tax Harmonisation and Production Efficiency', *European Economic Review*, vol. 39, no. 9, pp. 1657–82.

Eisner, R., Albert, S. and Sullivan, M. (1984), 'The new incremental tax credit for R&D: incentive or disincentive?', *National Tax Journal*, vol. 37, no. 2, pp. 171–85.

Griffith, R., Sandler, D. and Van Reenen, J. (1995) 'Tax Incentives for R&D' *Fiscal Studies*, 16, 2, 21–44.

Grossman, Gene and Helpman, Elhanan (1991), *Innovation and Growth*, Cambridge, Mass: MIT Press.

Hall, B. (1993) 'R&D Tax Policy During the 1980s: Success or Failure?', *Tax Policy and the Economy*, 1–35.

Hall, B. (1995) 'Effectiveness of Research and Experimentation Tax Credits: Critical Literature Review and Research Design' Report to Office of Technology Assessment, Congress of the United States.

Himmelburg, C. and Peterson, B. (1994) 'R&D and internal finance: A Panel study of small firms in high tech industries' *Review of Economics and Statistics*, 76(1), 38–51.

Hines, J. (1994) 'No Place like Home: Tax Incentives and the location of R&D by American Multinationals' *Tax Policy and the Economy* 8, 65–104.

Keen, M. J. (1991) 'Corporation tax, foreign direct investment and the single market' in L. A. Winters and A. J. Venables (eds) *The Impact of 1992 on European Trade and Industry*, Cambridge: Cambridge University Press.

King, M. A. and Fullerton, D. (eds) (1984), *The Taxation of Income from Capital: A Comparative Study of the United States, the United Kingdom, Sweden, and West Germany*, Chicago: University of Chicago Press.

Leydon, D. and Link, A. (1993) 'Tax Policies Affecting R&D: An International Comparison' *Technovation*, 13:1, 17–25.

Mairesse, J. and Sassenou, M. (1991) 'R&D and Productivity: A Survey of Econometric Studies at the firm level' NBER Working Paper No. 3666.

Mansfield, E. (1986) 'The R&D Tax Credit and Other Technology Policy Issues' *American Economic Association Papers and Proceedings* 76: 190–194.

Mayer, C. (1992) 'The Financing of Innovation' in Bowen, Alex and Ricketts, Martin (eds) *Stimulating Innovation in Industry*, London: Kogan Page.

OECD (1991), *Taxing Profits in a Global Economy: Domestic and International Issues*, Paris.

OECD (1996) *Main Science and Technology Indicators*, DSTI, Paris.

Van Reenen, John (1997) 'Why has Britain had slower R&D Growth?', *Research Policy*, 26: 493–507.

Worda, J. (1994) *Canadian R&D tx treatment: an International Comparison* report No. 125–94, Ottawa: The Conference Board of Canada.

9
Reconstructing the Local and the Global: Europeanisation, Regulation and Changing Knowledge Relations

Henry Rothstein and Alan Irwin

Introduction

The management of regulatory affairs by pesticide companies is now very different to that of thirty years ago. Talk to a manager of a pesticide company's 'regulatory affairs' department today and you will learn that, until at least the 1970s, there was probably no such department. In the UK until the mid-1980s, there were no statutory regulations for pesticide approval. Instead, a voluntary scheme operated on the principle that only pesticides approved by government experts would be supplied. Meanwhile, obtaining approval was given a low priority by companies, typically 'tacked-on' at the end of the innovation process and overseen by ex-field trials officers towards the end of their careers. The scheme was sufficiently informal and the network of professional contacts so small that, in the words of one manager, it was possible to 'take out the MAFF (Ministry of Agriculture) representative for a couple of beers and everything would be all right'.

Today pesticide approval is a very different matter. The European Plant Protection Product Directive (Council of the European Communities, 1991; Scharpe, 1992) requires European-wide approval of new pesticide active ingredients. Pesticide products must also be approved and mutually recognised by national authorities according to commonly-agreed European rules. In addition, the new regime has instituted a rolling review of existing pesticides to remove inefficient or more harmful compounds from the available chemical inventory. In this new European context, the large multinational R&D-intensive

161

agrochemical companies have departments dedicated to regulatory affairs, staffed by personnel trained in environmental and toxicological science, agronomy and law, with extensive knowledge and understanding of regulatory developments and politics. Given that the list of data requirements necessitates documentation typically weighing three-quarters of a tonne, it is abundantly clear why this has come to be the case.

Building upon the particular example of pesticides, a number of wider questions become highly relevant. If it is indeed the case that we are living in a society increasingly concerned with risk, and that regulation is the foremost tool of government for the control of risk, what sorts of demand does this place upon the provision of knowledge and expertise? As regulators struggle to deal with a plethora of risks from BSE and GMOs to mobile phones and environmental oestrogens, what kinds of knowledges and practices are developing to meet the demands of regulation – often under conditions of extreme uncertainty? At the same time we need to enquire, amongst *which* institutions are these knowledges and practices distributed? Finally, and especially for this study, as risk regulation becomes increasingly globalised, is it possible to witness a parallel 'globalisation' of regulatory–scientific knowledges or can countervailing and 'localising' tendencies be observed? We will argue that these questions are of significance both for the whole topic of the 'Europeanisation' of regulation and for science and technology policy more generally.

Studies of the role of science in policy making have previously considered whether we are witnessing the emergence of a new and distinct body of what has been termed 'regulatory science'. This concept has either been related to the uncertainties of the subjects with which it must deal or to the, often politicised, environments in which it is practised (see Jasanoff, 1990; Shackley and Wynne, 1995; Irwin *et al.*, 1997). However, in this study we argue that the increasing significance accorded to supranational science-based regulation suggests that a fresh examination of this domain is required.

We, therefore, consider the character and dynamics of developing regulatory knowledges in the context of contemporary and, in particular, European risk regulation. Taking as our central case the European regulation of pesticide approvals, we sketch out the evolving institutional complex of actors and organisations involved in these processes. We examine how differing types of knowledge-producing activities are distributed throughout the regulatory network and the consequent implications for the character of contemporary knowledge production.

And finally, we consider the relevance of the social relations of these activities in determining the local conditions of regulatory understanding, practice and enactment.

This study is based upon an extended series of interviews with industrialists holding special responsibility in this area (including toxicology, R&D and regulatory affairs managers) within R&D-intensive multinational agrochemical corporations with a base in the UK. We have also interviewed government officials from the relevant departments and agencies (including the Pesticides Safety Directorate, PSD), officials of the European Commission and scientists (working in university and industrial contract laboratories). In addition, we have made full use of documentary sources. Whilst the focus of the research was on the impact of harmonisation within the UK, it should be pointed out that all our interviewees by virtue of their position and work, have had considerable experience of the regulatory system in Europe and the rest of the world.

Pesticide registration and regulatory science

Increasing environmental concerns have undoubtedly driven the huge growth in information requirements concerning pesticides – for example, by expanding testing into the fields of ecotoxicology and environmental fate. As these environmental sciences themselves develop, new issues are inevitably placed on the regulatory agenda. Other regulatory regimes, such as those concerned with water quality, have also had significant impacts on pesticide control. At the same time, the requirement for producers to undertake their own 'risk assessments', nominally to encourage self-learning and speed the regulatory process, has further increased the workload.

Pesticide regulation has therefore been characterised by increasing demands on science to assess and minimise impacts on humans, wildlife and the environment. A brief discussion of the impacts of this new regime on regulatory scientific capacities illustrates both the diversity of *activities* that are undertaken and the variety of *institutions* which those activities tie together (for a fuller discussion see Irwin *et al.*, 1997). For the purposes of this discussion, we consider just three out of many possible areas of activity: drafting the directive; national implementation of the European regime; and regulatory compliance testing.

In *drafting* the pesticides registration directive the European Commission has – where possible – borrowed from existing regimes in member states, North America or international organisations such as the OECD. The concern has been to ensure that whilst standards of environmental protection are raised, the new regime should accord as much as possible with existing regimes and regulatory developments inside and outside the EU. It should be emphasised that there is no public sector regulatory science institute either nationally or in Brussels for consultation on such matters. Instead, the European Commission (EC) co-ordinates these developments through committees of representatives of member states, which have (on the stated grounds of superior technical expertise) predominantly consisted of northern European representatives.

Many toxicological test methodologies are well established and have been unproblematically incorporated into the test requirements. In some cases, however, there has had to be negotiation over which testing methodologies to adopt. This negotiation typically involves balancing differing member states preferences and views on the policy need for *standardisation and simplicity*, and the scientific need for *similitude to real-life conditions*. However, where no suitable testing methodologies have existed, particularly those for ecotoxicity and environmental fate, the EC has liaised with the OECD or contracted-out research to various organisations across the EU. This has drawn upon the diverse institutional framework of government, commercial organisations, a small number of academic laboratories and professional associations. In so doing, this also provides opportunities for interested groups to feed forward into the regulatory process. For example, in the case of beneficial insects, an industry group co-organised a conference (with EC funding) which produced test guidelines that are now utilised by the EC (Barrett *et al.*, 1994).

The *implementation* of the Directive by member states is not just a technical–legal question of transposing the Directive into national legislation. The new regime places considerable demands on the national regulatory authorities of member states, either acting as rapporteurs for the European approval of active ingredients, or as approval authorities for pesticide products containing those active ingredients. This national tier of activity has been explicitly included in the new regime to deal with the effect of regional ecology on pesticide efficacy, safety and environmental impact (Scharpe, 1992). Whilst the regime has attempted to harmonise registration activities across member states, to the extent of attempting to establish uniform principles of interpretation, regulatory authorities have an important role in fleshing out the character of the regime through its implementation. As no list of regulations can in practice be exhaustive – covering every conceivable kind of agrochemical, its intended application and all ecological conditions – there is always some need for professional judgement. This is particularly the case where discretion has been accorded to national authorities on certain environmental issues in the absence of established rules or guidelines.

For some member states such as the UK, the implementation of the Directive has been relatively straightforward and has not necessitated too many changes. In part, this reflects the influence that the UK has brought to bear in negotiating the details of the regime. It also reflects the strength of the UK's own approval system – especially given the considerable administrative expansion following the introduction of domestic pesticide approval regulations in the mid-1980s (House of Commons Agriculture Committee, 1995, 210). Even so, MAFF's Pesticides Safety Directorate (PSD), which administers approvals, contracts out some initial reviews of approval applications to commercial laboratories (which might themselves be conducting testing) to deal with the still heavy workload. At the same time, for other member states that have no or only minimal prior experience of pesticide approval, the implementation of the regime is more problematic requiring a considerable expansion of bureaucratic and technical capacities.

Regulatory compliance testing to support applications for approval is conducted entirely in the private sector. In general, regulatory compliance testing is repetitive and highly-standardised, governed by fixed protocols and test procedures, and amenable to auditing and scrutiny in accordance with the requirements of Good Laboratory Practice. This work is undertaken either by the agrochemical company using in-house facilities or is contracted out to commercial laboratories specialising in such work. Few British university laboratories get involved, generally being considered (with a few notable exceptions) by industry as an irrelevance in this domain. Only where more specialist investigative research is required, such as when a test produces a positive result, is work organised on a more case-by-case basis, occasionally bringing in more specialist expertise from academic institutions.

In contrast to regulatory compliance testing, the completion of the in-house risk assessment and compilation of the dossier for submission is a multi-disciplinary process combining technical, regulatory and managerial inputs, sometimes working closely with consultancies and contract laboratories. In the UK, the PSD may also play a role in offering constructive advice and general guidance on the often-complex, and sometimes open-ended, requirements.

This broad outline of regulatory scientific work illustrates the variety of activities and institutions that have evolved to meet regulatory demands. Some of the activities accord with conventional representations of academic science, whilst others are undoubtedly highly bureaucratised. Some activities are undertaken in research intensive and academic environments, others are conducted in 'conveyor-belt' and commercial settings. Some activities are driven by fundamental scientific questions, some by political and bureaucratic demands. It therefore does not appear to be possible to categorise regulatory science as a unified set of activities. However, we can observe the significance of such regulatory–scientific activities at every stage in the development and control of pesticides.

Instead of any simple characterisation, the often hybrid nature of regulatory scientific practices can be identified, crossing conventional disciplinary boundaries and bringing together a variety of scientific and bureaucratic demands and practices. Furthermore, these activities interconnect a range of institutions and indeed are often cross-institutionally located. Overall, it is important to recognise the degree to which regulatory science in this area is dominated by business and government. From our perspective, regulatory science represents an important field of 'changing knowledge relations' – a field made all the more important by the ubiquitous character of contemporary risk concerns.

The global and local relations of regulatory science

Prior to the introduction of the new European regime, pesticide companies had to apply for approval in each country within which they wished to market their product. This meant that companies had to comply with a wide range of national rules. This also provided a national character to regulatory science in that, for example, tests would have to be conducted to specific national requirements, and possibly in the country where approval was sought. The harmonisation of pesticide registration requirements was intended to change this. By establishing a common core of requirements, the EU has attempted to reduce the problems of duplication, eliminate the use of national rules that restrict the European market in pesticides and raise environmental standards. This has been accompanied by what might be termed a globalisation of regulatory science in the domains of activity discussed in the previous section. In this section, however, we will argue that the processes of globalisation are by no means as unidirectional as the prevailing rhetoric suggests (see also Rothstein *et al.*, 1999).

Global dimensions

The *drafting* of a common set of rules for assessing and approving pesticides is based upon the principle that the creation of common scientific requirements will provide a universal basis for assessing risk throughout the EU. However, reconciling the wide variety of scientific requirements that exist across the EU has a social as well as a scientific character. Questions of how best to test for particular hazards and how the results should be interpreted have until recently been decided on a national basis within the constraints of available scientific knowledge and specific regulatory practices.

In creating the new European regime, nationally-based decision-making or advisory institutions and organisations are no longer accorded primacy. Decisions have to fit European requirements for pesticide manufacture and use. Furthermore, moves towards harmonising rules with regimes outside of Europe mean that decisionmakers in Brussels will look anywhere in Europe or even beyond for advice and guidance. As a result, organisations and state institutions that have played a key part in developing their indigenous regulatory regimes can find themselves in competition with their European counterparts in influencing decisions on the details and profile of scientific requirements. At the same time, there is an increasing trend towards the international organisation of professional groups to feed into European decisionmaking, as with the new guidelines on beneficial insects noted in the previous section.

The *implementation* of the regime has also internationalised regulatory approval. Active ingredients are approved at the European level, and approval of pesticide products in one country should be mutually recognised in other countries, ecological variation excepted. In principle, therefore, it makes no difference which member state reviews a pesticide product (although it might be reasonable to expect products to be approved by a member state with relevant agronomic and ecological conditions). Indeed, it is possible that a European market in pesticide registration is developing as national agencies look for business outside of their previous national ambits.

At the same time, the implementation of the regime has provided opportunities for national learning and co-operation. This is a significant development both for those member states with well established regimes as well as for those member states that have little or no experience of pesticide registration. In this latter case, especially in order to aid the principle of mutual recognition, more experienced agencies have been enlisted by the EC to aid less experienced member states in their implementation and operation of the regime (House of Commons Agriculture Committee, 1995, 57).

It is possible to identify a similar Europeanisation of *regulatory compliance testing*. The assumption of scientific of scientific universality means that tests performed in a French toxicological laboratory can satisfy the regulatory authorities in Athens and Copenhagen. An important premiss of the new European regime, therefore, is that a test or trial competently carried out in one member state should have validity elsewhere, ecological variation excepted. This contrasts with the previous situation whereby certain national agencies demanded tests to be undertaken within their country as a precondition of approval. As a result, there is a burgeoning international market in regulatory compliance testing with specialist laboratories (one has even been based in a multinational pesticide company) offering services across Europe.

In these different domains of regulatory scientific activity, therefore, it is possible to portray Europeanisation as being characterised by a globalisation of regulatory scientific requirements, methodologies and interpretative rules as well as the international transformation of previously national institutions and organisations providing regulatory scientific services. Yet despite these changes, it is also possible to identify countervailing (or centrifugal) tendencies that suggest the persistence of national characteristics in the implementation and enactment of the regime.

Local dimensions

In the *drafting* of the Directive, it is possible to identify ethnocentric approaches of member states towards potential testing and assessment regimes. For example, the competition between member states wanting the new regime to adopt their test methodologies and assessment criteria suggests commitments to beliefs and practices that cannot be explained by scientific rationales (at least as narrowly defined) alone. In some cases, member states have been concerned not to have to deal with unfamiliar rules and methods: familiarity and certainty being especially important to national agencies in successfully implementing the new regime. In other cases, because some tests require specialised and scarce laboratories and expertise, the outcome can directly favour regulatory scientific facilities in certain countries over others. Importantly, decisions also reflect political variation amongst member states towards environmental protection, particularly on the extent of testing required to demonstrate absence of harm. And finally, decision making concerning the details of scientific requirements has, in general, been dominated by the more experienced northern European member states, with southern European member states playing only a marginal role. Harmonisation therefore has tended to be based on the transfer of northern European practice across the EU.

Whilst the regime has internationalised regulatory approval, its *implementation* retains national characteristics. This is, in part, a direct consequence of the institutional architecture of the regime which places responsibility on national authorities for product approval. However, this is not simply a matter of rote rule-following. As has already been observed, there is considerable scope for professional judgement and interpretation of the rules. For example, this is the case where discretion has been given to national authorities on certain eco-toxicological tests pending future agreement. Regional ecological variation across member states also presents particular problems for interpretation. Judgements of similarity and difference of regional ecology and agronomic conditions can have significant consequences for the mutual recognition of member states' approvals.

Such problems are representative, however, of the broader point that despite attempts to create a universal scientific basis for regulatory approval, regulatory science requires contextual interpretation and situation specific modifications. The assessment of ecological variation or the adequacy of a few test species to substitute for the wider ecosystem are not just 'technical' issues but have social and institutional dimensions also. National authorities are liable to interpret these issues differently, taking into account national specificities and traditions.

From a practical point of view, this presents pesticide companies with a number of dilemmas when considering how best to proceed with product registration. For example, are some national authorities likely to view certain products more favourably than others? Do some authorities carry greater weight by virtue of their experience and expertise? Will some authorities be more open to dialogue or more 'straightforward' in their requirements? Even within a harmonised setting, there is likely to be considerable national variation in what is deemed to be acceptable and to be sufficient in tests.

These questions are intimately tied into pesticide companies' strategies for *regulatory compliance-testing*. Such are the heavy investments in new pesticides that pesticide companies need to know as early as possible whether or not the product they are developing is likely to be approved. This is one reason why pesticide companies often undertake their own compliance testing so that they are fully aware of problems and issues as they emerge. Where testing is contracted out to external laboratories, the development of trust between laboratory and company is seen to be of paramount importance, so that local laboratories are often used to enable such relationships to develop. Contact with the government agency during the testing phase is also critical in ensuring that the correct tests are undertaken and that the potential concerns of the regulatory authority eventually reviewing the pesticide are second-guessed as much as possible. Consequently, ex-government employees are valued both by pesticide companies and contract laboratories for their 'insider knowledge' and contacts, to the extent that contract laboratories may be quite open about their employment of ex-government personnel who are able to 'get on the phone' to their former colleagues in the agency as soon as a problem arises.

In the UK, the relatively small and informal character of the institutional network enhances this situation. Given that there are fewer than ten R&D active companies with a base in Britain, an equivalent number of larger contract laboratories and, in PSD, a high-profile government agency, it is not surprising that close personal links have developed over time as people move between institutions. One consequence of this is that, even in the European context, national regulatory networks still have a role to play in fostering mutual understanding between national regulatory authorities, pesticide companies and contract laboratories. For this reason, it may pay a pesticide company to use a contract laboratory in the member state in which it wishes to have its product approved, if it is not itself well connected to the national regulatory network. In other words, despite moves towards the Europeanisation of regulatory science, the *local relations* of regulatory science are still significant.

Reconstructing the global and local relations of regulatory science

In certain ways, this discussion of the globalising and localising tendencies of regulatory science is distinctly misleading. After all, the pesticide market has been international in character for many years, dominated as it is by relatively few research-intensive multinational companies operating across various national settings of product development, manufacturing and distribution. In that sense, pesticide companies, both national and multinational, have always had to act internationally and understand the different national dimensions of regulatory scientific requirements and practices within their diverse product markets. In trying to understand how harmonisation has changed regulatory science across Europe, it is important to recognise that the global and local have long been inseparable within such organisations.

Rather than trying to decide whether industries such as these are 'local' or 'global' in character, it seems more appropriate to consider them as embodying both elements – and as actively constructing themselves as either (or both) within different settings. For example, it can suit a specific company politically to represent itself as either 'British' or 'European' (or indeed 'global') depending upon the situation at hand. Certainly, the UK-based companies at which we conducted interviews were fully-internationalised in terms of their operating practices and market appreciation – even as they also demonstrated a close personal knowledge of British regulatory officials and their colleagues in other companies (with comparative golf handicaps a particular topic of conversation). In this combination of the local and the global, we begin to identify the inseparability of such elements within modern industrial and scientific practice.

Similar points can be made about the governmental agencies which increasingly need to work across national boundaries. In that way, it becomes ever more difficult to decide how a 'British' perspective on any issue can be separated from those of European colleagues with whom all such points will inevitably have been debated (at least in general terms). Thus, a self-awareness of the global setting of even very local procedures makes a difference to the individual decisions taken – and also to the manner in which these are subsequently presented and legitimised. In such a situation, we find an intriguing relationship between the local and the global in operation. The Europeanisation of regulation has not dissolved local ties and informal understandings – on the contrary, it seems to have reinforced their significance in terms of negotiating the new regime and its regulatory scientific implications. Meanwhile, Europeanisation – alongside commercial pressures towards globalisation – provides the framework within which regulatory scientific decisions must be enacted and, ultimately, defended.

These cross-cutting tendencies are also evident in scientific terms. Whilst international regulatory regimes claim justification on the basis of the 'universal' character of science, similar pressures towards both the local and the global can be identified. Thus, the acknowledgement of ecological variation as a legitimate source of national and local differences can conceal the extent to which local regulatory scientific practices vary for reasons that are not simply 'ecological' in nature.

British industrialists were particularly fond of characterising the 'pragmatic' manner in which technical decisions were seen to be taken in the UK with the 'bureaucratic' (or 'box-ticking') approach taken in certain other countries. In that way, local variations are not just explained by 'natural' variation but also by differences in local scientific interpretation of what, for example, constituted a valid test of 'real world' conditions. Here again, we see elements of both the local and the global in simultaneous operation. Whilst scientific authority might be based on its 'global' status, local operating practices and cultural assumptions seem not to have been swept away by the new regime. Equally, trust relations – based both on 'international' scientific competence (otherwise, scientific testing would be worthless) and also upon known links and previous relations – seem to embody this sense of the local and the global in simultaneous operation.

Whilst, therefore, it may be tempting to present 'Europeanised' regulatory systems as sweeping away local differences, our research suggests a more complex picture (see also Waterton and Wynne 1996; Yearley 1996; Rothstein *et al.,* 1999). Moreover, the lingering significance of the local within global systems implies that these are not simply transitional factors that will eventually lose significance as the system 'beds down' (as one form of European rhetoric currently suggests). Instead, we see such inter-cutting relations of the local and the global as fundamental to the operation of regulatory science. Whilst one element or the other may be emphasised at different points, it is upon their *interaction* that attention might more productively focus.

At the same time, it must be noted that terms such as 'local', 'global', and 'European' are not fixed points but instead are open to differential interpretation and reconstruction. The definition of both the 'local' and the 'global' depends very much upon the social and institutional perspective adopted. Within a discussion of globalisation, for example, the 'local' and the 'national' may appear very close to one another – but this would not apply within every consideration of regulatory systems (especially if one begins from the specific sites of pesticide application and usage). Rather than attempting to reify terms such as 'local' and 'global', therefore, it is important to be sensitive to their changing meanings within scientific and policy discourses.

Meanwhile, the challenge for European policymakers is to achieve a degree of uniformity (essentially, for commercial reasons) whilst also retaining a sense of the different levels at which regulation must not only be enacted but also negotiated and developed. Our argument here is that the 'local' represents not just a series of specific sites for the application of centralised policies but also a very important context within which decisions over pesticide safety are actively taken.

Similarly, 'Europeanisation' can be taken as representing both a denial of local differences but also – through the principle of subsidiarity – a recognition of the fundamental significance of such differences. In the area of regulation, therefore, the debate may be less over whether or not Europeanisation occurs but more over *which forms* of this concept are applied – and also over the varying meanings and significances which are attached to terms such as the 'European' and the 'local' within policy debates. In the case of regulatory science, the practical question concerns whether or not legitimate social and technical differences will be explicitly recognised by emerging regulatory regimes – or whether the meaning of 'Europeanisation' is defined in such a way as to conceal scientific, institutional and 'local' assumptions of the kind discussed here.

Discussion

In this chapter, we have suggested something of the new demands on regulatory institutions and on regulatory science which have emerged under the broad label of 'Europeanisation'. We have briefly sketched the hybrid character of these demands – both in terms of the institutions involved and of the intellectual challenges being raised across a range of disciplinary areas. We have also observed the interconnection of cultural and technical assumptions in this field of scientific practice – so that it becomes impossible to separate 'ecological' from 'institutional' variation when seeking to reach specific technical decisions. In particular, we have noted the complex relationship between 'global' and 'local' practices in this area.

Paradoxically, standardised systems seem to re-emphasise the significance of local relations of expertise and trust. At the same time, local and national activities become transformed by their larger framework of significance. In this situation, the precise meaning which is given to the 'Europeanisation' concept becomes highly significant – will the emerging regulatory systems simply view local variation as a challenge to further standardisation or will they build upon a sense of difference as well as uniformity? In that sense, Europeanisation represents a test-case for the development of global institutional processes which can remain sensitive to important local, institutional, ecological and cultural differences.

For scientific practice, this European policy framework raises a number of possibilities. Certainly, there is the danger that significant matters of scientific uncertainty and local variation will be swept aside by the emphasis on cross-national standardisation. Equally, peer review and external scrutiny can be jeopardised by remote institutional processes that do not allow the opportunity for localised discussions. The domination of regulatory science by government officials and industrialists causes further problems for academic – and public – oversight. At the same time, however, international frameworks can serve to break up what might appear to be excessively-cosy links between national regulators and the regulated – and offer new challenges in terms of achieving best practice for environmental protection.

In summary, our argument is that the development of European regulatory regimes represents a series of substantial challenges both to the academic interpretation of a dynamic and internationalised field and also to policy making. Rather than simply representing an unglamorous and low-grade area of technical activity, regulatory science appears to embody many of the major characteristics of contemporary scientific research: cross-institutional, industry-led, intellectually diverse, closely related to practical concerns and international in character. At the same time, regulatory science embodies many of the tensions and cross-cutting characteristics of the relationship between science and environmental concerns. In examining the relationship between the local and the global in this setting, therefore, we are also addressing a far wider set of issues about science and regulation, and about the development of technical and policy institutions capable of dealing with the scientific and cultural uncertainties of modern risk issues.

References

Barrett, K. L., Grandy, N., Harrison, E. G., Hassan, S. and Oomen, P. (1994) *Guidance document on regulatory testing procedures for pesticides with non-target arthropods*. Society of Environmental Toxicology and Chemistry – Europe.

Council of the European Communities (1991) 'Council Directive of 15 July 1991 Concerning the Placing of Plant Protection Products on The Market' (91/414/EEC) *Official Journal of the European Communities* No. L230.

House of Commons Agriculture Committee (1995) *Pesticides Safety Directorate and Veterinary Medicines Directorate*, Vol. II, 391–II. London: HMSO.

Irwin, A., Rothstein, H., Yearley, S. and McCarthy, E., (1997) 'Regulatory Science – Towards a Sociological Framework' *Futures* 29 (1): 17–31.

Jasanoff, S. (1990) *The Fifth Branch: science advisers as policymakers*. Cambridge, MA: Harvard University Press.

Rothstein, H., Irwin, A., Yearley, S. and McCarthy, E. (1999) 'Regulatory Science, Europeanisation and the Control of Agrochemicals'. *Science, Technology and Human Values*, Vol. 24, No. 2, pp. 241–64.

Scharpe, A. (1992) 'New Legislation on the Authorisation of Plant Protection Products', in Commission of the European Communities (DG XI) *Chemicals Control in the European Community* Cambridge: The Royal Society of Chemistry.

Shackley, S. and Wynne, B. (1995) 'Global climate change: the mutual construction of an emergent science-policy domain' *Science and Public Policy* 22(4): 218–30.

Waterton, C. and Wynne, B. (1996) 'Building the European Union: science and the cultural dimensions of environmental policy' *Journal of European Public Policy* 3(3): 421–40.

Yearley, S. (1996) *Sociology, Environmentalism, Globalization: reinventing the globe* London: Thousand Oaks, New Delhi: Sage.

IV

Regulation in Practice

10
The Globalisation of Environmental and Consumer Protection Regulation: Resources and Accountability

Erik Millstone

Introduction

Trade liberalisation, especially under the provisions of the Single European Act and the Uruguay GATT Treaty, has shifted the locus of responsibility for setting regulatory standards covering the protection of the environment and public health from the governments of nation states firstly to European Community wide institutions, and more recently to global bodies such as the Codex Alimentarius Commission (Codex) and the World Trade Organisation (WTO). Those shifts, however, have not merely changed the location of decision making from the local to the international and global, but they have also involved a progressive shift from relatively well resourced to relatively poorly resourced organisations, and from institutions amenable to some democratic checks and balances to organisations unrestrained by checks or balances.

Prior to the signature of the Single European Act (SEA) in 1986, the locus of responsibility for all those matters of environmental and consumer protection which were not covered by international treaty, in other words the vast majority, was entirely within the separate jurisdictions of national governments. Such checks and balances as existed were provided by particular national constitutions. We have yet to create institutional mechanisms with which to check the decisions and actions of international institutions. Recent events, however, suggest that opportunities to such mechanism may be emerging.

The example of regulating toxic hazards

The main changes in the ways in which regulatory policies are decided, as a consequence of trade liberalisation, can be illustrated by the example of controls on the use of food additives and pesticides. When additives and pesticides were regulated by individual countries the process has normally been divided into three relatively discrete stages.

- The first consideration is whether or not there is any technical economic or social need for a particular type of chemical, if so the question of safety or toxicity would arise.
- Evaluating the safety of a compound is a task usually performed by toxicologists and other relevant medical specialists. Governments developed the practice of asking the scientists to estimate the quantity of each particular compound which an average consumer should be able to ingest on a regular daily basis without suffering, or at any rate exhibiting, any adverse effects. That figure is typically referred to as an 'acceptable daily intake' or ADI. Setting an ADI, however, does not by itself determine the levels at which the compounds may be used.
- In the light of the toxicological evaluation, commercial and industrial judgements have to be made as to the types of foods and food products into which particular chemical additives may be incorporated, and the maximum levels at which they may be used. For pesticides, once ADIs have been set, the next stage involves setting so-called Maximum Residue Limits or MRLs, specifying not so much the levels at which they may be used in farming, but rather the quantities of particular toxic ingredients which may remain in particular foods at the eventual point of sale.

A comparative analysis of national regulatory regimes covering the regulation of food additives prior to the implementation of the SEA, indicated that the British system provided a lower level of consumer protection than that of the USA and of some EU member states (Millstone and Abraham, 1989). Under antecedent conditions, the UK had the longest list of chemicals permitted in the food supply of all EC member states, and compared with that of the USA. At the start of 1992, the UK permitted 299 compounds, while the Germans allowed approximately 150 compounds, and the Greeks allowed just 120 (Millstone, 1991, 1992). At the same time the USA was allowing approximately 130 compounds (Jacobson, 1976). Permissible levels of use in the UK have, moreover, frequently been more generous than those in the USA and Germany.

Accounting for international differences

There is evidence indicating that these differences could be explained, at least in part, by reference to specific institutional and political factors (Food Policy, 1985; Abraham and Millstone, 1989). One of the defining characteristics of British institutional structures has been that typically the responsibilities for regulating and sponsoring particular industrial sectors are vested in one and the same department. That arrangement creates the conditions in which regulatory capture is almost inevitable.

Regulatory capture

Regulatory capture describes a state of affairs in which a body that is supposed to regulate some industrial sector so as to protect, for example, the environment or public health from the actions of firms in that sector becomes covertly subordinated to the commercial interests of such firms (Bernstein, 1955). When a government department with responsibility for protecting environmental and/or public health from the actions, products and processes of some industrial sector is also charged with responsibility for looking after the commercial interests of that sector, it is probable that considerations of the latter type will predominate over the former.

It is, moreover, not difficult to specify in general terms other structural arrangements which increase the risk that regulatory capture will be established and maintained. If policymakers are advised by experts who are allowed to act as paid consultants to the companies whose products they are evaluating, or if they are allowed to have some other kind of commercial links with the relevant companies then the opportunities for regulatory capture will be enhanced.

A declaration of interests on the part of members of expert advisory committees can be important because public confidence in the probity of the regulatory process requires a belief that vested interests are not directly influencing the selection and/or interpretation of the scientific evidence. Evidence that commercial organisations can and do attempt to buy influence over scientific experts can be obtained in many ways, but rarely have industrialists articulated their strategy as frankly as in 1978 when Owen and Braeutigam published a remarkable book in which they provided a practical manual for industrial executives describing how to most effectively subordinate regulatory institutions to their interests; they gave advice on how to achieve and sustain regulatory capture. In their book they say:

> Regulatory policy is increasingly made with the participation of experts, especially academics. A regulated firm or industry should be prepared whenever possible to co-opt these experts. This is most effectively done by identifying the leading experts in each relevant field and hiring them as consultants and advisors, or giving them research grants and the like. This activity requires a modicum of finesse; it must not be too blatant, for the experts themselves must not recognise that they have lost their objectivity and freedom of action. At a minimum, a program of this kind reduces the threat that the leading experts will be available to testify or write against the interests of the regulated firms. (1978, 7)

In the USA it subsequently became unlawful for a scientist who works for, or advises, federal agencies such as the Food and Drug Administration (FDA) or the Environmental protection Agency (EPA) to act as a paid consultant, or otherwise to have a direct or indirect commercial interest in the companies whose products they are called upon to evaluate. The FDA and the EPA will, of course, receive scientific advice from a wide range of outsiders, but they are always expected to declare any relevant commercial links they may have. That is not to say that regulatory capture does not or cannot occur in the USA, but merely that the opportunities are rather more narrowly circumscribed (Epsteim, 1990; Castleman and Deim, 1988; Millstone, 1994).

Declarations of commercial interests

From the time of the establishment of the UK's Committee on Toxicity of Chemicals in Food, Consumer Products and the Environment (CoT) until the early 1990s, expert advisers in the UK were not expected or required to declare any commercial interest which they may have had. During the mid-1980s the position changed slightly as members of expert committees were told that they should provide some indication of their interests to the civil servants servicing their committee, and that such declarations would be shown only to the chair of the committee, but would not be disclosed to the other members of the committee nor to the general public (Erlichman, 1987).

In a remarkably frank interview held in 1987, Dr Francis Roe, then a member of the CoT, asserted that: '...he earns consultancy fees from so many companies and organisations that he is effectively beholden to no one employer'. Roe explained that: 'At any one time I am involved with 30 to 40 companies. I don't feel any need to defend one, to be truthful'. When asked why he did not step aside when a topic in which he had an interest was being discussed he said: 'I asked the chairman if he wanted me to leave the room or not, but the fact is that on many occasions with the CoT I would have to declare an interest in every item on the agenda'.

Until 1992 members of the British government's expert advisory committees, such as the Food Advisory Committee (FAC) and the CoT were not expected or required publicly to disclose their relevant commercial interests. Following sustained pressure from consumer organisation and public interest representatives, reforms were initiated. The position in the UK has improved to the extent that the committee members are required to provide a public declaration of their interests, although some declarations remain rather vague. In 1995, the most recent year for which information is available, the CoT consisted of 16 people (Department of Health, 1995). Only three of those 16 indicated that they had no commercial links whatsoever with relevant companies. Eleven members, including the chair, had direct personal financial interests in companies which either manufacture food additives or market products containing them. Between them the members of the CoT held 28 consultancies with relevant firms, and 12 earned 'occasional fees' from them. No information is provided indicating how much they received for their services. The chairman of the CoT explains, moreover, that through his university department, as opposed to his personal finances, he has interests in a '...wide range of national and international food and chemical companies'. Since the names of those companies are not even given, that disclosure is singularly uninformative. The 1996 Annual Report of the FAC indicates that of the 16 members, seven report no personal interests in relevant commercial organisations, while six members report having indirect interests in 'a wide range of national and international food companies' (Ministry of Agriculture, Fisheries and Food, 1997).

Confidentiality of scientific evidence

Regulatory capture is also especially likely to be achieved and sustained under a regime of secrecy and confidentiality of the type which generally prevails in the UK and in most other EU member states. For example, until 1986 in the UK, when evaluating the safety and/or toxicity of chemicals the Committee on Toxicity would accept and review data which were unpublished, and then subsequently keep those data confidential (Horton and Steadman, 1986). Not merely were the details of the conduct and results of the studies kept out of the public domain, the CoT would even not disclose the scientific nature of some or all of the studies. A scrutiny of CoT reports for that period shows that such information as was disclosed was released in strictly homeopathic doses.

Not merely were the data kept confidential, except where the companies involved chose to publish them, the CoT would also keep confidential the criteria by reference to which those data were selected and interpreted. That might, at first sight, seem a relatively marginal consideration, but in some cases it is of the utmost importance. Consider, for example, the case of saccharin.

The case of saccharin

Saccharin has been in use since the 1880s, although there have been doubts about its safety since 1890 (Arnold *et al.*, 1983). The central focus of the contemporary debate about toxic hazards from saccharin dates from the early 1970s and has concentrated on the issue of its putative carcinogenicity. To cut an extremely long story short, by the mid-1970s there was clear and consistent evidence from at least four rat feeding studies that, when saccharin is incorporated into the animals' diet there is a significant dose-related increase in bladder cancer rates amongst the males. The experimental evidence from laboratory animals is, however, equivocal, because not merely do male and female rats exhibit different patterns of response, but such patterns also vary as between different varieties of rat, moreover when various species are compared the differing patterns show even less consistency. This lack of consistency readily provokes the pivotal question of which type(s) of animals, if any, provide suitable models accurately to represent the effects saccharin may have on people?

While that question has not been directly addressed, two other lines of potentially relevant inquiry have been pursued. First, since there are good reasons for supposing that one route by which carcinogens can initiate or promote tumour growth is by causing a mutation (that is to say by damaging the genetic material in the nucleus of cells) it can be useful to test materials to see whether or not they cause mutations in bacteria and/or in tissue culture systems *in vitro*, that is to say in glass dishes. *In vitro* mutagenicity tests yield some information, but their evidence is not necessarily decisive. Since some carcinogens may act through non-genotoxic routes, a compound might show no *in vitro* mutagenic activity, and yet be a genuine carcinogen.

Appropriate human epidemiological studies are extremely difficult and expensive to conduct, and the evidence which they generate may also be inconclusive. It is, nonetheless, possible to conduct epidemiolgoical studies with human populations to try to establish whether or not any correlation can be found between saccharin consumption and the incidence of cancers, not just in the bladders of human males, but maybe at other sites too.

There are at least two ways in which potentially pertinent epidemiological studies can be conducted. Firstly, one might study a group of male bladder cancer sufferers to try to establish whether they were more or less likely than an otherwise comparable group to have consumed saccharin. Alternatively, one could study diabetics and try to establish whether or not they have elevated rates of cancer of the bladder, since typically diabetics use more artificial sweeteners than other groups, and for most of this century that has meant consuming saccharin. Since it is well known that compounds can cause cancer at one site in one species but at a different site in other species, a failure to discover significantly higher rates of saccharin consumption amongst adult human male bladder cancer suffers would not be conclusive. On the other hand, even if there is a higher rate of cancer amongst diabetics we could not be certain that it was the artificial sweeteners or even the saccharin that was responsible, because it might have been causally related directly to the diabetes, but independent of saccharin consumption.

All those caveats notwithstanding, numerous epidemiological and bacterial mutagenicity tests have been conducted, but their combined results have been profoundly equivocal. Bacterial mutagenicity testing started in the early 1970s (Ames *et al.*, 1973). The early test systems use *salmonella* bacteria cultured in a standardised growth medium, but by the end of the 1980s a very wide range of different kinds of bacteria, in a variety of differing growth media, were being used. When the putative mutagenicity of saccharin has been investigated, it emerges that while saccharin is not evidently mutagenic in some bacteria under some conditions, it does appear to be mildly active in other bacteria under certain conditions (Arnold *et al.*, 1983).

More than 20 epidemiological studies on saccharin had been conducted by the early 1980s, but all of them on relatively small samples, using relatively poor control for possible confounders, and while some of them found no significant correlation, a few of them did yield evidence of a possible link between saccharin consumption and bladder cancer (Arnold *et al.*, 1983).

Given the uncertainties and equivocation both within and between animal feeding studies, *in vitro* mutagenicity tests and human epidemiology, a bold attempt was made in the early 1980s by the US National Academy Sciences panel to estimate the upper and lower bounds of the hazard that saccharin might pose to the US population. They estimated that if, on average, the population of the USA were to ingest some 120 milligrams of saccharin daily for a period of 70 years (which corresponded to the average level of consumption in the USA in the early 1980s) it was unlikely that fewer than 0.22 deaths from bladder cancer would occur throughout the entire US population over that period, while on the other hand it was unlikely that more than 1 144 000 extra deaths would be caused (Wilkinson, 1983). In other words, estimates of the potential carcinogenicity of saccharin for humans are characterised by uncertainty of six orders of magnitude.

The response of the regulatory authorities in Britain, the European Community/European Union and many other countries has been to assume that, while saccharin is an animal carcinogen it is not a human carcinogen, and its use has continued to grow – despite the fact that there is no evidence that artificial sweeteners help consumers lose weight, and evidence from at least ten separate studies indicating that it may be counter-productive because it can function as an appetite stimulant (Sheffield and Roby, 1950; Friedhoff *et al.*, 1971, Holman, 1980; Sclafani and Xenakis, 1984; Tordoff, 1988a, 1988b; Tordoff and Friedman, 1989a, 1989b, 1989c, 1989d; Ramirez, 1990). In other words, both the British CoT and the European Commission's Scientific Committee for Food (SCF) have interpreted the evidence in a way which awards the benefit of the doubt to the compound and to the food and drink companies, and not to the consumers, assuming saccharin to be safe in the absence of definitive proof of human toxicity.

Can we generalise from the example of saccharin?

Saccharin is exceptional only in that an attempt has been made to provide a quantitative estimate of the range of uncertainty, but not otherwise. The pattern exhibited by the saccharin case is typical of hundreds of others in that the CoT and SCF typically interpret the results of toxicology tests on animals that indicate no adverse reactions as providing a good model for the likely effects on humans, while adopting the opposite tack when they interpret positive evidence that a compound is toxic to animals. In those cases they typically and opportunistically invoke reasons for thinking that the animals do not provide good models for the likely effects on humans (Millstone, 1988).

In April 1977 the FDA responded to the evidence of saccharin's carcinogenicity by proposing to ban saccharin from all processed food, in soft drinks and as a table-top sweetener. Despite the explicit provisions of the so-called Delaney Amendment, which obliges the FDA to ban all known carcinogens from the permitted list of food additives, the proposal to ban saccharin in the USA has never been implemented because it has repeatedly been overridden by Congress. Until very recently that anomaly has been difficult to explain.

It was evident that, at the behest of the American food, drink and additive industries, a substantial and successful campaign was organised to persuade Congress to overturn the FDA's proposed ban. In the autumn of 1977 Congress passed a temporary moratorium which prevented the FDA from banning saccharin, and this has subsequently been renewed at least three times (Miller and Frattali, 1989). Instead of banning it, Congress only required that all products containing the chemical must carry a warning label to the effect that: '...the use of this product may be hazardous to your health. This product contains saccharin which has been determined to cause cancer in laboratory animals.'

That this has occurred might be cited as evidence that contradicts my analysis. I am arguing that the greater the involvement of democratic institutions in policy making, and the greater the openness and accountability, the more likely it will be that public policy will prudently protect public health. The US experience seems to suggest that Congress, as a democratic institution, undermined the protection of public health, by overriding the advice of the FDA's experts and officials. In March 1996, however, evidence emerged in a New York Court which casts doubt on that interpretation. Top officials of the Cumberland Packaging Company, a firm which manufactures and sells saccharin-containing products under the Sweet 'N Low brand label, pleaded guilty in a Federal court in Brooklyn to charges of funnelling more than $200 000 in illegal contributions to political campaigns to try to persuade members of Congress to vote to block the ban on saccharin which had been proposed by the FDA (Mokrycki, 1995). As Mokrzycki explains: 'Among the recipients of the illegal largesse were the presidential campaigns of Bob Dole in 1988 and George Bush in 1992, as well as campaigns by Senator Alfonse D'Amato, Republican of New York, former Senator Lloyd Bensten, Democrat of Texas, and former Representative Geraldine Ferraro, Democrat of New York, who ran for Vice President in 1984' (Mokrycki, 1995). Given that officials of contractors of the Cumberland Packing Company pleaded guilty, we are entitled to assume that plea bargaining may have taken place and, therefore, that not all the facts have been publicly disclosed. Whatever took place when members of Congress voted to block the FDA's proposed ban on saccharin, it can hardly be counted as having been a purely democratic decision.

These examples, and others too, indicate that although American institutions are far from perfect, and while regulatory capture can and does occur in the USA as well as in EU member states, and at the European Commission too, the provisions of the US Freedom of Information Act provide a mechanism which makes it harder to achieve and easier to uncover regulatory capture in the USA than in Europe. In Whitehall and at the Commission the presumption of confidentiality shields the policymaking process from any proper scientific and/or democratic scrutiny. Freedom of information does not guarantee that political institutions function democratically, but when decisions are taken in secret the risks of undemocratic collusion and corruption are massively greater. Furthermore, the greater the commercial interest, the more important it is, from a democratic point of view, that policy making takes place openly.

The case of saccharin, and the class of other examples it represents, serves to illustrate the importance for environmental and public health policy of ensuring that the public domain contains not merely the scientific evidence by reference to which expert advisory committees and policymakers base their judgements and decisions, but also the criteria by reference to which the scientific evidence is selected and interpreted.

The example of saccharin serves to dispel the myth that regulatory judgements in public health and environmental policy are purely scientific. It shows, on the contrary, that often commercial, social and political considerations masquerade as purely scientific. Since these decisions are irredeemably both socio-political and scientific it follows that the mechanisms of accountability and the kinds of checks and balances need to be richer than might be the case if considerations of one sort alone were involved.

The structure of EC/EU institutions

The shift of responsibility from EC/EU member states to the Commission following the implementation of the Single European Act has been important for several reasons. As far as the key variables outlined above are concerned, it is noteworthy that responsibility for food safety regulations in the EU lies with Directorate General III (DG-III), which is the part of the Commission responsible for sponsoring European industry. In this sense, European institutions have been constructed on the British model because the responsibility for regulation has not been assigned to what was formerly known as the Consumer Protection Service, which is now part of Directorate General XXIV with responsibility for Consumer Policy and Health Protection. On matters of food chemical safety, the Commission is advised by the Scientific Committee for Food (SCF). Until 1997 the group in DG-III which had responsibility for regulation also provided the SCF with its secretariat. In the wake of the BSE crisis the Commission decided to reassign the SCF and its secretariat to DG-XXIV, although responsibility for regulatory policy remains in DG-III.

There is, however, an important respect in which the EU's post-1992 regulatory system is even more permissive than the previous national system in the UK, and the same applies to the Codex–WTO global regime. As previously explained, national regulatory regimes typically required evidence that there was a 'need' for some proposed new additive before the question of safety or toxicity was even addressed. If there was already an adequate range of permitted compounds for some technological function then new materials were not allowed, however safe they might be. Under the EU-wide post-1992 regime, 'need' ceased to be a criterion. As long as an additive had some industrial utility, the Commission would allow it to be used throughout the EU, if it was deemed to be acceptably safe. Consequently the number of additives permitted for use throughout the EU rose to approximately 420 at the end of 1992, a number which was substantially higher than those for any of the member states. The SCF (and at the global level, JECFA (the UN Food and Agriculture Organisation's Joint Expert Committee on Food Additives) too) are only asked to evaluate the safety of compounds without any consideration being given to the issue of whether or not there is any need for these compounds.

The SCF accepts unpublished data from industry, and undertakes to keep it confidential unless and until the industrial firms choose to publish it. SCF members can and do act as paid consultants, without any declarations of interest. At a meeting in Westminster of the Parliamentary Food and Health Forum on 28 June 1988, Paul Gray, then Head of Foodstuffs in DG-III, seemed to accept the force of some of those arguments and indicated that: '...it was essential to have greater disclosure of information for greater public confidence when there was a freer circulation of foodstuffs. The Commission was moving in that direction and those submitting data were now warned that this would eventually be published' (Parliamentary Food and Health Forum, 1988). A decade later no progress whatsoever in that direction has been achieved. While there has been some limited domestic progress within the UK, the concessions have been made within an increasingly unimportant forum, while the forum with greater decisionmaking power functions in a relatively archaic and unaccountable fashion.

The post-GATT global regime

Under the provisions of the GATT Treaty, responsibility for setting food safety standards for internationally traded commodities has been assigned to the Codex Alimentarius Commission (Codex), which is in turn advised by two main expert committees, both of which are part of the International Programme on Chemical Safety (IPCS). In respect of food additives, Codex receives advice from the World Health Organisation and JECFA; in relation to pesticides the comparable committee is called the Joint Meeting on Pesticide Residues (JMPR). As the Canadian Environmental Law Association has said, these developments have created '...procedural impediments towards environmental protection...by allowing politically unaccountable trade representatives to have future decision-making power over ... food safety and animal and plant protection' (Makuch, 1993).

Part b of Article XX of the GATT Treaty allows exemptions from normal GATT trade rules for laws to protect '...plant, animal and human life or health...' and this is referred to as Sanitary and Phytosanitary Measures. The Agreement on Sanitary and Phytosanitary Measures, which is part of the GATT Final Act, states that '...no member shall be prevented from adopting or enforcing measures necessary to protect human, animal or plant life or health subject to the requirement that they are not applied in a manner which would constitute a means for arbitrary or unjustifiable discrimination between Members where the same conditions prevail or a disguised restriction on international trade'.

The Agreement on the Application of Sanitary and Phytosanitary Measures states that: 'Members shall ensure that any sanitary or phytosanitary measure is applied only to the extent necessary to protect human, animal or plant life or health, is based on scientific principles and is not maintained without sufficient scientific evidence, except as provided for in paragraph 22'. The main problem with this provision, as the case of saccharin shows, is that all environmental and consumer protection decisions are taken against some of the evidence. The wording of the GATT Treaty presupposes that the scientific evidence is unequivocal, that it can be interpreted unproblematically and without recourse to non-scientific considerations. That supposition is, however, entirely unrealistic.

Paragraph 22 states that: 'In cases where relevant scientific evidence is insufficient, a Member may provisionally adopt sanitary or phytosanitary measures on the basis of available pertinent information, including that from relevant international organisations as well as from sanitary or phytosanitary measures applied by other Members. In such circumstances, Members shall seek to obtain the additional information necessary for a more objective assessment of risk and review the sanitary or phytosanitary measure accordingly within a reasonable period of time'. Even though scientific uncertainties can be diminished, it is unrealistic to think that they can be eliminated altogether, or even if they could that regulatory policy decisions could be taken solely by reference to scientific considerations.

The GATT Treaty states, moreover, that measures to protect sanitary and phytosanitary health are to be based on international standards where they exist. 'To harmonise sanitary and phytosanitary measures on as wide a basis as possible, Members shall base their sanitary or phytosanitary measures on international standards, guidelines or recommendations, where they exist...'. In any challenge the burden of proof lies with the country wishing to defend its higher standards. This creates a mechanism, therefore, through which food additive and pesticide standards can be expected to descend to the level of the lowest common denominator, or to those levels set by Codex.

Accountability of Codex and its advisory committees

Members of JECFA and the JMPR are even less accountable scientifically and politically than those on the FAC, CoT or the SCF. It is possible to question Ministers in Parliament about the decisions of the FAC or CoT, and the European Parliament and the Council of Ministers have at least the possibility of exercising some oversight of the SCF, but JECFA and the JMPR are entirely unaccountable. Both JECFA and the JMPR accept and review unpublished data, and keep them out of the public domain in the name of commercial confidentiality. There are no restrictions on members of those committees acting as consultants to, or otherwise having commercial interests in, companies whose products they are evaluating. Members of JECFA and the JMPR are not asked whether or not they have any such interests, and were they to volunteer such information to the secretariats provided by the WHO and FAO, the information would remain confidential, and would not even be shared with the other members of those committees. In correspondence and discussions with the secretariat, I have been told that all is well because the secretariat have confidence in the integrity of their members. What matters, however, is not *their personal levels* of confidence but the presence or absence of formal institutional safeguards which can provide some reassurance to the general public (Herrman, 1996).

Once the JMPR and JECFA have set ADIs, those figure are then used by Codex to set maximum permitted levels of use for additives in specific food products, and to set maximum Residue Limits for pesticides. The Codex Alimentarius Commission was established in 1963 primarily '...because of a widely perceived need to facilitate trade in foods' (Codex Alimentarium Commission, undated), while a concern about proper standards of consumer protection was at best a secondary consideration.

Avery, Drake and Lang (1993) have analysed the membership of Codex and reviewed the participants in Codex meetings from 1989 to 1991. Codex is a curious hybrid body and attendance at meetings depends on the composition of national delegations. Member states of Codex normally send some civil servants, but they are entitled to incorporate into their delegations representatives of other interests, such as firms, trade associations and consumer groups. Avery, Drake and Lang analysed in particular the participation in the 19th session of Codex in 1992 and their main conclusions were that: '26% of all participants on Codex committees represented industrial interests. In contrast, public interest organisations comprised only 1% of total participation. On several committees that dealt with topics of particular concern to consumers the percentage of industry participation was even higher. For instance, in...meetings of the Committee on Food Additives and Contaminants, industry comprised 41% of total participants. Industry comprised 46% of participation on the Committee on Nutrition and Foods for Special Dietary Uses'. They explained, moreover, that: 'The vast majority of non-governmental participants on Codex committees represent industry: 445 (81%) non-governmental participants on national delegations represented industry. Only 8 (1%) non-governmental participants on national delegations represented public interest groups. The rest were consultants and academics.'

The influence of industrial interests was most conspicuous in the Swiss delegation, almost two-thirds of which consisted of industrial representatives and their consultants, while representatives of the Swiss government accounted for just 36 per cent of the size of the delegation. It would therefore be misleading to talk about the role of industrial interest as acting as a lobby at Codex meetings, since the notion of a lobby is to represent forces outside the lobby trying to influence decisions being taken on the inside. In Codex industry is a direct participant in the decisionmaking process on the inside, and not outside the lobby. In this sense, food safety and environmental standards are being set by a body comprising representatives of many of the firms whose products are being evaluated, and they are entirely unaccountable.

How do Codex standards compare with national standards?

An analysis conducted by the US General Accounting Office showed that Codex pesticides standards are frequently lower than those set in the US and Canada (US General Accounting Office). As Makuch explains: '...among pesticides identified by the US EPA as probable carcinogens, the US EPA has lower maximum residue levels in 55 per cent of the cases. Codex Alimentarius has done so for only 27 per cent of these substances. In addition, Codex standards have permitted residues in food substances of pesticides which have long been banned in both Canada and the United States – including DDT, endrin and aldrin – while allowing higher residue levels for such toxic substances as heptachlor and aldicarb' (Makuch, 1993). DDT was banned in the UK in October 1984; aldrin was banned in the UK in May 1989; endrin is also not allowed in the UK.

Some examples are given in the table below, which compares CODEX standards with those set by the US EPA, representing this as a ratio of the size of the residue of particular compounds in specific foods.

A slightly different example is provided by the use and regulation of synthetic hormones in beef production. In the USA, these compounds are permitted, and their use has been sanctioned by JECFA and Codex, but their use is prohibited under EU legislation. Since their use is sanctioned by JECFA and Codex, the US government is proposing to take the EU to a GATT/WTO dispute procedure. The ways in which that

Table 10.1: The ratio of Maximum Residue Levels (MRLs) set by Codex and the US EPA for selected foods and compounds

Crop	Pesticide	Ratio of codex MRL to US EPS MRL
Carrotts	benomyl	25
Apples	permethrin	40
Strawberries	lindane	3
Potatoes	diazinon	5
Bananas	aldicarb	1.6
Broccoli	heptachlor	5
Grapes	DDT	20
Milk	endrin	3
Peaches	dieldrin	50
Lettuce	aldrin	3.3

Source: Lang and Clutterbuck, 1991, 99–100.

dispute will be decided will provide an indication of how global policy-making under the WTO and Codex is likely to unfold.

Resources

Not merely has power and responsibility shifted from relatively more accountable to relatively less accountable institutions, it has also shifted from relatively well resourced to markedly less well resourced institutions. The FDA is far and away the best resourced of all the institutions discussed in this study. The FDA's Centre for Food Safety and Applied Nutrition employs several hundred scientists to work on the collection, analysis and interpretation of safety and toxicity data. In the UK, the Food Advisory Committee and Committee on Toxicity are in a position to draw upon the labour of no more than a dozen in-house experts, and they have hardly any resources to devote to external consultants. Moreover, the UK has a policy of not spending public funds on the conduct of safety or toxicity tests with commercially marketable materials. The Scientific Committee for Food at the European Commission is serviced by a very small secretariat, currently numbering some three individuals. The JMPR is serviced by a secretariat of two full-timers and 17 part-timers seconded from national regulatory agencies, while JECFA has 16, of whom all but two are part-timers. One indication of the under-resourcing of the IPCS, and its close links with commercial interests, is the fact that when in 1994, a comprehensive list of JECFA's evaluations was eventually published, it emerged as an enterprise sponsored by the

International Life Sciences Institute (ILSI) which is a thinly disguised front organisation representing many of the larger companies in the food and chemical industry (JECFA, 1994). Consumer organisations are unlikely to be confident about the judgements of IPCS committees until they cease to be financially dependent on industrial and commercial organisations such as ILSI. Neither the SCF, JECFA nor the JMPR has any resources with which to commission any independent research. Although JECFA and the JMPR have rather more resources than the SCF at Brussels, their responsibilities are correspondingly far greater as they now make judgements on a far wider range of compounds, and do so with reference to the entire global market.

Summary and conclusion

The main thrust of the argument in this study is summarised in Table 10.2.

The analysis provided above shows first that the completion of the Single European Market entailed a marked increase in the opportuni-

Table 10.2: **International comparison of key features of regulatory institutions**

	Separation of regulation from sponsorship?	Public access to unpublished scientific data?	Are the criteria of interpretation disclosed?	Declaration of interests?	Judicial oversight?	Legislative oversight?
USA	Yes	Yes	Yes	Yes	Yes	Yes
UK <1986	No	No	No	No	No	In principle, but not in practice
UK >1992	No	No	No	No	No	In principle, but not in practice
EU	No	No	No	No	No	In principle but not in practice
Codex regime	No	No	No	No	No	No

ties and scope for regulatory capture in the regulatory policy institutions of the EC/EU when compared with the situation in member states prior to the implementation of the Single European Act. The completion of the single European market produced a marked deterioration in standards of consumer protection in those sectors because the liberalisation of trade was not complemented by regulatory policies to protect consumers and the environment.

Second, the Uruguay GATT treaty contains provisions that entail a shift of responsibility for these regulatory matters to bodies in which the opportunities and scope for regulatory capture are even greater, and which have a history of setting weak consumer protection standards. The IPCS committees, JECFA and the JMPR, operate in a secretive and unaccountable fashion. They accept and review unpublished studies and fail to place unpublished data in the public domain. They do not articulate principles of analysis or interpretation of those data, and the members of those committees can, and some do, act as paid consultants to the companies whose products they are evaluating, without any disclosure of those interests. Codex committees are, moreover, richly peopled with industrial representatives, who are directly participating in setting the standards governing their own companies and products. There is a complete absence of checks or balances, and this democratic deficit brings with it many risks, both to public and environmental health, and to public support for trade liberalisation and for multinational trade agreements.

Unless some fundamental reforms are introduced to make expert advisory committees and the Codex decisionmaking bodies more open, accountable, and less poorly resourced, a decline in standards of consumer and environmental protection seems probable. If that occurs, it is almost inevitable that this will eventually backfire by provoking public outcries against liberalised trade because of the failure to provide proper protection for public and environmental health.

The BSE crisis, which began on 20 March 1996 when it emerged that a new variant of Creutzfeld-Jakob disease appeared to have emerged as a consequence of people in the UK having eaten contaminated beef, has had very profound repercussions on food safety policy in the UK and the EU. The Labour government, which was re-elected in June 2001, is committed to diminishing the scope for regulatory capture, in food safety policymaking. The government has decided to separate regulation from sponsorship by relocating political responsibility for food safety policy to the Department of Health, taking it away from the Ministry of Agriculture, Fisheries and Food. The government has established the Food Standards Agency to insulate those who provide expert scientific advice on public health and safety from direct political and commercial control; indications have also been given that the Food Standards Agency will operate with a freedom of information regime. If those commitments are fully honoured, and if my analysis has been correct, then UK domestic food chemical safety policy will change radically.

The changes which the European Commission have subsequently recommended are almost as radical, but the pace of change in Brussels will be slightly less rapid. The Commission wants to reform food safety policymaking in the EU so as to try to reduce the likelihood of further disruptions on the scale provoked by the BSE crisis. Responsibility for providing the secretariat for the SCF has already been relocated from DG-III to the Directorate General for Consumer Policy and Health Protection, DG-XXIV. Responsibility for setting regulations remains in DG-III, but there are indications that that may be only a temporary arrangement; in the medium-term the logic of separating industrial sponsorship from regulation will be accepted in the EU as it has been in Whitehall. The European Parliament's criticisms of the handling of the BSE crisis by the UK government and by the Commission have focused, amongst other things, on their lack of openness, and unacceptable closeness with commercial and industrial interests (Ortega, 1995). The pressure for freedom of information in EU regulatory institutions is bound to grow, and a requirement that expert advisors should disclose their commercial interests has already been articulated.

If the British and EU authorities are both successful in this reform process, attention will inevitably shift to the global level. The most probable scenario, however, is one in which a sharp disparity will develop. On the one hand Europe can expect rising food safety standards while the most likely trajectory of the Codex–WTO regime is for standards to decline towards the lowest common global denominator. As the disjunction between those two trends sharpens, something will have to change. Either European authorities will have to dilute hard won improvements, or the global regime administered by the WTO and Codex will have to be reformed. In the autumn of 1997 it is not possible to predict which outcome is the most likely; further research will be required.

References

Abraham, J. and Millstone, E. (1989) 'Food additive controls: some international comparisons', *Food Policy*, Vol. 14, No. 1, Feb. 1989, pp. 43–57.

Ames, B. N. *et al.* (1973) 'Carcinogens are Mutagens: A Simple Test System Combining Liver Homogenates for Activation and Bacteria for Detection', *Proceedings of the National Academy of Sciences*, Vol. 70, 2281 ff.

Arnold, D. L. *et al.* (1983) 'Saccharin: A Toxicological and Historical Perspective', *Toxicology*, Vol. 27, Part 3–4, July-August, pp. 179–256, esp. p. 181.

Avery, N., Drake, M. and Lang, T. (1993) *Cracking the CODEX: an analysis of who sets world food standards*, National Food Alliance, London.

Bernstein, M. (1955) *Regulating Business by Independent Commission*, Princeton University Press, 1955.

Castleman, B. I. and Diem, G. E. (1988) 'Corporate influences on threshold limit values', *American Journal of Industrial Medicine*, 1988, Vol. 13, pp. 531–59.

Codex Alimentarium Commission (undated) *Introducing the Codex Alimentarium Commission*, Joint FAO/WHO Food Standards Booklet, Rome, undated.

Department of Health (1995) *Annual Report of the Committee on Toxicity of Chemicals in Food, Consumer Products and the Environment, 1994*, pp. 13–14, HMSO.

Epstein, S. (1990) 'Corporate Crime: Why we cannot trust industry-derived safety studies', *International Journal of Health Services*, 1990 Vol. 20, No. 3, pp. 443–58.

Erlichman, J. (1987) 'Food watchdog denies conflict of interest', *Guardian*, 28 July, p. 4.

Food Policy (1985) 'Food Additive Regulation in the UK', in *Food Policy*, Vol. 10, No. 3, August, pp. 237–52.

Friedhoff, R. *et al.* (1971) 'Sucrose Solution vs. No-Calorie Sweetener vs. Water in Weight Gain', *Journal of the American Dietetic Association*, 1971, Vol. 59, pp. 485–6.

Herrman, J. (1996) Personal communication with Dr John Herrman, WGO Joint Secretary of JECFA, September 1995 and January 1996.

Holman, E. W. (1980) 'Irrelevant-incentive learning with flavors in rats', *Journal of Experimental Psychology: Animal Behavior Processes*, 1980, Vol. 6, pp. 126–36.

Horton, J. and Steadman, J. (1986) *Availability of toxicological data on food additives*, Letter to All Interested Parties, from J. Horton (Secretary to the Food Advisory Committee) and J. Steadman (Medical Secretary to the CoT), Ministry of Agriculture, Fisheries and Food, London, 11 July.

Jacobson, M. F. (1976) *Eater's Digest: the consumers factbook of food additives*, Anchor Doubleday, 1976.

JECFA (1994) *Summary of Evaluations Performed by the Joint FAO/WHO Expert Committee on Food Additives* ILSI Press, 1994.

Lang, T. and Clutterbuck, C. (1991) *P is for Pesticides*, London: Ebury Press, p. 96.

Makuch, Z. (1993) 'Environmental regulation and natural resource implications of the Draft Final Act of the GATT Uruguay Round of Multilateral Trade Negotiations', Ch. 5 of *The Environmental Implications of Trade Agreements*, Canadian Environmental Law Association, prepared for the Ontario Ministry of Environment and Energy, Queen's Printer for Ontario.

Miller S. and Frattali V. P. (1989) 'Saccharin', *Diabetes Care*, Vol. 12, No. 1, Suppl. 1, January, pp. 75–80.

Millstone, E. and Abraham, J. (1989) 'Food Additive Controls: Some International Comparisons', *Food Policy*, Vol. 14, No. 1, February, pp. 43–57.

Millstone, E. (1988) *Additives: a guide for everyone*, Harmondsworth: Penguin Books.

Millstone, E. (1991) 'Consumer Protection Policies in the EC: The Quality of Food'. Ch 20 of C. Freeman *et al.* (eds), *Technology and the Future of Europe*, Frances Pinter, p. 339.

Millstone, E. (1992) *Food additives: look before you eat!*, Channel Four Television and BBC Good Food, 1992, p. 2.

Millstone, E. (1994) 'Sweet and Sour: The Unanswered Questions about Aspartame', *The Ecologist*, Vol. 24, No. 2, March/April, pp. 71–4.

Ministry of Agriculture, Fisheries and Food (1997) *Food Advisory Committee, Annual Report 1996*, July, Annex III, pp. 32–4.

Mokrzycki, M. (1995) *Saccharin Maker Admits Illegal Contributions to Block Ban*, Associated Press, 14 March 1995.

Owen, B. M. and Braeutigam, R. (1978) *The Regulation Game: strategic use of the administrative process*, Ballinger Publishing Co. 1978.

Oreta, M. M. *et al.* (1995) *Report on alleged contraventions or maladministration in the implementation of Community law in relation to BSE*, European Parliament, 7 February 1997, DOC EN\RR\319\319544 European Commission Decision 95/273/EC 6 July 1995, *Official Journal* L 167, 18 July.

Owen, B. M. and Braeutigam (1978) *The Regulation Game: strategic use of the administration process*, Ballinger Publishing Co.

Parliamentary Food and Health Forum (1988) *Food Labelling, Additives and the Consequences of EEC Harmonisation on Food Legislation in the UK*, minutes of the meeting of the Parliamentary Food and Health Forum, 28 June, House of Lords, p. 6.

Agreement on the Application of Sanitary and Phytosanitary Measures, GATT Final ACT, MTN/FA II-AIA-4, p. 1.

Ramirez, I. (1990) 'Stimulation of energy intake and growth by saccharin in rats', *Journal of Nutrition*, Vol. 120, pp. 123–33.

Sclafani, A. and Xenakis, S. (1984) 'Sucrose and polysaccharide induced obesity in the rat', *Physiology & Behavior*, 1984, Vol. 32, pp. 169–74.

Sheffield, F. D. and Roby, T. B. (1950) 'Reward value of a non-nutritive sweet taste', *Journal of Comparative and Physiological Psychology*, Vol. 43, pp. 471–81.

Tordoff, M. G. (1988a) 'How do non-nutritive sweeteners increase food intake?', *Appetite*, Vol. 11, Suppl., pp. 5–11.

Tordoff, M. G. (1988b) 'Saccharin and Food Intake', Ch. 10 in, G. C. Birch and M. G. Lindley (eds), *Low Calorie Products* Elsevier Applied Science, pp. 127–46.

Tordoff, M. G. and Friedman, M. I. (1989a) 'Drinking saccharin increases food intake are preference: I. Comparison with other drinks', *Appetite*, 1989, Vol. 12, pp. 1–10.

Tordoff, M. G. and Friedman, M. I. (1989b) 'Drinking saccharin increases food intake are preference: II. hydrational factors', *Appetite*, 1989, Vol. 12, pp. 11–21.

Tordoff, M. G. and Friedman, M. I. (1989c) 'Drinking saccharin increases food intake are preference: III. sensory and associative factors', *Appetite*, 1989, Vol. 12, pp. 23–35.

Tordoff, M. G. and Friedman, M. I. (1989d) 'Drinking saccharin increases food intake are preference: IV. cephalic phase and metabolic factors', *Appetite*, 1989, Vol. 12, pp. 37–56.

US General Accounting Office (1991) *International Food Safety: Comparison of U.S. and Codex Pesticide Standards*, August.

Wilkinson, C. (1983) *Proceedings of the 10th International Congress of Plant Protection*, 1983, Vol. 1, p. 46; cited in Graham-Bryce, *Chemistry and Industry*, 17 December, p. 864.

11
Science and Technology in the Defence Industries: the Growing Influence of Transnational Industrial–Governmental Networks

John Lovering

Introduction: defence spending, the defence industry and the national innovation system

It has long been recognised that defence spending is a major element in the science and technology activities of some industrialised nations (Malecki, 1991; Nelson, 1993; Kaldor, 1990). Defence spending – in countries where it is proportionately large relative to GDP – can have a major influence on the trajectory of economic development, influencing technological–industrial developments, geographical patterns, corporate structures and government–industry relations (Sen, 1988; Chenais, 1993; Hebert, 1995; Lovering, 1994). This chapter[1] draws attention to some aspects of the current restructuring of the defence industry in Britain and Europe which are likely to have significant implications for science and technology (S&T).

In Britain and France a large share of publicly-funded S&T has been dedicated to defence objectives. In addition, defence companies are amongst the leading business spenders on Research and Development (R&D) (in Britain in the mid 1990s GEC's total R&D budget exceeded that of the Office of Science and Technology, the official sponsor of the British science base). Since the end of the cold war, public defence R&D spending has fallen. However, the issues at stake are more than quantitative. Government defence-related departments, and companies involved in defence markets, have been learning to behave in new ways. The result is a qualitative change in the nature of the S&T effort in defence.

Up to the mid 1990s it was common for observers of the defence scene to point out – and to advocate – that defence R&D is increasingly interwoven with civil R&D. What became known as the 'dual-use' debate stressed the growing dependence of defence upon civilian technologies. It was claimed that the 'civil–military' technological divide was being eroded (Alic, 1992; Walker, 1992; Walker and Gummett, 1992). The role of civilian sources of technology was highlighted during the 1991 Gulf war when US journalists discovered that American military aircraft relied heavily on Japanese 'chips'. Influential insiders, such as Jack Gansler, later to become head of Pentagon procurement, argued that a systematic new relationship between civilian and military S&T needed to be developed, and that this would ideally also have an international (i.e. transatlantic) dimension (Gansler, 1996).

Since then, however, the on-going and global restructuring of the defence industry has taken a somewhat different course – rather than seeing the emergence of diverse civil and military producers, the restructuring has been characterised by the emergence of 'pure play' defence specialists. This is prominently the case in the USA, but also applies in Europe. Thus in the 1980s British Aerospace attempted to become a diverse manufacturer, producing civil and military aircraft, ammunition, cars and construction. Daimler Benz also acquired other companies in an attempt to position itself at the apex of a range of civil as well as military technologies. In the 1990s both companies reversed these strategies and focused more narrowly. BAe sold off many of its civil divisions, ranging from cars to executive jets, while Daimler sought to specialise more clearly in civil activities. In 1998 it was announced that the military aircraft activities of these two companies would probably be merged, thereby laying the basis for the first large trans-border European defence company.

These development reflect a fundamental feature of the modern – post-cold war – defence industry which has wider implications for S&T. I refer to the fact that for all intents and purposes the defence industry is no longer nationalised, whether *de jure* or *de facto*. By the same token, a growing part of defence R&D is effectively becoming privatised. The result, I suggest below, is that the relationship between defence companies and governments is changing. In effect, no less than a new framework of *de facto* industrial governance is being developed in defence-related activities. Governance operates in this realm through a complex set of networks, which bring together public and private actors, national and overseas authorities. There is an idiosyncratically European dimension to this, for nowhere else in the world is there an equivalent set of major defence producers working ever-more closely together, in the absence of a unitary overarching state. The only producers of similar size, or larger, are in the USA, which has one government, one defence department and one procurement agency. Europe at present, and for the foreseeable future, lacks any such focus. This is a result of the distinctive trajectory of the development of the European 'proto-state apparatus' represented by the European Union (together with related organisations such as the west European Union – discussed below). The overall effect, I suggest, is that a significant part of European S&T effort is moving beyond the regulatory influence of any accountable body, and in particular the elected politics which supposedly represent the peoples whose taxes find their way into this new network of actors. This curious combination of what has in another context been called 'governance with government' (see Lovering, 1995) may have invidious implications. These relate not only to the economic aspects of S&T effort, notably the social and geographical impacts of defence–industrial spending, but also possibly to security and defence questions.

Background: the defence industry in Western Europe during the cold war

Aggregate West European defence spending peaked in the late 1980s at just over half that of the USA, roughly the same as the USSR, or ten times that of the whole of Asia (Deger and Sen, 1990). In some countries and many regions the defence sector formed an important sub-set of industry. In Western Europe as a whole, it employed a workforce of the same order of magnitude as the car industry. Its significance for science and technology cannot be quantified (since it involves intractable evolutionary questions) but was clearly enormous. In the mid 1990s European defence industry output was around 60 billion ECU (the UK, France, Germany and Italy accounting for some 90 per cent of the total) (CEC, 1996). Although this corresponded to only about 2 per cent of Union industrial output, it represented a higher proportion of what most would regard as 'high-technology' activity and employment, as Jacques Delors noted in his (largely ignored) call for a co-ordinated policy for high-technology-based competitiveness (CEC, 1994a).

The winds of change began blowing in the defence sector, however, long before the cold war came to an end. They were driven not by new

defence strategies but by new 'neo-liberal' economic policies and constraints on government spending. Thus real defence spending in
Britain under the later Thatcher administrations fell more rapidly than
at any time since the late 1940s. In the 1990s, German defence spending collapsed as a result of the disappearance of the Soviet Union and
German reunification. West European defence spending fell almost
17 per cent in six years, and equipment expenditure fell almost twice
as rapidly (SIPRI, 1994). The decline was greatest and fastest in
Germany, least and latest in France, where it only began to be felt in
the late 1990s.

As a result defence R&D spending in Britain fell, while it continued
to grow in other European countries (Table 11.1). UK government
defence R&D spending is expected to have fallen by up to a further 50
per cent over the decade. French spending patterns are likely to show a
similar trend, but at a less extreme level. German defence R&D spending is at a much lower level and is set to remain broadly static. In
general, Europe's defence industry found itself in the mid 1990s having
to provide a higher proportion of defence-related R&D from sources
other than host governments.

Restructuring in the defence industry is a far more complex matter
than a simple linear contraction in line with aggregate government
defence budgets. The defence industry is dominated by a small and
increasingly interwoven group of large corporations. Concentration
has intensified rapidly in the 1990s, initially on the national level, so
that by 1998 there was one major supplier in each sector in each
country – BAe/GEC in Britain, Daimler Benz in Germany, with measures announced to consolidate. Aerospatiale, Matra (the defence arms
of the Lagardere group) and Dassault in France. In December 1997 the
defence ministers of Britain, France and Germany issued a high-profile
statement insisting that Europe's defence industry had to rationalise if
it was to survive the growing challenge of the giant American corporations. In October 1998 the first fruits emerged in the form of the
proposal to merge BAe and Daimler Benz military aircraft.

**Table 11.1: Changes in government spending on Defence R&D (constant
prices) 1985–92**

UK	–25%
France	+36%
Germany	+24%
USA	+7%

Source: Technology Foresight Panel 12 Defence and Aerospace.

A critical but often overlooked element in this restructuring has been the transformation in corporate behaviour as a result of the privatisation or *de facto* 'marketisation' of the leading defence companies. Between the late 1980s and late 1990s British Aerospace, Aerospatiale, Thomson-CSF, Daimler Benz Aerospace, and even, in convoluted form, the Italian Finnmeccanica group have all been shorn of governmental ownership, or (in the French and Italian cases) been granted substantially more autonomy at corporate management level. Compared to their cold war predecessors, Europe's defence companies now enjoy an unprecedented degree of decisionmaking power. Partly as a result of this empowerment of managers, the cost pressures arising from declining home markets and the growth of competition in home and foreign markets have been translated – broadly speaking – into less Research and more Development, and also into a series of reforms in the production process, such as the adoption of lean production, closer management of slimmer supply chains, more tightly controlled employment practices, large-scale job losses, flatter management hierarchies and a reshaping of the employment profile (CEC, 1992; Lovering 1993; Hebert 1995). The defence sector, in other words, has taken on many of the habits of civilian manufacturing (Delbridge and Lowe, 1998).

Towards a European defence industry?

From the late 1980s it was widely expected that the renewed energy devoted to European integration would lead to stronger European technology and industry policies in general (Middlemass, 1995). At the same time the promise of closer political union was thought by many to imply the development of a common regime governing security and defence (Allebeck, 1993; Deger and Sen, 1990; Delors, 1991). The official ending of the cold war, coming on top of these tendencies, encouraged the Commission to urge upon member states measures to bring the restructuring of the defence industry within the framework of European industrial and technology policy. The Commission call was to be ignored.

In the 1985 White Paper laying the basis for the Single European Act, Lord Cockfield and Jacques Delors had suggested that the defence sector should come under the same single market regime as civilian industry (RUSI, 1990, p. 12). Six years later Delors tried to forge a link between this theme and the security and defence dimension. If the European Community was 'to act as a community' he insisted, 'it needed not only a military capacity, but also a coherent defence–industrial strategy' (Delors, 1991 p. 102). In 1991–92 European Commissioners toured member countries assuring local authorities, defence companies and trades unions that they regarded a policy for the defence industry as vital not only to compensate for job-losses but also to harness Europe's military–technological assets to its industrial competitiveness in the new world of global high-technology driven competition. These ideas were directly influenced to a significant degree by the incoming Clinton administration's declared strategy to encourage concentration and diversification in the US industry as an aid to US competitiveness.

Laura Tyson, before becoming Clinton's economic advisor, had argued in an influential book that a strategic approach to the US defence industry as a national technological resource was necessary to address growing global competition (Alic, 1992; Tyson, 1992). The new Vice-President Al Gore championed a strategy for promoting 'dual-use' (military and civil) technologies as a means to develop both defence industrial-capacity and competitiveness (Misheloff, 1994). These considerations found expression in the Technology Reinvestment Programme (RTP) administered by the Advanced Research Project Agency (from which the former prefix 'Defence' was dropped). Viewed from Europe, these were powerful new instruments for harnessing the S&T capacities hitherto locked up in the defence sector to US industrial regeneration. In the event, they would turn out otherwise (Markusen, 1997), but Commissioners and industrialists in Europe were not to know this in the early 1990s.

Accordingly, European Commissioners, with defence industrialists (especially German ones) looking over their shoulders, pondered how to link defence–industrial policy to technology, industry and regional goals in the context of the 'Delors II' agenda for a proactive and integrated industry and technology strategy (Middlemass, 1995). In 1991 the Commission proposed the adoption of a common policy for defence research and production. It also, as an enabling condition, proposed the suppression of Article 223, the clause in the Treaty of Rome which allows member governments to exclude European Community institutions from matters of national security.[2] In 1992 Martin Bangemann (Commissioner for Industrial Policy) proposed extending the new EC regulations on open public procurement to the defence industry (Allebeck, 1994, p. 201). In 1993 the Commission's White Paper on Competition included a few sentences hinting at the need to make the most of the technological potential of the European defence industry (CEC, 1993).

But Euro-scepticism was on the rise, and national governments (especially in Britain and France) rejected Commission efforts to play a role in defence–industrial matters. In 1992 the Council of Ministers rejected Commission proposals to promote restructuring in the aerospace industry. In Lisbon the following year Ministers debated the arms industry, but issued no official press release, being unable to agree (Allebeck, 1993). Even the modest KONVER scheme (which provided 'mopping-up' funds for localities affected by defence job losses) drew criticism from the central governments of Britain and Germany.

The Commission's defence–industrial ambitions were scaled down and eventually became little more than rhetorical. Article 223 remained in place, and was invoked by the British to exclude European intrusion into GEC's acquisition of the Vickers submarine yard at Barrow, and later (1998) to fend off inquiries into the merger of GEC and the Italian Alenia Difensa group. The Commission stood back, confining itself to issuing pronouncements urging more assistance to restructuring defence companies, and abandoning its earlier hopes of incorporating the defence industry into a coherent holistic European technology strategy (see CEC, 1995a, 1995b, 1996, 1997). The European Parliament did not debate the defence industry restructuring between 1992 and 1996 (EP, 1995). The action was taking place elsewhere.

Intergovernmentalism and the reinvention of NATO

In 1995 the *Economist* correctly observed that 'the slower the EU has gone, the more it has seemed as if NATO is forcing the pace'. Two years later NATO was clearly the leading actor in defence and related fields, whether in the Bosnian tragedy, or the entry of Poland, the Czech Republic and Hungary into the West European 'family'. The reconstruction of NATO reflected the reassertion of national government influence over the 'Euro-federal' thrust of the Delors era.

All EU governments, especially the 'Big Three' in defence (Britain, France and Germany), wished to sustain institutions which would maintain the US military commitment to Europe. The most important of these is NATO. Second to this is the Western European Union (WEU), which came into existence in the mid-1950s as a result of attempts to legitimise German rearmament in the context of the cold war. It was dormant until 1984 when it was reanimated as a forum to promote European defence co-operation as a complement to NATO (Grosser, 1987; Cahen, 1989). In 1990 France and Germany urged that the WEU should play the main role in the European Union's forthcoming security and defence activities (Middlemass, 1995, 187). An annexe to the Maastricht Treaty declared that the WEU would become the defence component of the European Union.

Ostensibly, the WEU became the formal framework within which the future of the European arms industry would be worked out. In 1994 WEU spokespersons boldly declared that the organisation was developing 'an industrial armaments policy ... an arms export policy; a joint European equipment procurement mechanism; and means for further opening the European market'. It was also examining 'how to establish a common European defence science and technology base' (Reed, 1993). In fact, although the WEU was proliferating a maze of new organisations, they would have virtually no impact on the development of the defence industry.

The formal structures: the Western European Armaments group (WEAG)

In 1992 the WEU took over the work of the Independent European Programme Group (IEPG), an informal association of European NATO members founded 16 years earlier with the aim of strengthening co-operation in defence equipment production. The IEPG transmogrified into the Western European Armaments Organisation a formal body under a Treaty, with a permanent staff in Brussels, claiming to be a putative co-ordinated European Armaments Agency.

There have been many proposals to establish a European Armaments Agency since the 1960s, all floundering on the reluctance of the continent's many Armed Forces and competing producers to work with common equipment, along with suspicions that the bulk of the benefits of closer transatlantic co-operation would go to the US (Grosser 1987). But in the 1990s, as the restructuring accelerated, the scope for greater integration of the marked increased and the prospect of a European Armaments Agency of some form or other was revived. However, the WEU and WEAO were not alone in the field. In 1996 another body – known from its French initials as OCCAR – was created to supervise procurement relating to the Franco-German 'Eurocorps' and a number of major new military equipment programmes. As a result, there are currently two organisations aspiring to be the embryo of a future European Armaments Agency.

The real significance of these Byzantine developments in the corridors of transnational bureaucracies is that neither organisation has had the slightest influence on the transformation of the defence industry.

In researching the leading defence companies in the mid 1990s, it was soon clear that not a single company regarded the proliferation of these formal bodies as significant for corporate strategy. Some industry and government interviewees said they regarded these developments as little more than 'fig-leaves to cover the lack of commitment of member governments' to a European defence strategy and European defence–industrial policy. Others indicated that 'the companies can't get all that they are looking for there', so they are busy elsewhere. This 'elsewhere' is made up of webs of trans-border networks through which individual companies, procurement agencies and armed services devise and institute new weapons development programmes.

Since most defence companies are also high-technology civil producers, they are also involved with civilian industry support at national and European levels. Many received funding through the ESPRIT programme. Less formally the major players also have good informal access to European Commissioners, notably in the Directorates for Industrial Policy and Technology, where it is said that the door is 'always open to the handful of leading companies'. But the first and most important port of call remains a company's national government. The defence industry influences national procurement decisions, arms trade policies, and national research priorities through a range of trade, lobbying and campaigning networks. Its relationship to national government departments is changing, but remains vital. In Britain the election of the Labour government in 1997 has improved government–industry relations, to the immediate satisfaction of the latter, which received two massive contracts within weeks of the election – confirmation of the Eurofighter programme, and of UK participation in the bidding for the future American Joint Strike Fighter (JSF) programme (Lovering, 1998a).

The marginal significance of the formal institutions

The institutional environment and policy agendas impacting on European defence companies is very different from that of the cold war era, even in France where persisting state control is looked at askance by British and German companies and politicians (Hebert, 1995; Serfati, 1996). It consists of a plurality of interacting institutions, including long-established and embryonic pan-European organisations, national and intergovernmental institutions, and numerous formal and informal networks. For an outsider, this system is infuriatingly complex, and is probably fully understood by only a minority of insiders. But it appears to be clear to all that increasingly the key industrial decisions are being made outside the formal European institutions (WEU, EU, WEAO and OCCAR) and the national polities they represent. It would appear that the real significance of these bodies is that they will eventually provide post hoc public legitimisation of decisions that will have been arrived at through more shadowy corporate–governmental negotiations on a transnational scale.

Industrialists interviewed in 1995 suggested that it may take 20 years of such 'policy cascading' before the degree of openness in the European defence industry approximates that of civilian industries. But it should be born in mind that civilian industries characterised by lumpy investments, monopolist purchasers, and the presence of transnational companies are also far removed from the open markets imagined in economics textbooks, and misleadingly invoked in much of the current discussion of the virtues of 'globalisation'. Chomsky (1988) has recently reminded us that perhaps only 15 per cent of USA trade is really 'free'.

Where the real action is: towards 'new model' cross-border collaborations

In this context, defence firms like other transnational operators adapt as best they can to the pressures and opportunities they can perceive. This is the reason why the restructuring of the European defence industry in the 1990s has a markedly *ad hoc* and piecemeal character, in contrast with events the other side of the Atlantic where a unitary state and procurement agency sat down with the companies to agree a design for – and subsidy for – restructuring (Markusen, 1997). Amongst the more competitive and politically-well placed firms, which generally but not exclusively means the larger ones, the most auspicious adaptations consist of cross-border collaborative strategic alliances and development agreements which bring together selected companies and governments around specific programmes (Skons, 1993). Virtually all the leading European defence producers are engaged in a range of collaborative defence R&D projects.

Some of these originated before the end of the cold war (for example, Aerospatiale with DASA in Eurocopter, DASA with BAe, FIAT, and CASA on Eurofighter, etc). Typically these older programmes were government-led, driven by the rising costs of advanced weapons technology, growing constraints on national defence budgets, the desire to sustain 'strategic' industries or companies, and the wish to cement international alliances. 'Traditional' collaborations were notoriously inefficient, resulting in duplication of facilities and training, and over-runs on costs and timetables (Willett *et al.*, 1994; Sandler and Hartley, 1995).

The collaborations which are now being constructed are very differ-ent from those inefficient – and often, for the firms – frustrating fore-runners. The ideal towards which the industry hopes to move is a system in which groups of customer governments commit themselves to long-term development support for a particular weapon, system, or technology. A consortium of companies is then left to arrange how best to meet this demand, allocating work between themselves (and subcontractors) according to the kind of criteria which would be famil-iar in major civilian technology developments (Lovering, 1998b). A research and development phase would be followed by a separately negotiated production phase in which a separate process of work allo-cation takes place. Prime contractors are thus increasingly acting as autonomous, rational, companies in ways quite unlike those of the cold war era of national Military Industrial Complexes, subject to home government direction. Such collaborations promise firms a new freedom to develop rational investment strategies of the scale and duration required by modern defence technologies. They allow them to chose how best to exploit their technological capacities, and the skills of their workforces (including civilian applications).

Companies expect this ideal to be realised progressively through a sequence of collaborative projects over the next ten to 20 years.[3] In 1996–99 a number of such projects came on line. Between 1981 and 1990 the number of consortia involving European firms remained at around 20. Between 1991 and 1994 it rose to 38. The number of looser strategic alliances has also increased. In the post-cold war round of defence–industrial collaborations which is now underway, national gov-ernments increasingly accept that defence research and product devel-opments should be industry – rather than government – driven (see for example Barrie, 1995). The growth of collaboration is such that defence R&D is now 'more internationalised' than is civil R&D: overseas funds account for around less than one–seventh of all business expenditure on civil R&D in Britain, but almost one quarter in defence R&D.

The 1995 decision of the British government to join the Future Large Aircraft (FLA) programme, rather than rely entirely on buying US Hercules aircraft, and the possible creation of Airbus Industrie Military Aircraft around the FLA project, was one landmark along the road towards these New Model collaborations.[4] Work on FLA wings is being competitively fought out between Daimler Benz Aerospace and British Aerospace. Development work for the HORIZON frigate (Britain, Italy, France), and the merger of the munitions and missiles systems divisions of Daimler Benz and Thomson in TDA Armements were also cited as exemplars of elements of the New Model (Reed, 1995). In addition, some longer-established collaborative programmes, such as Eurofighter, are being modified in ways which incorporate New Model features. The signing of the contracts for the new European 'battlefield taxi' in 1998 was seen as a major step further along the road.

Collaboration as insurance against political risk

Collaboration makes economic sense because it makes possible larger-scale projects than individual national governments could afford, and thereby enables defence companies to gain access to longer production runs, standardisation, and incremental development. But collaboration also has other advantages.[5]

In the post-cold war environment defence spending is widely regarded as unpopular. In Germany in particular the debate over defence spending, especially major programmes such as Eurofighter, has been intense (Albrecht *et al.*, 1994). In Britain the dominant parties have prevented the widespread public cynicism towards defence spending finding expression. Only in France is there still a general public consensus in favour of high defence spending, and even here it is less firm than in the past, especially since the public spending crisis of 1995 brought demonstrators onto the streets. France and Britain, which account for perhaps 80 per cent of European defence R&D spending, have been growing closer on defence issues; however there remains a lack of consensus at the European level and sustained opposition to major defence spending in many EU member countries.

In this hostile climate, collaborative programmes help to 'depoliticise' defence industrial decisions. For the industry, they make it possible to overcome what is seen as the primary problem of 'fickle national politicians, anxious to please electorates in the short-term and uneasy about defence spending in the absence of an agreed Threat'. For the companies, and also for segments of the armed services who hope to acquire their products, 'technical problems are not the issue, the fundamental point is the unreliability of politicians'. Collaboration provides protection against political risk by surrounding defence programmes with both legal–technical formalities (subject to withdrawal penalties) and foreign policy agreements.

In addition to supporting cross-national company collaborations on a negotiated case-by-case basis (Reed, 1995), the governments of Britain, France, Germany, Italy, Spain, Sweden and the Netherlands agreed in 1994 to form a new organisation to co-ordinate their aerospace research establishments. One commentator noted that 'In a decade from now... the research establishments links with industry will increasingly be interwoven with transnational working relationships' (Moxon, 1994). From what has been said so far, it follows that these arrangements are unlikely to be subject to much national scrutiny.

The system of economic governance in the European defence industry: transnational neo-corporatism?

The construction of a distinctive pattern of economic governance in the European defence industry is underpinned by the absence of a wide public consensus in favour of high levels of defence spending, the reassertion of intergovernmentalism (FCO, 1996), and the growing *de facto* autonomy of the companies. Companies and governments (and through them the armed services) interact in formal and informal ways, some visible, others obscured from public view. This nexus apportions influence unevenly. Within the defence industry the larger companies can exert considerable influence on governments (consumers) through a range of fora. But within the business sector the actors are markedly uneven in their access to resources for fruitful negotiation.

There are clear parallels here with trends on non-defence high-technology industries in Europe. In his study of the Europeanisation of the telecommunications industry Alan Cawson noted that 'existing political practices have tended to exhibit a dualism between corporatism for the powerful and pluralism for the powerless' (1990, 117). Much the same could be said of the trend within the defence industry. While many smaller European defence companies still hope for a continuation of previous patterns (and cling to Article 223 as a means to this), their more powerful brethren are able to actively influence their future through negotiations with a multiplicity of actors, both governments and companies. While the official European institutions labour to respect the wishes of the less powerful companies, regions, and governments, the defence industry is being transformed as a result of less formal, and accountable, processes.

This represents a significant 'normalisation' of the defence industry in Europe. The reduction of straightforward protectionism, increased exposure to competition, and infusion of new managerial styles, has pitched it into 'informal politics' and the more advanced companies have responded energetically and effectively. These emergent structures are perhaps too informal and ad hoc to justify the title of transnational neo-corporatism. But they echo some of the features of corporatism this time on a transnational scale. They differ from the stereotype also in that they lack any participation of organised labour.

As Schmitter and Streek (1995, 174) have stressed in another context, Europe's 'weak, fledging pseudostate' has sufficient resources to attract the attention of organised interests, but it lacks resources to influence their organisational design. If the fledgling Euro-state is taken to refer not just to the EU but to the nexus including EU, WEU and NATO institutions, their assessment applies equally to the defence sector. The commanding heights of the industry are becoming moments in new transnational circuits of research and development, and production, beyond the design or regulation of any unitary overarching public body.

The distinctiveness of the influences on European defence industrial restructuring

The distinctiveness of the contemporary European defence industry is rooted in the absence of both a powerful unitary state, and a cultural and corporate consensus. This contrasts sharply with its major competitor.

The US defence industry is subject to a uniquely militarised and unitary state which spends around ten times as much on defence R&D as does Europe. The US state has assisted the corporate restructuring of the arms industry with a view to strengthening both its global competitiveness and its military edge. The US case highlights the dilemmas posed for companies in Europe by the absence of the kind of developmentalist defence–industrial strategy which Delors proposed. If the USA example highlights the amorphousness of the European state system, a comparison with the Japanese example highlights the significance of the cultural and ideological diversity within Europe. It was suggested above that a key factor driving the piecemeal 'restructuring from below' of the European defence industry is the construction of corporate-driven strategies to reduce 'political risk'. A comparison with Japan throws an interesting light on this. According to Samuels (1994) risk in the Japanese case is minimised through corporate structures (Zaibatsu) and governmental behavioural protocols norms (such as the sequential sharing out contracts amongst companies) both of which derive from a 'cultural consensus'. As a result the Japanese defence industry has been able to grow within a nurturing environment of effective 'techno-nationalism' (Ostrey and Nelson, 1995). Samuels (1994, 31) claims that the cultural consensus as to the desirability and purposes of technology ultimately derives from Japan's military tradition. Samuels account highlights the salience of the cultural characteristics of Europe.

Europe lacks both the unitary defence-oriented state apparatus of the USA and the integrative ideology of identity and concertative institutions of Japan. This is why the European defence industry is becoming subject to a uniquely complex new system of *de facto* international governance. This involves national, intergovernmental and international determinations, but it lacks a single overriding authority. The European defence at the end of the twentieth century is characterised by 'governance without government' (Cox, 1992, 30; Lovering, 1995). One effect of this is that there is no consistent pressure to ensure that firms internationalise within, rather than out of, European economic space.

In the search for new corporate, and thereby geographical, linkages 'Europe' is not necessarily the key entity shaping corporate planning. Most collaborative programmes include only a small selection of European companies and countries, and many also include non-European suppliers. The USA connection remains dominant, trade in defence equipment with the USA long having been far larger than intra-European trade (Hartley and Cox, 1992). Over 230 British companies contract to USA suppliers to the Pentagon. Despite fears that alliances with US firms may turn European companies into mere subcontractors (*Economist*, 1996) it has long been clear that the next round of mergers in the US defence industry may 'spill across the Atlantic' (Gold, 1994). British participation in the JSF looks like being a major case in point.

On present trends the core of the reconstructed European defence industry in the new century will be a small set of high-technology defence-dual-use companies based in a small number of key locations in Europe's relatively advantaged regions, interacting with a co-ordinated network of European research laboratories. A major part of this nexus will be formally linked through a new European Defence Company – probably based on the BAe–Daimler merger announced on October 1998. But the experimental nature of 'piecemeal collaboration' along with unregulated restructuring lower down the supply chain, leaves open the possibility that many individual companies and capacities may be lost, with possible domino effects. The future of the more competitive companies may be secure, but not that of the 'European Defence Industrial Base' as a whole. Indeed, the concept may cease to have much content.

Conclusion

Judging by current trends and the expectations of many industrialists, new forms of transnational agreement will pervasively influence the defence-related industries. It follows that key decisions as to defence R&D, and the use of high-level S&T manpower, are increasingly likely to depend on the strategies of companies, rather than governments as in the recent past.

Despite the involvement of what is still a large amount of public funds, the governance of the defence industry through a network of networks devised by companies and a sub-set of government departments seem bound to diminish the transparency and accountability of decision-making (Blunden, 1990). This may have important implications in the S&T field. Contrary to the ritual incantation of politicians as to national sovereignty in defence matters, a significant part of national defence-related S&T activity in some countries (especially Britain and France) is likely to move beyond the purview of national polities. The on-going reorganisation of the defence industry suggests that the economic, social and security effects of the European S&T effort are slipping out of control of the agencies that fund them, the taxpayers who ultimately provide those funds, and the employees and regions dependent on the work they provide.

Notes

1. This study draws on an ESRC-funded research project (Grant No. R000 23 4420 The Restructuring of the European Defence Industry and European Community Policy). Interviews were conducted in 1994–45 with 70 industrialists, trade organisation representatives, government officials, trades unionists, and researchers in Britain, France, Germany, the Netherlands, Belgium and Italy. In view of the subject matter, the research drew heavily on semi-structured discussions on a 'Chatham House Rule' basis. As a result, the text here includes some verbatim quotations which are not attributed to identifiable individuals.
2. Article 223 of the Treaty of Rome, unaltered in the 1992 Maastricht revision, states '(a) no member states shall be obliged to supply information the disclosure of which it considers contrary to the essential interests of its security; (b) Any Member State may take such measures as it considers necessary for the protection of the essential interests of its security which are connected

with the production of or trade in arms, munitions and war material...'. In practice, the list of items to which this applies has been a matter of contention, the British and French governments leaning to a generous if vague definition, the German government adopting a more restrictive and precise list of 'warlike goods'. Hartley and Cox (1992) estimated that about two-thirds of European procurement is of Article 223 'warlike items'.

3. One reason for the emphasis on collaboration is that other routes to internationalisation are problematic. Direct foreign investment is constrained in the defence industry, for security reasons (Gold, 1994, 5). Although foreign shareholdings in European defence companies have increased, they have generally been subject to a governmentally-imposed ceiling.

4. This appears to have been suspended following the change of direction in Daimler Benz, and the related collapse of Fokker in 1996.

5. The neo-classical economic literature suggests that the savings arising from collaboration, due to economies of scale and competition effects, may be offset by the 'collaboration premium' arising because collaboration also gives firms special influence over governments (Sandler and Hartley, 1995, 234–8; Hartley and Cox, 1992).

References

Albrecht, U., Lock, P. and Cohen, J. (1994) 'Germany The Reluctant Eurofighter Partner' in Randall Forsberg (ed.) *The Arms Production Dilemma: Contraction and Restraint in the World Combat Aircraft Industry*, Cambridge Mass: MIT Press 177–92.

Alic, J. A. (1992) *Beyond spin-off: Military and commercial technologies in a changing world*, Boston: Harvard Business School Press

Allebeck, A. C. (1993) 'The European Community' in Herbert Wulf (ed.) *Arms Industry Limited* SIPRI, Oxford University Press, 191–221.

Barrie, D. (1995) 'A Minister for Europe' *Flight International* 15–21 March, 28–9.

Blunden, M. (1989) 'Collaboration and Competition in European Weapons Procurement' *Defense Analysis*, 5, 291–304.

Cahen, A. (1989) *The Western European Union and NATO* London: Brassey's Atlantic Commentaries No 2.

Cawson, A. (1992) 'Interests, Groups and Public Policy-Making: the case of the European Consumer Electronics Industry' in Justin Greenwood, Jurgen R. Grote and Karsten Romit, (eds), *Organised Interests and the European Community*, London: SAGE.

CEC (1992) *The economic and social impact of reductions in defence spending and military forces on the regions of the Community Study* Economists Advisory Group, Commission of the European Communities, Brussels.

CEC (1994a) *Growth, Competitiveness, Employment: the Challenges and Ways Forward into the 21st Century*, White Paper, Commission of the European Communities, Brussels.

CEC (1994b) *Communication to the Member States fixing the guidelines for operational programmes or global grants that the Member States are invited to propose within the framework of a Community initiative concerning defence conversion* (KONVER) Brussels, 17 February.

CEC (1995a) 'The defence-related industry in the European Union Commission of the European Communities', DGIII, Discussion Paper, 20 January.

CEC (1995b) 'The Industrial Base for the production of Defence Equipment in the European Union Commission of the European Communities', DGIA, Document prepared for the Informal Group on Cooperation in the Area of Armaments, January.

CEC (1995c) 'The Community research and Technological development policy and its potential relevance to the technological base of the defence sectors Commission of the European Communities', Document prepared for the Informal Group on Cooperation in the Area of Armaments, March.

CEC (1996) *The Challenges facing the European defence-related industry: a contribution for action at European level Commission of the European Communities*, Brussels COM (96) 10 final.

CEC (1997) *Implementing the European Union strategy on defence-related industries,* European Commission COM (97) 583 final.

Chenais, F. (1993) 'The French National System of Innovation' in Richard R. Nelson (ed.) *National Innovation Systems* Oxford University Press, 192–229.

Chomsky, N. (1998) 'Power in the Global Arena' *New Left Review* 230, 3–28.

Cox, R. W. (1992) 'Global Perestroika' *Socialist Register* London: Merlin.

Deger, S. and Sen, S. (1990) *Military expenditure: The political economy of international security* SIPRI, Oxford University Press.

Delbridge, R. and Lowe, J. (1998) *Manufacturing in Transition* London: Routledge.

Delors, J. (1991) 'European integration and security' *Survival* XXXIII 99–109.

Economist (1995) 'The making of modern Europe' 13 May 16–17.

Economist (1996) 'American monsters, European minnows' 13 January 69–70.

EP (1995) 'Report on progress made in implementing the common foreign and security policy' European Parliament, Session documents A4-0083/95 24 April.

FCO (1996) *A Partnership of Nations: The British Approach to the European Intergovernmental Conference 1996*, London: Foreign and Commonwealth Office, Cmnd 3181.

Gansler, J. S. (1996) *Defense Conversion*, Cambridge Mass: MIT Press.

Gold, D. (1994) 'The Internationalisation of Military Production' *Peace Economics, Peace Science, and Public Policy,* 1.3, 1–12.

Gray, B. (1995) 'France and Germany offer UK a role in arms group' *Financial Times* 28 March.

Grosser, A. (1987) *The Western Alliance: European-American Relations since 1945* Translated by Michael Shaw, London: Macmillan – now Palgrave.

Hartley, K. and Cox, K. (1992) *The Costs of Non-Europe in Defence Procurement: Executive Summary Commission of the European Communities*, DGIII, Brussels, July.

Hebert, J.-P. (1995) *Production d'armement: mutation du systeme franciais* Paris: Etudes de La Documentation Francaise.

Kaldor, M. (1990) *The Imaginary War: understanding the East–West conflict,* Oxford: Blackwell.

Lovering, J. (1993) 'Restructuring the British defence industrial base after the Cold War: Institutional and geographical perspectives' *Defence Economics* 4 123–39.

Lovering, J. (1994) 'After the Cold War: The defence industry and the new Europe' in Brown, P. and Crompton, R. (eds) *A New Europe? Economic restructuring and social exclusion,* London: UCL Press, 175–95.

Lovering, J. (1995) 'The production and consumption of the "means of violence" after the Cold War: implications of the reconfiguration of the state and economic internationalisation' *Geoforum* 25, 4, 471–86.

Lovering, J. (1998a) 'Labour and the defence industry: an alliance for further globalisation' *Capital and Class* no. 65, Summer, 9–20.

Lovering, J. (1998b) 'Opening Pandora's Box: de facto industrial policy and the British defence industry' in Manufacturing in Transition edited by Rick Delbridge and James Lowe, London: Routledge 151–68.

Lovering, J. (1999) 'Which way to turn? The European defence industry after the cold war' in Ann Markusen and Sean Costigan (eds) *Arming the Future* Washington: Washington DC, Council on Foreign Relations, 334–70.

Markusen, A. (1997) 'How We Lost the Peace Dividend' *The American Prospect* July–August, 86–96.

Markusen, A. and Yudken, J. (1991) *Dismantling the Cold War Economy* Basic Books.

Middlemass, K. (1995) *Orchestrating Europe: the informal politics of European Union 1973–1995* London: Fontana Press/HarperCollins.

Misheloff, J. (1994) 'Economic Competitiveness, and the Future of the Military Industrial Base' *The Journal of Strategic Studies* 17, 3, 209–37.

Moxon, J. (1994) 'European researchers agree to join forces' *Flight International* 11–17 May.

Nelson, R. R. *(ed.) (1993) National Innovation Systems* Oxford University Press, 158–91.

Ostrey, S. and Nelson, R. E. (1995) *Techno-nationalism and Techo-globalism,* Washington DC: Brookings Institution.

Reed, C. (1995) 'European minds look to meet on mergers' *Jane's Defence Weekly* no. 6 11 February, 23–4.

RUSI Working Group (1990) '1992: Protectionism or Collaboration in Defence Procurement Royal United Services Institute for Defence Studies', Whitehall Paper Series (written by Ron Smith, Keith Hayward, Richard Mills, Mark Harvey and David Bolton).

Samuels, R. (1994) *Rich Nation, Strong Army: National Security and the Technological Transformation of Japan,* Ithaca and London: Cornell University Press.

Sandler, T. and Hartley, K. (1995) *Cambridge Surveys of Economic Literature: The Economics of Defense,* Cambridge University Press.

Schmitter, P. C. and Streeck, W. (1991) 'Organised interests and the Europe of 1992' reprinted in Brent F. Nelson and Alexander C.-G. Stubb (eds) *The European Union,* Boulder, London: Lynne Rienner 169–87.

Sen, G. (1988) *The Military origins of Industrialisation and Trade Rivalry,* London: Pinter.

Serfati, C. (1996) *Les industries europeeennes diarmament,* Paris: La documentation franciaise.

SIPRI (1994) *SIPRI Yearbook 1994* Stockholm: International Peace Research Institute.

Skons, E. (1993) 'Western Europe: Internationalization of the arms industry' in Herbert Wulf (ed.) *Arms Industry Limited* Stockholm International Peace Research Institute (SIPRI), Oxford University Press 160–90.

Tyson, L. dfA. (1992) *Who's bashing whom? Trade conflict in High-Technology*, Washington/Longmans, London: Industries Institute for International Economics.

Walker, W. (1992) '"Defence" in Technology and the future of Europe' in (eds) Freeman C., Sharp M. and Walker W. Pinter Publications/Science Policy Research Unit 365–382.

Walker, W. and Gummett, P. (1993) 'Nationalism, internationalism and the European Defence Market' Chaillot Papers 9 Paris: WEU Institute for Security Studies.

Willett, S., Clarke, M. and Gummett, P. (1994) 'The British Push for the Eurofighter 2000' in Randall Forsberg (ed.) *The Arms Production Dilemma: Contraction and Restraint in the World Combat Aircraft Industry*, Cambridge Mass: MIT Press, 139–160.

12
The Political Economy of Medicines Regulation in Britain

John Abraham

Introduction

The regulation of technologies and especially technological risk is often approached by scrutinising contemporary case studies of product hazards or by contemporary international comparative analysis (Gillespie *et al.*, 1979, p. 265–301; Brickman *et al.*, 1985; Jasanoff, 1990). Such studies provide detailed knowledge about the actions of regulators, but tend to neglect how political and economic factors may have generated regulation in the first place partly because of the limited time frame utilised. As Ronge notes, this can be a limitation because 'the political system is by no means autonomous in choosing its tasks and ends. .... Safety and risk are at least to a high degree problems of a particular structural relationship between State and economy' (Ronge, 1980, pp. 209–38). It follows from this that attempts to analyse or influence regulatory policy about technological risk might be fruitfully informed by greater insight into the factors that shape the political trajectory of regulation. To that end, in this chapter about pharmaceuticals and the safety of medicines I take a political economy approach which examines where in the British State regulatory policy is made, and the interactions between the State, capital, industrial interests and other social groups *over a substantial time period*. Before discussing these matters, however, it is instructive to consider what theories and data can assist in this task.

Theorising regulation

There has been no shortage of attempts to theorise how the State regulates industrial activity, but three enduring and distinct theoretical propositions can be identified. Bernstein's 'life-cycle' theory of regulatory commissions is the classic example of capture theories. Bernstein postulates that a regulatory commission is typically established as a result of compromise legislation designed to protect certain groups against the abuses of the regulated industry. Initially the commission tends to be aggressive and adversarial towards its regulatees, but becomes isolated as its enthusiasts tire and retire. Eventually it is progressively 'captured' by, and comes to share the perspectives of, the regulated industry (Bernstein, 1955). From this stage onwards, argue capture theorists, the regulatory authority favours industrial interests unless, and until, a scandal highlighting the failures of regulation trigger a new drive for adversary, and consequently, the commencement of a new cycle. Arguments of this genre are often referred to as public interest theories because they assume that from the outset regulation is established in order to serve the public interest against industry, and that its proper role is to continue to do so. (Mitnick, 1980, pp. 95–109). Such assumptions are common in studies of regulatory science. For example, Brickman *et al.*, (1985) concentrate on how the chemical industry adapts to, or opposes. State regulation without much attention to the possibility that industrial interests might generate regulation.

Some traditional Marxist theories of the State stand this view on its head by claiming that regulation is an instrument of working class oppression propped up by capitalist interests, although modern Marxists tend to argue that the State has some 'autonomy' from the capitalist class, and that it is necessary to distinguish between the interests of capital reproduction and particular capitalist interests (Offe, 1983, p. 669; Miliband, 1983, pp. 57–68). Nevertheless, the main focus of Marxist theories of State regulation remains class interests so that the exercise of State power is generally interpreted in terms of class struggle within or outside State apparatuses. One obvious drawback with these Marxist approaches is their insensitivity to regulatory processes not reducible to class interests with the consequence that they may be insufficiently discriminating to detect intra-class conflicts of interest and cross-class common interests. This problem is compounded by the dearth of empirical research designed to substantiate Marxist theories of the state. As Jessop (1990, pp. 167–8) puts it, 'much theoretical work remains to be done but concrete studies are also urgently required'. Furthermore, both capture and Marxist theories of regulation tend to represent the State as rather passive.

The third position considered here is corporatist theory, which assumes neither that regulatory authorities serve capitalist or public interests nor that all interests are reducible to class (Cawson, 1986). Rather, following neo-Weberian closure theory, (Murphy, 1988) the role of the State is defined in relation to the power of organized interests to monopolise socioeconomic or status advantages by closing off opportunities to other groups defined as ineligible (Cawson, 1985, pp. 1–21). Such closure may manifest itself along class lines, but not necessarily so.

Given the grand nature of these theories it is necessary to examine their relevance to medicines regulation by reference to an extended period of time. The period from the late nineteenth to the twentieth century has been chosen because that is when State regulation of medicines has been of most significance. Before then it was virtually non-existent. The strategy in this chapter is not to try to make the empirical materials fit one or other of the above regulatory theories but rather, in the light of the empirical findings, provide an historically grounded assessment of modern medicines regulation in Britain using the regulatory theories as a guiding framework. Such an assessment is timely as regulators, industrialists, doctors and consumers brace themselves for the increasingly globalised markets and therapeutic standards for medicines in the 21st century.

Data sources

Frequently the literature on the development of medicines regulation in Britain is constituted by little more than a cursory chronological listing of major legislation. Nevertheless, a computer search of published literature and a manual search of the British index to theses from 1950 did reveal a number of sources of varying substance. Unfortunately almost all those sources share one major drawback, namely, that their account of regulatory developments centres around the use and hazards of medicines (Jenkins, 1987, pp. 56–7; Hodges, 1987, pp. 119–22; Mann, 1988, pp. 725–8, 1984; Penn, 1979, pp. 293–305). The result is that the political and economic contexts of regulation, such as the political economy of the pharmaceutical industry, are entirely unexplored. Even Penn's substantial thesis on the subject falls short in these respects (Penn, 1982). One major exception is Stieb (1966), but his analysis is confined to the 19th century.

In addition to the above publications, the main empirical materials on which this chapter is based are the *Pharmaceutical Journal* from 1900–1990 (a major press for the British pharmaceutical profession and drug trade), British ministerial and other government papers held at the Public Record Office from 1900 to 1960 (when public records ceased to be available under the 'thirty-year rule'), the Association of the British Pharmaceutical Industry (ABPI) Annual Reports from 1961 to 1990, ABPI News from 1975 to 1990, Scrip (World Pharmaceutical News Press) from 1975 to 1992, and the *British Medical Journal, Chemistry and Industry, New Scientist* and *Hansard* all from 1950 to 1990.

The 19th century context

As the Industrial Revolution swept across England in the late 18th and 19th century the foundations for extensive urbanisation were laid. During the Middle Ages the craft guilds, of which apothecaries were a part, had exercised some control over adulteration practices by setting standards of quality, inspecting shops, confiscating substandard goods, and punishing offenders in order to prevent 'unfair' competition between guild masters. In addition, since 1540 the Royal College of Physicians had been empowered to inspect local apothecaries' shops for 'faulty wares'. Urbanisation, however, created sufficient distance between producer, physician and consumer that these traditional village-based controls collapsed (Burnett, 1966; Penn, 1979, pp. 295–9; Steib, 1966). The government made no attempt to replace them with State controls. As a result, drug adulteration, that is, 'any procedure that produces an alteration in strength or purity, or both, from the avowed standard of a drug, whether through intent or neglect' (Steib, 1970), rose dramatically at the beginning of the nineteenth century.

In his startling *Treatise on Adulterations of 1820* Frederick Accum concluded that 'nine tenths of the most potent drugs and chemical preparations used in pharmacy are vended in a sophisticated [i.e. adulterated] state' (Steib, 1966, p. 114). At this time the patent medicine business co-existed alongside the 'ethical' pharmaceutical firms. Unlike the patent medicine makers these 'ethical' companies, which were later to form the basis of the modern pharmaceutical industry, concentrated on selling higher quality medicines to doctors (Tweedale, 1990). Neither of these elements of the medicines trade showed an interest in combating drug adulteration. Despite his efforts Accum's work had no direct impact on the control of adulteration, not only because his methods were scarcely used by most apothecaries to check for drug quality, but also because the political climate did not favour social reform which extended the regulatory powers of the State. The old Tory orthodoxy remained in power virtually uninterrupted from 1783 to 1830. It held that government should, as far as possible, leave society how it found it. This traditional anti-reformist view commanded substantial support if only because there was a common fear that social change could lead to uprisings similar to the French Revolution, and in the wake of the English wars against France such a scenario was perceived by the propertied classes and others as most undesirable (Somervell, 1929, pp. 3–16).

As the fear of change *per se* subsided in the 1820s, Tory traditionalism gave way to the laissez-faire doctrine of liberalism. Theorised by Adam Smith in 1776 and successfully championed in government by Jeremy Bentham during the 1830s and 1840s, it viewed legislative interference with private business as abhorrent and resisted State control of product standards (Bruce, 1961, pp. 42–55). The 1850s, however, marked a turning point, the beginning of a quarter of a century of unmistakable economic prosperity as symbolised by the international superiority of Britain's enterprise and expertise in manufacturing and engineering evident at the Great Exhibition of 1851. Substantial sections of the working classes for the first time tasted the fruits of industrial capitalism as wage-increases more than kept pace with inflation (Bedarida, 1976, pp. 3–35; Burnett, 1966, pp. 91–112).

As the Chartist opposition to industrial capitalism went into retreat and extra-parliamentary political agitation withered, the public increasingly looked to the House of Commons for legislative change. The parliamentary parties, in turn, vied to win public support for their legislative programmes. By the late 1860s legislative reforms, including ones to regulate trade, were gathering pace and tempered according to the interests of the significant newly emerging professions (Bruce, 1961, pp. 89–153). It is in this context that the campaign to control drug adulteration can be seen as classic political activity of the period.

In 1850 the physician Arthur Hill Hassall was the first to realise full and systematic application of microscopy to the detection of adulteration even though the microscope had been introduced to analytical chemistry as early 1747 (Steib, 1966, pp. 68–9). Microscopy made possible for the first time the detection of adulteration in many organic substances for which chemical tests remained unavailable (Steib, 1966, pp. 51–68). However, Hassall's endeavours might have been confined to one isolated article had it not been for Thomas Wakley who, as a zealous proponent of medical reform in Parliament and editor of the *Lancet*, offered Hassall the opportunity to publish his detailed reports of microscopic examinations of foods and drugs in the journal between 1851 and 1854 (Forrester, 1978, pp. 1360–2). Of equal importance was the campaigning of Birmingham's John Postgate for government control of food and drug adulteration. He gained the support of Birmingham MPs, one of whom was to chair the 1855 and 1856 House of Commons Select Committee on Adulteration of Food, Drinks, and Drugs. This Committee was able to turn to Hassall for substantive testimony and scientific evidence as well as using the debate generated by Wakley's *Lancet* as a foundation from which to build further testimony (Steib, 1970, pp. 21–2).

The Committee heard how drugs such as chloroform, opium and scammony were adulterated (House of Commons Select Committee on Adulteration of Food, Drinks and Drugs, 1856, pp. 56–7, 253). Many witnesses, including physicians, chemists and druggists testified that drug adulteration was extensively practised and advocated legislation to discourage it (House of Commons Select Committee on Adulteration of Food, Drinks and Drugs, 1856, pp. 142–9). All were agreed that competition to meet the demand for low priced medicines was the cause of adulteration yet so powerful was the ideology of laissez-faire that Bell, the editor of *The Pharmaceutical Journal* felt able to argue that market forces could be relied on to put an end to adulteration (House of Commons Select Committee on Adulteration of Food, Drinks and Drugs, 1856, p. 253). A corollary to this state of affairs was that the poorer classes suffered most from drug adulteration. No-one disputed that the rich who could resort to higher classes of retail druggists were relatively safe (Home of Commons Select Committee on Adulteration of Food, Drinks and Drugs, 1856, pp. 91–100). As one witness euphemistically put it:

> ... still genuine opium can be obtained by those who like to go to the market and give the price for it; it is chiefly a question of price (House of Commons Select Committee on Adulteration of Food, Drinks and Drugs, 1856, p. 253).

In its Report the Committee admitted that adulteration arose because there were many chemists and druggists who yielded 'to the hard pressure of competition forced upon them by their less scrupulous neighbours' (House of Commons Select Committee on Adulteration of Food, Drinks and Drugs, 1856, p. v). However, the Committee was clearly reluctant to move forcefully against the ideology of free trade and wished merely to define the boundaries of 'honest competition' as illustrated by its remark:

The great difficulty of legislation on this subject lies in putting an end to the liberty of fraud without affecting the freedom of commerce. (House of Commons Select Committee on Adulteration of Food, Drinks and Drugs, 1856)

The Committee finally recommended that local authorities should be empowered to appoint inspectors who could examine any food or drug item they supposed to be adulterated (House of Commons Select Committee on Adulteration of Food, Drinks and Drugs, 1856, p. vii). By contrast, the dominant attitude of the medical and pharmacy professions was a preference for voluntary control rather than regulations imposed by government and law. That these professions were successful in persuading the government is evident from the fact that the 1860 Adulteration Act, the first piece of legislation following from the 1856 Committee Report, left it up to local authorities whether or not to appoint inspectors and applied only to food and drinks, but not drugs (Steib, 1970, pp. 20–2).

The pharmacists' profession, as represented by the Pharmaceutical Society of Great Britain (PSGB), were much more concerned with achieving public recognition than with the control of drug adulteration *per se*. In particular the Society sought legal recognition of qualified practitioners and the elimination of unqualified competition. Its emphasis on the need to educate the profession in order to control adulteration was partly a strategy for achieving this goal. In pursuing this strategy, however, the Society became drawn into legislation which would not only advance its professionalisation but also government regulation of adulteration (Steib, 1966, pp. 143–53).

After lobbying the House of Commons for four years to restrict those who could compound or sell prescriptions to pharmaceutical chemists, the Society succeeded in establishing the Pharmacy Act of 1868 which marginally extended the 1860 Adulteration Act to medicines (Hodges, 1987, p. 119). This enabled the Society's leadership to dissociate itself from adulteration practised by quacks and other non-registered vendors not least because it empowered the PSGB to keep a register of those who had passed its examinations. Nevertheless, for the rest of the century, the Society complained that the extensions of government controls incorporated in the Adulteration Act of 1872 and the 1875 Sale of Food and Drugs Act impinged upon their professional prerogatives and failed to tackle the supposedly more important problem of educating the public to demand higher quality drugs (Steib, 1966, pp. 153–4).

By contrast, the profession of public analysts sought single-mindedly to extend and strengthen legislative control of drug adulteration. Indeed, the successful operation of the anti-adulteration Acts depended largely on the appointment and expertise of such analysts. In 1874 the Society for Public Analysts (SPA) was formed to develop the profession and exerted consistent influence on the form of anti-adulteration law during the last quarter of the century. For example, the 1899 Amendment to the Sale of Food and Drugs Act increased the regulatory powers of the local government, including the authority to enforce the operation of the Act in areas where it had been neglected (Steib, 1966, pp. 204–9).

The SPA was not the only force pressing for regulation of drug standards. As the growing 'ethical' pharmaceutical industry took over the task of preparing medicines it was forced to provide drugs of a sufficient standard to satisfy pharmacists and prescribing doctors. The pharmaceutical industry looked favourably upon the standardisation of drugs through modest regulation because of the competitive manufacturing advantage over the small pharmacists it would create (Penn, 1979, p. 299).

Yet incredibly there were no drug standards in law during the last quarter of the 19th century. The 1875 Sale of Food and Drugs Act and all its amendments avoided completely the term 'adulteration'. Instead they defined as an offence the sale 'to the prejudice of the purchaser' a drug 'not of the nature, substance and quality of the article demanded' (Steib, 1966, pp. 129–30). In practice most practitioners probably felt obliged to use the *British Pharmacopoeia* (*BP*) as the standard even though it had no legal status. Hence any person asking for a preparation in the BP and not receiving it could consider him or herself 'prejudiced' in the transaction (Steib, 1970, pp. 23–5, 1966, pp. 131). In cases where the defendant attempted to argue that there was a sufficient commercial standard different from that of the *BP* the court ruled against the defendant (Bell, 1910, pp. 26–7). As William James Bell concluded in his interpretation of the 1875 Act:

> ... the standard of the *British Pharmacopoeia* is not conclusive, but ... very strong evidence is necessary to displace it. (Bell, 1910, p. 27).

For some scientists, however, this was a less than satisfactory situation. For example, the SPA claimed that the *BP* lagged so far behind scientific methods for establishing purity that it effectively sanctioned drug adulteration. During the last quarter of the 19th century the SPA consistently argued for the drawing up of stringent standards to be used in law. That the legislature did not support their efforts is testimony to the success of the pharmaceutical trade in persuading the government that, on the whole, self-regulation should be adopted (Steib, 1966, pp. 204–7).

Regulatory reforms: 1900 to 1945

The first five decades of the 20th century saw far more government activity in the regulation of drugs than had been evident in the previous century. The reasons for this lie partly in the reformist politics which came to dominate the period. As the 19th century drew to a close domestic profits fell, unemployment became a persistent feature and poverty widespread (Hall, 1984, pp. 7–49). By the beginning of the 20th century the entrepreneurial vigour of the manufacturing classes, which had sustained Britain's economic growth was giving way to the powerful financial, imperialist and investment sectors. Indeed, Britain's involvement in the Boer War resulted from the growth of imperialism as a strategy to restore Britain's economic prosperity at home. Britain's defeat in this war led to the view in elite circles that the country's fortunes could only be safeguarded by a more active and efficient State.

Whereas Britain's commercial command of world markets in the 19th century had been accomplished by laissez-faire principles now it seemed that the imperium had to be positively organized. Moreover, the new Liberals, also known as the social imperialist's, led by Chamberlain, argued with considerable success that more effective imperialism was required to finance the needed social reforms at home. Whilst the new Liberals may have genuinely believed in the moral desirability of assisting the poorer classes and establishing universal citizenship, Chamberlain hoped that the formula of imperialism plus social reform would provide the basis for national consensus and integration thus improving national efficiency and warding off the burgeoning support for the labour and suffragette movements. After a landslide victory in 1905 the new Liberal reform programme, motivated by this amalgam of factors, began in earnest (Hay, 1975).

At the centre of the Liberal reforms was the 1911 National Health Insurance Act (NHI). In 1909 Lloyd George, the Chancellor of the Exchequer, introduced the famous 'People's Budget' which in his own words aimed 'to wage implacable warfare against poverty and squalidness' (Bruce, 1961). NHI was made possible by the 1909 budget, but Lloyd George looked upon the scheme particularly favourably because it gave the poor some relief at minimal cost to the State. In effect people below a certain income level could receive 'medical benefit' via a national system of insurance for sickness funded by statutory contributions from the employer, the State and the employed – of which the State paid less than a quarter (Bruce, 1961). This was a popular policy, an important condition for political success due to the recent extensions of the electoral franchise to the masses. Simultaneously, however, official secrecy designed to control the civil service and the unauthorised release of information to the public was intensified. The Official Secrets Act of 1911 was instituted to help ensure that the way in which government conducted its business could not be scrutinised by the public (Robertson, 1982, pp. 1–91). This principle of secrecy has characterised British medicine regulation ever since with significant consequences for the conditions under which governments have constructed regulatory policies.

As a result of the NHI the government became the purchaser of many drugs and prescriptions from pharmacists to the tune of £550 000 per year (PRO, 1921a). Such State involvement was accompanied by new government interest in the quality of drugs. During the First World War the PSGB and others made representations to the government arguing that health services were in a chaotic condition and needed the establishment of a Ministry to improve them. In particular, shortages of supply due to the war situation meant that some drug prices for retailers and consumers rocketed. For example, between July 1914 and January 1918 the price of aspirin rose more than sixfold (PSGB, 1939).

Lloyd George declared his support for the idea and in 1919 the Ministry of Health was born into a particularly close relationship, and shared sense of purpose, with the PSGB (PSGB, 1920a, 1920b). As an editorial in the *Pharmaceutical Journal* marking the end of the Ministry's first year noted:

> The Advisory Committee are bound to serve as salutary deterrents from bureaucratic tendencies, and the Ministry of Health Committee of the Council [of the Pharmaceutical Society] and the Federation of Medical and Allied Societies, of which the [Pharmaceutical Society] is a constituent member, hold watching briefs for the medical, pharmaceutical, and allied interests likely to be affected by the policy and operations of the Ministry (PSGB, 1920c).

Attempts to regulate the pharmaceutical sector were intensified in the early 1920s as the British government faced a grave political and economic situation. Not only had it incurred a huge national debt through financing the war but the onset of a severe recession was accompanied by industrial unrest and rising unemployment (Aldcroft, 1986, pp. 1–43). The government responded by making cuts in public spending and implementing a budgetary clampdown. It was in this context that the Treasury became concerned about the efficiency of drug services and in autumn 1920 the Ministry of Health asked the Committee on the Supply of Drugs to Insured Persons (CSDIP) to advise it on the 'arrangements for securing that the drugs for insured persons supplied by chemists are of proper standard, quality and quantity' (PRO, 1921a). In 1921 the CSDIP expressed 'grave doubt' that the expenditure on the insured was being well spent because the Insurance Committees, which had been established by the 1917 Insurance Act to oversee the supply of medicines to insured people, had no special staff for checking that the drugs supplied were of proper quality (PRO, 1921a). Moreover, the CSDIP concluded:

> Where reports were submitted by Insurance Committees, the results of the tests made were somewhat disquieting. ... Certain additional machinery will be necessary if an effective check in the matter of drug supply is to be secured. While much can undoubtedly be done by testing medicines actually dispensed, no provision has hitherto been made for the sampling of crude drugs, medicines and appliances found on the stock shelves of the chemist. (PRO, 1921a)

The CSDIP recommended two major extensions of drug testing for regulatory purposes. First, the empowerment of inspectors with special pharmaceutical knowledge to enter chemist's premises and sample stocks of drugs. And second, the establishment of a centralised Pharmaceutical Section of the Ministry of Health with £10 000 of annual funding in order to control and co-ordinate local arrangement for drug testing (PRO, 1921a). On 18 February 1921 Sir Arthur Robinson, the Minister of Health, responded by agreeing that the CSDIP had revealed 'a serious state of affairs', but he expressed reservations as follows:

> The doubts which I feel about it are to some extent political, and based on the present general position of the Ministry which makes it wise to avoid ground of public controversy if we can. It seems to

me that the chemists would be likely to raise an outcry against inspectors with such extremely wide powers as those proposed .... this would be a real case of an 'inquisition' and we might have difficulty maintaining it. Is there no way out? (PRO, 1921b)

The Ministry's desire to avoid public controversy at this time is explained by the crisis which faced the government as a whole and it had a profoundly dampening effect on regulatory reforms of drug testing. Almost four months later the CSDIP proposed compromise measures involving only half the annual expenditure of the original and confidential discussions with the representatives of chemists before making any formal proposals with a view to minimising objections from the pharmacy profession. The weak nature of the drug testing finally adopted is all too obvious from the Committee's comment:

We are all in favour of a not too ambitious scheme being launched at the outset, and we recommend that amended proposals of a tentative character should be put forward .... (PRO, 1921c)

Nevertheless, even the compromised scheme represented the first systematic testing of dispensed medicines.

During the 1920s the British drug manufacturing industry continued to expand but also became more concentrated (PSGB, 1929a, pp. 23–4). Prior to this period British pharmaceutical firms had been characterised by the traditional practice of importing and refining raw materials and packaging them for distribution to chemists and druggists (Tweedale, 1990, p. 120). However, by the late 1920s pharmaceutical companies sought to use developments in 'scientific medicine' as a way of differentiating their products as superior to patent medicines. Technological innovations and organisational changes verging on the oligopolous contributed to the achievement of that goal. Notably in 1929 a large number of manufacturing firms amalgamated to form the Wholesale Druggists Trade Association (WDTA). The declared purpose of the new Association was to advance the interests of its members through improved organisation especially regarding departmental or parliamentary legislation affecting the drug trade (PSGB, 1929, p. 486, PSGB, 1945, p. 223).

The sustained growth of the pharmaceutical industry during the late 1920s and 1930s owed much to the structural changes brought about by the First World War. At the outbreak of war the UK was cut off from supplies of pure chemicals and synthetic medicinal chemicals for which it had formerly been dependent on Germany. The chemical and pharmaceutical industries proved crucial to the war effort in their endeavours to render the UK independent of foreign supplies and drew considerable investment and status from government as a result. The success of these industries depended crucially on the sympathetic attitude of the Board of Trade to manufacturers and as early as 1921 the government passed the Safeguarding of Industries Act which imposed tariffs on imported manufactures in order to assist 'key' British industries including the fine chemicals industry (Aldcroft, 1986, pp. 55–78; Hill, 1935, pp. 533–4).

Ironically by the mid-1930s the pharmaceutical industry suffered from an overproduction of drugs and a declining demand on the home market as public health legislation began to have long-term positive effects on the health of the nation. Moreover, prices and profits in the drug trade were dwindling because of the operations of small distributors who were able to undercut the prices of the mainstream manufacturers and retailers by employing unqualified staff for low wages (Anon, 1934, p. 335). Under these conditions drug adulteration persisted and even grew during the 1930s with small-scale enterprises apparently using 'sheds' or 'backyards' as premises and 'oddments of apparatus and utensils valued at a few shillings' as plant (PSGB, 1934, p. 117). In response the 'ethical' industry attempted to develop self-regulation. In 1934 the National Pharmaceutical Union (NPU) and the WDTA established a joint committee to find a means of 'checking the all-too-free sale of drugs ... by unqualified and untrained vendors ... and controlling the innumerable wholesale channels through which at present the goods reach these vendors' (PSGB, 1934, p. 118).

Nevertheless, the patent medicines business continued to flourish. Some had thought that the 1911 National Health Insurance Act would reduce the sale of patent medicines because some of the poorer classes would receive assistance in purchasing medically approved drugs. However, in the immediate prewar period holders of patent medicine licenses numbered about 40 000, increasing to 60 000 in 1926. By 1935 the General Secretary of the Proprietary Articles Trade Association (PATA) and the Secretary of the NPU could boast that the figure was 140 000 (Chapman, 1935, pp. 544; Mallinson, 1935, pp. 535–7).

Yet as early as 1909 the British Medical Association (BMA) exposed the fraudulence of the 'secret remedies' in the patent medicine business juxtapositioning an analysis of their basic ingredients with the extravagant and unbelievable claims of efficacy made by their promoters. The BMA also criticised the Inland Revenue and the .existing Medicine Stamp legislation for helping to give credibility to 'secret remedies' by encouraging their sale under the Inland Revenue Stamp (BMA, 1909). Manufacturers and others who took advantage of the 'known, admitted and approved' exemption from stamp duty were forced to reveal the composition of their drugs but secrecy could always be bought with a stamp (Howells, 1941, pp. 140–1). Thus, a situation obtained in which the government had a vested interest in maintaining 'secret remedies'.

In 1914 the Select Committee on Patent Medicines published a report stating that 'for all practical purposes, British law is powerless to prevent any person from procuring any drugs or making any mixture, whether potent or without any therapeutic value whatsoever (so long as it does not contain a schedule poison), advertising it in any decent terms as a cure for any disease or ailment, ... and selling it under any name he chooses on the payment of a small stamp duty' (quoted in Chapman, 1935, p. 543). It recommended that there should be a special Commission with the power to prohibit the sale and advertisement of proprietary medicines, and that a statement of the ingredients of, and therapeutic claims for, such medicines should be furnished to the relevant government department (Penn, 1979, p. 302). A government Bill to give effect to these recommendations was introduced shortly after the First World War but did not pass into law due to strong opposition organised by the press who derived substantial income from the advertisement of proprietary medicines (PRO, 1940a).

It was not until the 1941 Pharmacy and Medicines Act that the government legislated against the sale of 'secret remedies'. However, as the origins of this legislation show, it was not derived primarily from a concern to protect the public interest, but rather from the conflicts of interest within the drug trade with respect to tax exemptions and related privileges. In fact, Ministry of Health correspondence reveals that the government specifically wished to avoid greater State regulation of proprietary drugs:

> As I understand the Chancellor's letter, the present proposal is to have an enquiry into the taxation aspects of the problem only and no doubt this is right since it would hardly be practicable to introduce legislation (which would probably be controversial) for the control of proprietary medicines at the present time. (PRO, 1940b)

The crux of 'the problem' to which the Ministry referred was that, though the Medicine Stamp Acts taxed medicines which were advertised as cures for everyday complaints, chemists, druggists or doctors were granted an exemption provided their medicines were 'known, admitted and approved'. Despite this the chemist was permitted to sell at the 'taxed price' with the 'unpaid tax' being split between the chemist and manufacturer according to mutual agreement. However, in the mid-1930s Woolworths, non-chemist retailers, began to sell *prima facie* taxable medical articles without stamp duty. When the Department of Customs and Excise instituted proceedings against Woolworths the company retaliated by launching an action against the Attorney-General who felt that it would be embarrassing for him to defend the government's position unless he could give an undertaking that the law would be amended to eliminate what he considered an unsatisfactory trading situation (PRO, 1941a).

Following Woolworths' action a Select Committee was set up to consider the subject in 1936. One year later the Committee recommended the repeal of the Medicines Stamp Duty (PSGB, 1941a, p. 18). In the immediate term nothing came of these recommendations due to opposition from chemists and pharmacists who claimed that the tax acted as a disincentive to unqualified vendors of quack remedies. Nevertheless, in 1939 Woolworths kept up the pressure by lobbying the Chancellor and the Home Secretary directly for the repeal of the tax. Moreover, in a Report to the Chancellor the Customs and Excise Department declared its position as administrators of the tax to be 'untenable' and argued that the existence of the tax did nothing to prevent the public from buying ineffective or deleterious drugs because that required regulatory control (PRO, 1941b, PSGB, 1941b, p. 1). Thus it was in response to wrangles within the trade that the issue of medicine regulation returned to the Government's agenda.

By January 1941 the Chancellor had instituted discussions regarding the Medicines Stamp Duty 'to try and get agreement amongst the interests concerned' (PRO, 1941c). Given the government's goal of achieving a consensus it was attracted to the idea of introducing strict regulatory control over 'secret remedies' because this would guarantee the support of the medical profession who stood to gain from the demise of quackery (PRO, 1941a). A month later the PSGB, WDTA, the Proprietary Association of Great Britain (PAGB) and the Scottish Pharmaceutical Federation pledged support for a Bill which repealed the tax and prohibited the retail sale of 'secret remedies' provided that legislation was introduced giving chemists and pharmacists the exclusive right to sell certain classes of proprietary medicines (PRO, 1941b, PRO, 1941d). Despite opposition from the NPU the Bill was passed into law (PSGB, 1941c, p. 86).

The Pharmacy and Medicines Act met with great approval from Customs and Excise. In a letter to the Secretary of Health, the department was candid about the government perspective on the legislations:

> Its effect is broadly to repeal the anomalies of the Medicines Stamp Duty, to abolish, for all practical purposes, the fiscal privilege at present enjoyed by chemists, and to give the chemists in return some sort of statutory recognition of their professional status. I doubt whether it could be held strongly that these proposals are contrary to the public interest, though they could scarcely be presented as required by the public interest. What they claim to be is an agreement made among the various interested parties which would enable them to accept the repeal of the Medicines Stamp Duty without making political trouble, and ... that might appear to the Chancellor and your Minister as an appreciable political point. (PRO, 1941e)

Indeed, the Ministry of Health described the legislation as no more than that which would 'give effect to the agreement between the organisations concerned with the sale of medicines' (PRO, 1941f).

The early postwar period

The introduction of the potent prescription drugs, such as salfa-drugs in the 1930s and penicillin in the 1940s, signalled the beginning of a transformation in the kinds of medicines produced by the pharmaceutical industry (Mann, 1984). Many companies sought to replicate those therapeutic breakthroughs creating a plethora of equally powerful drugs. As a result industrial promotion of drugs to doctors intensified. (Silverman and Lee, 1974) and the large high-technology firms used patents to command high monopoly prices for their drugs. With the introduction of the National Health Service (NHS) by the Labour government in 1948 following its NHS Act of 1946, the State became even more concerned with the control of medicines since the benefits of free medical care were extended to the whole population with the government footing the bill. The number of prescriptions under the NHS in 1951 had more than trebled to 220 million compared with the number given under the National Health Insurance Act (PRO, 1951). The main preoccupation of British governments in the early postwar period, therefore, was the excessive price of drugs prescribed under the NHS.

However, the control of drug prices by necessity had some implications for the regulation of drug standards.

In 1949 the Ministry of Health asked the Joint Committee on Prescribing (JCP), chaired by Lord Cohen, which was set up in July 1949 to consider whether it was desirable to restrict or discourage NHS doctors from prescribing 'medicines of doubtful value' or 'unnecessarily expensive brands of standard drugs' (HMSO, 1950).

In fact, the Ministry instigated a review of drug legislation in 1951 which claimed that:

> a major cause of the proprietary drug bill is the prescription of duplicate or doubtful medicines following skilful propaganda from the drug firms to the doctors in the service, and in some cases following advertising to the public which in turn results in pressure on the doctor by the patient. (PRO, 1951)

This review reveals that within the Ministry there was extensive concern about the inadequacies of drug control. For example, it was noted that the existing legislation was no longer adequate, not only because of the NHS, but also because of the rapid postwar progress in research which had led to a quick succession of new drugs. According to the Ministry one problem related to this was 'inadequate drug-testing to safeguard the consumer whether it be the public generally or the NHS patient in particular.'

The review concluded:

> (i) there is no effective control over the manufacture and sale of duplicate or dubious proprietary preparations (ii) there is no effective control over the advertising of proprietary medicines (iii) the existing provisions for the testing of drugs are inadequate. (PRO, 1951)

The review proposed that a register of prescribable NHS drugs should be established, excluding those drugs which the JCP thought lacked efficacy (PRO, 1951).

The Association of the British Pharmaceutical Industry (ABPI), the name adopted by the WDTA since 1948, was anxious about the Ministry's plans to rationalise drug prescribing especially under the Atlee Labour government whose new President of the Board of Trade, Harold Wilson, announced in 1947 that the essential needs of the home market, including public health requirements must come before exports (PSGB, 1950a; Lang, 1974). The importance of export markets became even more important to the industry when in 1950 the ABPI merged with the Pharmaceutical Export Group (PEG) which had been established during the Second World War at the suggestion of the Board of Trade (PSGB, 1950b). Not surprisingly, therefore the industry's fears mounted as the Chief Medical Officer at the Ministry of Health issued a circular in January 1950 asking doctors not to prescribe proprietary preparations unless 'satisfied that a standard drug or combination of standard drugs cannot be prescribed with equal effect' (PSGB, 1950c). Although the Ministry's primary concern was to reduce NHS costs these conditions meant that the JCP was effectively helping the doctor make judgements about the relative efficacy of drugs.

At the ABPI/PEG merger the President of the ABPI noted that the NHS was the industry's largest customer giving it considerable leverage over the plight of the industry and remarked pointedly that too much standardisation of the home trade could damage export abilities. As he put it:

> If the well-known branded names of preparations disappear they will no longer figure in the medical journals published here and be circulated widely overseas and this will make it more difficult for the export industry to develop. (PSGB, 1950b)

These were particularly influential arguments in the postwar period. Labour had swept to power in 1945 to form its majority government with the manifesto 'Let Us Face the Future'. This reflected the mood of the times. It was a clear vote for social reform and the prospect of something better than the return to mass unemployment and the inegalitarian society of the interwar years. However, the UK emerged from the war as the world's leading debtor country with badly depleted export potential and earnings. Despite this the UK economy did recover and this was led by the export boom of the sectors that had done well during the war such as communications and the chemical and pharmaceutical industries which took advantage of the temporary eclipse of Germany as a competitor in world markets (Aldcroft, 1986).

By 1950, when a Conservative government was returned, Labour had nationalised 20 per cent of all industry. This, together with the export success of the private sector, substantially reduced unemployment. The macro-economic landscape of the 1950s and 1960s, then, came to be characterised by almost full employment and a sizeable government budget generated by successful export trades. In this context high unemployment seemed to be electorally unacceptable and both Labour and Conservative governments of the period adopted Keynesian ideas of economic management which depended on the maintenance of virtual full employment. To do this, however, the governments needed to preserve a substantial budget with which to intervene in economic affairs (Thompson, 1984a).

The ABPI's view of the significance of macroeconomic factors for NHS drug regulation was astutely summarised in an editorial of the *Pharmaceutical Journal* reporting on the Association's annual report for 1955–56:

> the contribution of the industry should be taken as a whole – its help in reducing problems of the Chancellor of the Exchequer by maintaining the value of sterling abroad should be put alongside its ability to deliver the goods for our own Health Service. As many speakers have emphasised, the two sets of factors are inseparable and complementary. (PSGB, 1956a)

Such considerations affected the government's approach to drug regulation, which took account of more than the views within the Ministry of Health.

In meetings and correspondence with the Ministry of Health in June 1950 the ABPI and the PAGB argued that it would be undesirable for the JCP to publish a Report which classified drugs therapeutically because of the adverse effects on the export trade. Such a list, it was argued, would be used to keep British products out of foreign markets (PRO, 1950a, PRO, 1950b). One month later the Board of Trade also joined the fray and had clearly reversed the priorities proclaimed by Harold Wilson. In a letter to Sir William Douglas of the Ministry of Health a senior official of the Board of Trade pointed out that almost a third of proprietary drugs were exported and that the annual rate of export was valued at £4 million. The letter continued:

> ... there is a danger that certifying authorities or other import licensing authorities in other countries may gain access to the Ministry of Health list of 'banned' items and may refuse to grant authority to sell or import these proprietary medicines... Accordingly, I suggest that very great care should be taken to keep the list strictly confidential and, so far as possible, to avoid any undue publicity being given to the scheme as a whole. (PRO, 1950c)

Despite these protests the JCP lists were published, albeit discreetly, for, as Sir Douglas of the Ministry of Health pointed out, no cost-cutting benefit to the NHS could be derived from the reports if they were not circulated to doctors (PRO, 1950d).

By the mid-1950s the Ministry of Health had come to accept the basic philosophy that the export trade of the pharmaceutical industry was so precious that Governmental regulation of its affairs was to be avoided (PSGB, 1954, 1956b). However, following criticisms by the Hinchcliffe Committee the Minister of Health announced in 1959 that the whole question of drug control under the NHS was to be re-examined (PSGB, 1959). That the Ministry remained reluctant to embark on regulatory action is illustrated by the Parliamentary Secretary's comment in 1960 that 'unwelcome as restrictions were, there was a duty to safeguard the health of the public' (PSGB, 1960a, 1956b).

The Hinchcliffe Committee had recommended that all new drugs should be subjected to 'independent' clinical trials and that the government should set up a clinical trials committee to 'organise clinical trials of new drugs and preparations and interpret results' (PSGB, 1959b). Six months later the Working Party on Medicines Legislation of the Advertising Inquiry Council recommended that some administrative instrument should be established in order to review the trial and testing of every new drug, and the PSGB's submission to the Interdepartmental Working Party, set up by the Minister of Health in February 1960 to review drug legislation urged that control of medicines should be vested with the appropriate Ministers (PSGB, 1961, PSGB, 1962a). Indeed, the industry itself began to see some advantages in rationalising the legislative patchwork over therapeutic classes which had emerged since the Second World War. In 1959 the ABPI advocated the creation of an 'independent' voluntary trust to vet new drugs (Hancher, 1989). Thus, before the thalidomide disaster entered the public arena in late 1961 considerable pressure was mounting for greater regulatory controls on the testing of new drugs, even though it owed its origins to government concern with prescribing costs.

The thalidomide disaster illustrated the tremendous potential for harm that potent modern drugs possessed. Soon after the *Pharmaceutical Journal*, not renowned for radical criticism of the drug regulatory system, carried an editorial stating:

It is hard to imagine a more difficult choice than that which faces a manufacturer who has to decide whether or not to withdraw a profitable drug from the market on the basis of the evidence that, on the one hand the drug may be dangerous to a small number of patients and, on the other has valuable properties. So difficult must the choice be that it is questionable whether the manufacturer should be the one to make it. (PSGB, 1962b)

Lord Cohen was prompted to remark at a symposium in April 1962 that in the previous year more than half the drugs which had been issued had not been correctly clinically tested and that there was ample evidence of manufacturers supplying biased and unreliable information to physicians (PSGB, 1962c, PSGB, 1962d). In Parliament too the safety of drugs came to be extensively debated with some MPs advocating that new drugs should be issued under a positive system of licensing with the Medical Research Council made responsible for testing new drugs while others suggested the US FDA as an exemplary model for emulation (PSGB, 1962e, PSGB, 1962f).

The industry now became concerned that the thalidomide experience might have detrimental effects on the consumption of drugs generally. In May 1962 the ABPI set up a Study Group under its President with the purpose of examining arrangements for the toxicity testing and clinical trials of new drugs. Within a few months it concluded 'that to give greater assurance to the medical profession and the public, an independent body should be set up to review and offer advice on the evidence on safety submitted by manufacturers' (ABPI, 1963).

The committee on the safety of drugs

The response of the Conservative government to the thalidomide disaster was contradictory; accepting, on the one hand, that new legislation was needed to require the testing of all new drugs, while simultaneously arguing that it was against the commercial interests of any pharmaceutical company to market a drug, whose effects had not been subjected to the most relevant tests known (PSGB, 1962g, PSGB, 1963). Nevertheless, in June 1962 Enoch Powell, the Minister of Health, asked the Joint SubCommittee of the Standing Medical Advisory Committees under the chairmanship of Lord Cohen to advise on the testing and regulation of new drugs.

Despite Cohen's previous remarks about the industry's tendency to bias, in November 1962 his Committee gave the following interim advice: (i) that preclinical toxicity testing of drugs should remain the responsibility of individual firms because 'the industry, as a whole, discharges that responsibility effectively within the limits of contemporary knowledge of methods of testing; (ii) that the suggestion of a central drug testing authority was 'neither desirable nor practicable': and (iii) that there should be an advisory body to review the evidence and offer advice on the toxicity of new drugs (PSGB, 1962h; Wheeler, 1963, 1964). The industry, therefore, was to remain in control of drug testing operations. Powell accepted (i) and (ii) and awaited more detailed advice on (iii). Significantly the ABPI was to co-operate with the Cohen Subcommittee in consideration of the composition of the suggested advisory body (PSGB, 1962h).

It is not difficult to find plausible reasons for Powell's interest in closely consulting with the industry. As the President of the ABPI pointed out to the Minister of State at the Board of Trade at a luncheon on 25 October 1962, the Ministry of Health was the industry's sponsoring department and had responsibility for the industry's scientific and commercial progress (PSGB, 1962g). For its part the industry wanted some regulation to help rationalise its operations and to raise the standing of its products abroad, but it did not want a regulatory system too critical of its brand name products which were already established exports (Wheeler, 1964). It was in this context that the Cohen SubCommittee sat down in consultation with the ABPI to advise the Ministry of Health on the kind of regulatory body which should set the tone for modern drug safety control in the UK.

The ABPI argued that the regulatory body should be constituted as a Trust independent of the industry and the Government, comprising professional and trade associations. However, the Cohen Committee proposed that the Minister of Health should immediately and without legislation appoint an advisory Committee on the Safety of Drugs (CSD), which would depend on the voluntary co-operation of the industry. It also suggested that public opinion would require that the CSD should be entirely independent of industry (HMSO, 1963; PSGB, 1963b).

Accepting the advice of Cohen's Committee, the Health Minister appointed the CSD with Sir Derrick Dunlop as chairman and Powell pronounced that its membership was of such eminence that it was unthinkable that they would submit to any influence but the force of scientific consideration (PSGB, 1963c). Yet members evidently held strong views about the practice of industrial drug testing which could influence their interpretation of data submitted for examination. For example, in 1962 Professor Wilson, who had also been a member of the Cohen Committee, assumed:

> If a drug is shown to be harmful to animals, its use in Man is not contemplated, ... And every reputable pharmaceutical firm and clinical investigator ensure to the best of current knowledge that all the appropriate investigations have been done before the drug is given to Man. (Wilson, 1962)

Within its terms of reference the CSD was to invite reports on toxicity tests from the manufacturer, consider whether the drug should be put to clinical trial, obtain reports of such trials, and take into account the safety, efficacy and adverse effects of the drug (PSGB, 1963d). It began operations on 1 January 1964 and the ABPI and PAGB undertook not to market or submit to clinical trial any new drug against the advice of the Committee (PSGB, 1963e). Two months beforehand the CSD had pledged that information submitted to it by manufacturers about new drugs would be treated as confidential to the Committee ostensibly to ensure that the development of new drugs of therapeutic value was not hindered. Thus before it had even begun regulatory activity the Committee sealed itself off from public scrutiny (PSGB, 1963f). One can be confident that the industry was content with these arrangements since they provided it with valuable time and experience with which to gain strategic influence over the regulatory process and any forthcoming legislation (Wheeler, 1964).

Moreover, regulatory review was deliberately rapid averaging three months for new chemical entities and one month for novel reformulations (PSGB, 1966a). As the CSD commented in its annual report for 1966:

> it is fully recognised that a Committee such as this might exercise a detrimental effect on pharmaceutical research progress by unduly delaying the introduction of a possibly valuable drug or even by preventing its use altogether. (PSGB, 1967a)

Cahal, the CSD's medical assessor, revealed more about the CSD's activities when he recounted that in one submission an industry toxicologist had reached the conclusion 'no toxic effects were observed' regarding a drug which had caused severe tremors to the test animals on a low dose, convulsions to those on the intermediate dose and some deaths on the high dose. The discrepancy was not caused by the toxicologist trying to mislead the CSD, but because he had become so accustomed to these effects in toxicity tests, concluded Cahal. What the toxicologist had meant, assumed Cahal, was that no unusual toxic effects of the drug in question were observed. According to Cahal the importance of this anecdote was that nobody had noticed the discrepancy until the submission had been considered by an independent body which took a fresh look at the evidence (PSGB, 1966b). The implication of Cahal's argument was that gross errors could be made by industry toxicologists because they become jaded with their own data. This flatly contradicted the official statements by Powell and the Cohen Committee that the industry was subjecting its products to the most effective scrutiny contemporary knowledge could offer.

The ABPI hoped that any forthcoming legislation would emulate the CSD approach as follows:

> Difficulties have arisen .... but the satisfactory way in which these have been overcome has been largely due to the policy of the Committee in encouraging their staff to make the necessary contacts with manufacturers as informal as possible. The Association is anxious that this informality of approach and the flexibility of operation which are features of the present voluntary arrangements should be preserved under the new medicines legislation at present under consideration by the Government. (ABPI, 1966)

Significantly, in January 1965 Dunlop echoed these views, arguing that whilst legislation 'may well prove necessary and desirable, it is hoped that the Committee's present freedom will not be curtailed by a bureaucratic straitjacket' (ABPI, 1965).

The Sainsbury Committee, appointed by the government to advise on the relationship between the pharmaceutical industry with the NHS, was not so generous to the industry. It concluded in 1967 that some of the existing arrangements for promotion, including the extensive employment of manufacturers' medical representatives, were wasteful and lacking in the appropriate responsibility (HMSO, 1967a). The Sainsbury Committee recommended the abolition of brand names, the requirement that therapeutic classifications appear on all medicines, and the establishment of a Medicines Commission funded by, but independent of, direct control by the Ministry of Health with wide statutory powers to regulate the quality, safety, efficacy and promotion of drugs (HMSO, 1967a).

Predictably the ABPI opposed the idea of a regulatory Commission with substantial executive powers, and argued that a statutory system of classifying medicines according to therapeutic value and the abolition of brand names would be damaging to exports with consequent reductions in investment in pharmaceutical research at home (ABPI, 1968a, ABPI, 1968b). Evidently, the Sainsbury Committee provided the second postwar Labour government with a clear alternative to the industry viewpoint.

The 1968 Medicines Act

The government's 1967 White Paper on forthcoming medicines legislation outlined a product licensing system to regulate the quality, safety, and efficacy of new drugs but it rejected the Sainsbury concept of an independent Medicines Commission in favour of an advisory one which was to be appointed by, and ultimately accountable to, the Minister of Health acting as the licensing authority. The Medicines Commission was to advise the Minister on the appointment of expert committees who would advise the licensing authority on specific aspects of drug regulation (PSGB, 1968a, HMSO, 1967b). Indeed, the Government's Medicines Bill published in February 1968 stipulated that the Minister would.

During the period of drug legislation review in the 1960s the ABPI and the CSD maintained close liaison and their representatives responded with remarkable similarity to the issue of how the government should regulate drugs. The ABPI accepted the licensing system provided it was to be operated with the flexibility which characterised the CSD and did not impede the development of new medicines (PSGB, 1967b, ABPI, 1968b). In March 1968 Dunlop, chairman of the CSD, made a telling speech which indicated his approach to drug regulation (PSGB, 1968b). He began with the assertion that it was important that laws enacted to assure drug safety and efficacy did not impose unnecessary restraints on the prosperity of the pharmaceutical industry. The flexible approach which manufacturers appreciated, he explained, meant that contacts with companies were informal, good-humoured and often over the telephone rather than through official communications (Dunlop, 1971).

On the question of brand names he argued that their abolition was probably undesirable because it could place the major innovating companies in Britain at a competitive disadvantage overseas. He further noted that the medical profession depended on the industry's well-being, and warned:

> From this point of view *alone* we should be very chary of interfering with the reproductive processes of a goose which has laid so many golden therapeutic eggs. (emphasis added) (PSGB, 1968b)

As Cahal, the CSD's Medical Assessor explained, the Committee was dependent on the industry's co-operation:

> One is often asked how the Committee manages to comply with its terms of reference with so small a staff. The answer is 'decentralisation', which means, since there is nowhere else to which we can decentralise, decentralisation to industry. (US GPO, 1970)

Such extensive contact with industry, however, was not without impact on the way the CSD conducted itself as Wade, a former member, later explained:

> Looking back I see only one major error in our performance. We were so aware of the enormous co-operation that we received from the drug industry that the main Committee made every effort it could to see that submissions from firms were handled as rapidly as possible – as a result ... the Adverse Reactions subcommittee and ... the work of that subcommittee suffered. (Wade, 1983)

As the Medicines Bill was debated in Parliament and outside, the government's fundamental perspective on the new legislation became clearer. As early as 1964 Lord Newton, the Parliamentary Secretary to the Ministry of Health had told the ABPI that he hoped the manufacturers would look upon the government's efforts at new legislation as a codification of disciplines already recognised by the industry as being needed (PSGB, 1964). Following the publication of the government's 1967 White Paper the ABPI referred to its major underlying principle as being to codify the standards already adopted by most of the industry into up-to-date legislation (PSGB, 1967b). Such convergence of views increased as the Bill passed through Parliament. At Committee stage Julian Snow, Parliamentary Secretary to the Ministry of Health commented that the government was working towards a 'Dunlop type' speed of administration, whilst the Minister himself assured critics of the Bill that there was no need for clauses to safeguard industrial innovation because some of the members of the Commission would be drawn from the industry and it was unlikely that the Commission would use its influence to limit the introduction of new products by being unduly exacting in its requirements (PSGB, 1968c, PSGB, 1968d).

Furthermore, the World Health Organisation (WHO) had recommended that exported products should conform to home standards as a way of protecting consumers in, especially underdeveloped, countries whose regulatory systems were weak and the Bill proposed that the Labour government take a lead by implementing this recommendation in the UK. The industry was quick to oppose this, arguing that no international agreement to the WHO proposals had been reached and that unilateral action by the British government would only lose trade for the UK (ABPI, 1968b). In Committee stage the Ministry of Health accepted the industry's argument that such export regulations would be prejudicial to the UK's balance of payments and abandoned that part of the Bill (PSGB, 1968e).

The Bill's second reading won approval in the House of Commons on 15 February 1968 to become the Medicines Act (PSGB, 1968f). In May 1969, a few weeks after Dunlop had been appointed chairman of the new Medicines Commission, the ABPI and the PAGB were invited to have discussions with the Ministry of Health about the Commission's functions, structure and membership (ABPI, 1970). In April 1970 Dunlop outlined the regulatory philosophy he envisaged for the Medicines Commission, namely to find 'a happy medium' between the 'conflicting objectives' of maintaining the impetus of scientific advance and the well-being of the industry, on the one hand, and the control over the use of powerful drugs in the interests of public safety, on the other (ABPI, 1971a). Industrial interests, then, were to form an integral part of the Commission's concerns. So successful had the industry been in preserving a flexible regulatory approach by government that Harold Advise, a former chief pharmacist at the Ministry of Health who had been closely concerned with the new medicines legislation from 1962–67, felt able to predict that manufacturers would hardly notice the difference when the Medicines Commission took over from the CSD (PSGB, 1970).

Though the Cohen Committee on the safety of drugs had recommended that the CSD should be 'entirely independent of industry', members of the latter were permitted to, and did, retain consultancies with pharmaceutical companies (Ministry of Health, 1963). In 1970, however, the Department of Health invited the ABPI to consider a change of policy whereby persons holding consultancies in the industry would not be appointed to the CSD or its subcommittees. The ABPI refused to support such a change and it was never made (ABPI, 1971b). Indeed, all the major elements of regulatory organisations concerned with drug safety and efficacy have exhibited a close relationship with the pharmaceutical industry (Collier, 1985; Delamothe, 1989; SCRIP, 1991a).

Regulatory policy under the Medicines Act

During the 1970s the industry maintained its strategic influence over the DHSS and its advisory committees on drug safety through close consultation about regulations on data requirements for clinical trial certificates (CTCs) and product licences (PLs) (ABPI, 1972). Nevertheless, the regulatory authorities did demand increasingly detailed and complex preclinical data before granting a CTC. In 1977 just over one third of CTC applications were granted without requesting further information compared with 74 per cent in 1971 (HMSO, 1972, HMSO, 1978). Furthermore, it was claimed that the average time before clinical testing in the UK was four times that required in several other major Western countries (Cromie, 1980). Consequently, the number of CTCs issued fell from 170 in 1972 to 87 in 1980 and according to industrial representatives companies shifted investment in clinical trials to location outside the UK (ABPI, 1977a; Griffin and Diggle, 1981).

On the other hand, stricter regulatory controls during this period were associated with fewer new chemical entities, which ultimately failed to be of therapeutic value, reaching the British market (Steward and Wibberley, 1980). This implied that the new regulations were performing at least some consumer protective function. However, such controls, including the yellow card system pioneered by the CSD to track postmarketing adverse drug reactions, (Ministry of Health, 1963) did not prevent several thousand patients in Britain suffering serious adverse effects while taking ICI's beta-blocking drug practolol (eraldin) (Lesser, 1977). This was the biggest drug disaster recorded in the UK at that time and placed the regulatory authorities under close and critical scrutiny (PSGB, 1976a). This, then was a period of searching for more effective forms of regulating drug safety rather than one of deregulation (BMA, 1978, ABPI, 1977b).

In 1975 the Committee on the Review of Medicines (CRM) was established under the chairmanship of Scowen to comply with the EEC directive requiring all medicines to be reviewed and assessed according to modern existing licensing standards by May 1990. The task involved reviewing the 'licences of right' of some 36 000 medicinal products, including over 4000 proprietary prescription drugs, which had been allowed to stay on the market after the Medicines Act came into force without any independent scrutiny of the evidence of their safety or efficacy (Binns, 1980; BMA, 1977). Whilst the industry willingly co-operated with the CSD's successor, the Committee on the Safety of

Medicines (CSM) to obtain licences for new drugs it was reluctant to assist a body which threatened to restrict or revoke existing licences. Moreover, to accelerate the review process, the Minister of Health decided that consultation procedures with industry should be bypassed for products which the CRM thought to represent a special hazard. As a consequence the industry and regulatory authority drifted into 'an adversarial attitude' (Hurley, 1983). In particular the CRM was challenged unsuccessfully in the courts by the industry for recommending the revocation of a licence based on a comparison of a manufacturer's product with other products of the same therapeutic class (Hancher, 1989).

Extended regulatory activity occurred also in the context of Labour being returned to power under Harold Wilson in the February 1974 General Election with a manifesto containing for the first time proposals to take over sections of the pharmaceutical industry (ABPI, 1974a). At the 1973 Labour conference Wilson had specifically mentioned that the case for partial public ownership of the pharmaceutical industry 'needs no argument' (ABPI, 1974b). However, the pharmaceutical industry was not nationalised in any form. In fact, 1976 marked a change in the general political climate. The famous Keynesian-inspired Bretton-Woods system of fixed exchange rates collapsed in 1972 paving the way for rapid and destabilising fluctuations while the oil price explosion of 1973 led to a series of balance of payments problems for the government. To maintain its commitment to public expenditure the government opted for a programme of major overseas borrowing which resulted in a severe collapsed of sterling from $2.80 to the pound in 1973 to below $1.60 by the end of 1976. In an attempt to salvage the situation in 1976 Denis Healey, Chancellor of the Exchequer, obtained a £3.9 billion loan from the International Monetary Fund granted on the condition that the British government reduce its public expenditure and adopted monetarist policies in the form of stringent money supply controls in the economy (Thompson, 1984b).

The 1976 speech by James Callaghan, the then Prime Minister, at the Labour Party conference signalled the government's shift from a Keynesian approach:

> We used to think that you could spend your way out of a recession, and increase employment by cutting taxes and boosting government expenditure. I tell you in all candour that that option no longer exists. (Thompson, 1984b)

For Labour the necessary monetarist strategy involved less State intervention in the economy. Thus, in November 1976, Callaghan proclaimed that 'we must give absolute priority to industrial needs ahead
of even our social objectives' (Callaghan, quoted in ABPI, 1977c).
Similarly, in May 1977 Eric Varley, Secretary of State for Industry
argued:

> There is a new realisation in Britain that a profitable manufacturing
> industry provides the basis for all the social improvements we want
> to see. (Varley quoted in ABPI, 1977c)

In this context the Labour government not only abandoned any
thought of nationalising the pharmaceutical industry but also became
responsive to complaints from industries in general of excessive State
regulation (ABPI, 1977c). Throughout the late 1970s the ABPI complained about the extent of the DHSS regulatory activity concerning
preclinical data submissions for CTCs. Of particular significance the
National Economic Development Council's 'sector working party' on
the pharmaceutical industry, comprising six representatives from drug
industry, two from the government, two from trade unions and two
from the National Economic Development Office, concluded in 1976
that in order for the pharmaceutical sector to maximise its contribution to a positive UK balance of payments through expansion of direct
exports and import substitution the Department of Health should seek
to have the minimum impact on the industry's research by ensuring
that decisions regarding CTCs be reached within two months (BMA,
1976; PSGB, 1976b). Consequently, the CSM was asked to examine
ways in which its procedures for assessing CTCs could be expedited
(PSGB, 1976b).

In 1979 the Conservatives were elected with a positive monetarist
philosophy and a commitment to reduce state intervention in the
economy. By April 1980 Patrick Jenkin, Secretary of State for Social
Services, had announced the Government's intention to introduce a
clinical trial exemption (CTX) scheme (ABPI, 1980a). Thus, from
March 1981 under this scheme an applicant needed only to submit a
summary of the data relevant for a CTC to the Medicines Division who
then had five weeks to object to the proposed trials. If no objections
were made in this time then a CTX was granted without reference to
the CSM but if an exemption were refused then, as before the CTX
scheme, the applicant was required to submit all the data relevant for a
CTC for review by both the Medicines Division and the CSM (ABPI,

1980b, ABPI, 1981). The CTX scheme was much welcomed by the industry (Smart, 1981). In August 1981 senior representatives of the Medicines Division stated clearly that CTX scheme had become necessary 'because early development work on new drugs was going abroad to the detriment of British industry and with a loss of skill in our departments of pharmacology', thus indicating that the regulatory authority had adopted both the industry's interpretation of the effects of the CTC requirements and its suggestions for change (Griffin and Long, 1981).

The 1980s were dominated by a Conservative government determined to reduce public expenditure, especially on health and social services. During the postwar period up to the mid-1980s General Practitioners were able to prescribe virtually whatever medicines they pleased, confident that the NHS would foot the bill. However, in an attempt to cut the drug bill in 1984 Kenneth Clarke, the Minister of Health, and the DHSS introduced a Limited List of medicines, excluding approximately 1800 preparations which it was proposed the NHS would no longer pay for. Although the motivation for the Limited List was budgetary cuts, it also encouraged rational prescribing since nearly all the medicines excluded were therapeutically unimportant. Nevertheless, the pharmaceutical industry led a fierce campaign against the Limited List, gaining the support of the BMA and the Labour Party. For example, one company threatened to have MPs' views on the Limited List proposal posted on the notice boards in doctors' surgeries in their respective constituencies (Medawar, 1992). Consequently, the government gave ground and by the end of 1985 its Limited List was not so limited. Clarke also failed in his attempt to transfer the DHSS's role of sponsoring the pharmaceutical industry to the Department of Trade in the face of opposition from the industry, the Treasury and his own department (Medawar, 1992). Thus the fundamental tension between promoting the industry's trade performance and promoting public health remained within the DHSS, now the Department of Health.

The industry continued to complain about the delays in the licensing process throughout the early and mid-1980s. This prompted a government review of medicine control conducted by John Evans and Peter Cunliffe. In 1988 they proposed several organisational changes aimed at increasing the 'efficiency' of British medicine regulation. In particular they took up the pharmaceutical industry's suggestion that it would be willing to pay the cost of funding medicines approval if that were to result in a more 'efficient service' (SCRIP, 1988a). Obviously the regulatory authority under the Medicines Act, known as the Medicines Division, had been funded 65 per cent by licensing application fees from the pharmaceutical industry and 35 per cent by the government via taxes (SCRIP, 1988b). Following the Evans/Cunliffe Report in 1989 the Medicines Division became the Medicines Control Agency (MCA) almost entirely funded by industry fees. It is now essentially run as business selling its regulatory services to the industry and promoting itself as the fastest licensing authority in the world for new chemical entities (SCRIP, 1991b).

This certainly suggests that the pharmaceutical industry has been successful in obtaining from the government the kind of regulatory authority in the UK that it has campaigned for throughout the 1980s. However, because of the secrecy that surrounds the MCA's activities it is difficult to interpret the implications of these changes for consumers' interests. One interpretation is that much needed new medicines are now reaching consumers faster. Another is that the regulatory authorities manage to approve more new medicines faster without significantly more resources by undertaking less rigorous regulatory reviews involving greater trust in the industry and by permitting a larger degree of industry self-regulation. It is interesting to note that until mid-1988 product licences were suspended or revoked by the regulatory authorities at an average rate of about ten per year. Yet over the next three years no drug lost its licence until Upjohn refused to withdraw Halcion (Medawar, 1992). Certainly the switch to the business-like MCA does not seem to have improved public accessibility to the regulatory process for there is now a £250 admission fee to its annual meetings which are ostensibly held to 'hear and take account of the views of those whom it provides services' (Medicines Control Agency, 1991). Since that fee almost ensures that only company representatives will be able to attend this implies that the regulatory authority regards the industry, rather than consumers as its primary constituency of service.

Discussion and conclusion

The evolution of British medicine regulation is complex. Capture theories imply that when first established, and during subsequent periods of public pressure, regulatory reforms have primarily served the public interest, rather than industrial interests. Similarly, it is often claimed by representatives of the regulatory authorities themselves that public concern about the dangers of drugs has motivated the development of regulation, and that such regulation has been fundamentally aimed at protecting consumers' health. For example, in 1980 Penn, a representative of the Medicines Division of the DHSS stated:

> the regulatory agencies are concerned with the safety and protection of the public. I see these agencies as the logical and most recent development and expression of the anxiety long felt by the public and their elected representatives about the safety of drugs. (Penn, 1980)

Furthermore, critics of medicine regulation, such as Braithwaite, have accepted this account of history:

> The great lesson from the history of regulation in the international pharmaceutical industry is that massive reforms can occur following a crisis ... the world's regulatory systems are a muddle because they were born of hasty reactions to crises. (Braithwaite, 1986)

Undoubtedly sometimes drug disasters have contributed to the urgency with which proposals for reforms were passed into new legislation, but the supposition that major threats to public health have been the crucial motors of regulatory change in the UK is not supported by careful analysis of the available evidence. Rather the British government has been centrally concerned to negotiate with, and between, the interests of the drug trade. Consequently, so far as consumer protection is concerned, legislation has been consistently weak, compromised and not necessarily hasty. This is evident from the 1860 Adulteration Act, the 1875 Sale of Food and Drugs Act, the dilution of the proposals on drug testing made by the CSDIP, the origins of the 1941 Pharmacy and Medicines Act and the 1968 Medicines Act, and the ten year delay between the thalidomide disaster and the implementation of the Medicines Act in 1971. Further evidence that the British government has not given consumers' interests priority is provided by the fact that there is no trace of regulatory reform activity in the Ministry of Health after the 1937 Elixir Sulfanilimide disaster, even though the dire implications of that event for consumer safety applied no less in the UK than in the USA, where the tragedy occurred.

Policy studies of regulatory science frequently refer to the culture of 'flexibility' and 'confidentiality' within British regulatory systems (Beder, 1991; McCrea and Markle, 1984). However, explanations of that culture are rare. The foregoing sociohistorical analysis suggests that the primary reason for secrecy and flexibility in British medicines regulation is to protect industrial economic performance. The evidence fully endorses Gillespie *et al.*'s insightful comment that:

> Britain's weaker economic position has legitimated a continued stress on the promotion of economic development through technological change. British decision-makers have been very reluctant to encumber industry with unnecessary regulation, and this interest has continued to inform the British management of technological risks. (Gillespie *et al.*, 1979)

However, this link with regulation of technological risks also needs to be understood in the broader context of the use regulation serves. The improvement of regulatory standards for consumers has sometimes lagged behind even industrial support for it because the interests of the industry have changed and divided over time. The pharmaceutical companies were amongst the vanguard promoting the establishment of a Ministry of Health to help raise the standards of the trade, and the 1941 Pharmacy and Medicines Act brought incidental consumer protection by putting an end to patent medicines, even though it was motivated by the changing commercial interests of the industry. Hence, the economic performance of at least major elements of industry can be promoted by regulation in some contexts.

Moreover, one must take account of the requirements of the British State to maintain itself as a viable capitalist unit in terms of domestic budgets, balance of payments and social stability. How these three factors have affected medicines regulation has varied according to wider social circumstances. Balance of payments concerns have frequently allowed industrial export interests to dominate regulatory decisions. However, in periods of severe socioeconomic crisis, such as the early 20th century, the State has responded to increasing class antagonism with a tide of reforms having indirect effects on medicine regulation. Marxists theories seem to have some relevance here, especially Jessop's distinction between the State as a manager of capital accumulation and the State as negotiator with particular capitalist interests. Evidently medicine regulation may be influenced by both types of State role.

Though capture theories provide an inadequate account of the origins of medicines regulation, they do apply to certain aspects of regulatory organisations. Regarding incentives to capture, key regulatory personnel have assimilated the interests of the regulated industry, and this has affected regulatory policy as illustrated by the rapid approval philosophies adopted by the CSD in the 1960s and the CSM in the late 1970s and early 1980s.

The British medicines regulatory authorities are especially vulnerable to capture because of the large extent to which they depend on the pharmaceutical industry for expertise, as characterised by a heavy reliance on clientele sources and data to the exclusion of client-independent inputs.

Nevertheless, the most inviting theoretical construction that can account for development of British medicines regulation is what Middlemas (1979) refers to as 'corporate bias'. This involves regular bargaining between organized interests (in this case the pharmaceutical trade) and the State about the extent of regulation, and importantly goes beyond lobbying and pressure group politics:

> To put it simply, what had been merely interest groups crossed the political threshold and became part of the extended State; a position from which other groups, even if they too held political power, were still excluded. (Middlemas, 1979)

It is clear from the negotiations between the government and the pharmaceutical industry that the State does define its own interests and on occasions rejects the demands of the industry. Those uncommon occasions have led some commentators to mistake such behaviour as the norm. In an article entitled 'Drug famine', Smith, a senior official of the BMA, criticised the regulatory authorities for failing to approve enough medicines in the aftermath of eraldin. He concluded:

> introduced as they [regulatory agencies] were to prevent epidemics of drug-induced damage, their approach has inevitably been cautious. (Smith, 1980)

From the evidence adduced in this study Smith's account of British medicines regulations may be confidently rejected and the importance of avoiding too narrow an approach to the history of regulation can be noted.

Finally, as regards the impact of political parties on medicines regulation, it is clear that there have been some differences in sentiment. Under the Atlee Labour government the Board of Trade wished to prioritise domestic drug standards over the pharmaceutical industry's export profits and when Prime Minister, Harold Wilson, suggested nationalising parts of the industry. However, in practice, there seem to be few differences between Conservative, Labour and Liberal terms of office. All three parties attempted to reduce the government's medicine bill, but have been willing to compromise consumers' interests in the face of opposition from the pharmaceutical trade.

It might be argued that Labour governments have been unable to realise their consumer protective goals because of insufficient time in office. Yet that is implausible because one can point to the compromising of consumer protection and public access to information during the passing of the Labour government's 1968 Medicines Act and the regulatory retreat by Labour in 1976 midway through office. Such findings provide some support for the Marxist view that parliamentary parties can have only minimal political impact relative to the power of the more enduring machinery of the State and capitalist interests. Alternatively, they may imply that political parties need to ensure that they bring about radical structural and institutional changes in the nature of regulation in order to have an impact. It may be that the policy of the former Conservative government to have the British medicines regulatory authority run as a business funded by the pharmaceutical industry is just such a structural change. However, arguably that policy is more likely to be a road to regulatory capture than consumer protection.

References

ABPI (1963) 'Safety Testing and Clinical Trials', Annual Report 1962–63 London: ABPI, 10.

ABPI (1965) 'Safety of Medicines', ABPI Annual Report 1964–65 London: ABPI, 1965, 9–10.

ABPI (1966) 'Safety of Medicines', ABPI Annual Report 1965–66 London: ABPI, 13.

ABPI (1968a) 'Review of the Year: The Sainsbury Report', ABPI Annual Report 1967–68 London: ABPI, 1968, 6–7.

ABPI (1968b) 'Legislation: Medicines Bill', ABPI Annual Report 1967–68 London: ABPI, 1968, 9.

ABPI (1970) 'Legislation: Medicines Commission', ABPI Annual Report 1969–70 London: ABPI, 1970, 9.

ABPI (1971a) 'Annual Dinner', ABPI Annual Report 1970–71 London: ABPI, 1971, 15.

ABPI (1971b) 'The Medicines Act: Committees', ABPI Annual Report 1970–71 London: ABPI, 10.

ABPI (1972) 'Review of the Year Medicines Act 1968' ABPI Annual Report 1971–72 London: ABPI, 1972, 5.

ABPI (1974a) 'Review of the Year: Nationalisation or Public Ownership', ABPI Annual Report 1973–74, 6.

ABPI (1974b) 'Information and Services and Public Relations: Nationalisation', ABPI Annual Report 1973–1974 London: HMSO.

ABPI (1977a) 'Lessons of a Decade', ABPI News No. 164, January, 6.

ABPI (1977b) 'Sir Eric calls for Restricted Release', ABPI News No. 166 June 1977, 3.

ABPI (1977c) Annual Report 1976–77, London: ABPI, 9.

ABPI (1980a) 'Annual Dinner 1980', ABPI Annual Report 1979–80, 24.

ABPI (1980b) 'Medical and Scientific Affairs' ABPI Annual Report 1980–81, 6.

Aldcroft, D. H. (1986) *The British Economy: Vol. 1 The Years of Turmoil 1920–51* Sussex: Harvester, 1–43.

Anon (1934) 'The Other Side of the Medal' *Pharmaceutical Journa*, (22 September), 335.

Bedarida, F. (1976) *A Social History of England 1851–1975*, London and New York: Methuen, 3–35.

Beder, S. (1991) 'Controversy and Closure: Sydney's Beaches in Crisis', *Social Studies of Science* Vol. 21, 235.

Bell, W. J. (1910) *The Sale of Food and Drugs Acts 1875 to 1910*, London: Butterworth, 26–7.

Bernstein, M. (1955) *Regulating Business by Independent Commission*, Princeton: Princeton University Press.

Binns, T. B. (1980) 'The Committee on the Review of Medicines' *British Medical Journal*, Vol. 281 13 December, 1614–15.

Blake, J. B. (ed.) (1970) *Safeguarding the Public: Historical Aspects of Medicinal Drug Control*, Baltimore and London: John Hopkins Press.

BMA (1909) *Secret Remedies: What They are and what They Contain*, London: BMA.

BMA (1976) 'Pharmaceutical Industry', *British Medical Journal*, 4 December, 1397.

BMA (1977) 'Committee on the Review of Medicines: Testing the Golden Oldies', *British Medical Journal*, 17 September, 716.

BMA (1978) 'New Proposals on Surveillance of Drugs', *British Medical Journal*, 4 March, 588.

Braithwaite, J. (1986) *Corporate Crime in the Pharmaceutical Industry*, London: Routledge and Kegan Paul, 82.

Brickman, R., Jasanoff, S. and Ilgen, T. (1985) *Controlling Chemicals: The Politics of Regulation in Europe and the US*, Ithaca and London: Cornell University Press.

British Official Secrets Act (1911) *Criminal Law*, Vol. 8, 252–6.

Bruce, M. (1961) *The Coming of the Welfare State*, London: Batsford.

Burnett, J. (1966) *Plenty and Want: A Social History of Diet in England from 1815 to the Present Day*, London: Nelson.

Cawson, A. (1986) *Corporatism and Political Theory*, Oxford: Basil Blackwell.

Cawson, A. (1985) 'Varieties of Corporatism: The Importance of the Meso-Level of Interest Intermediation' in Cawson A. (ed.) *Organized Interests and the State: Studies in Meso-Corporatism*, London: Sage.

Chapman, H. E. (1935) 'Twenty-five Years of Patent Medicines', *Pharmaceutical Journal*, 4 May, 544.

Collier, J. (1985) 'Licensing and Provision of Medicines in the UK: An Appraisal' *The Lancet*, 17 August, 377–80.

Conrad, J. (ed.) (1980) *Society, Technology and Risk Assessment*, London: Academic Press.

Cromie, B. J. (1980) 'Testing New Drugs in the UK' *Journal of the Royal Society of Medicine*, Vol. 73, May, 379–80.

Delamothe, T. (1989) 'Drug Watchdogs and the Drug Industry', *British Medical Journal*, Vol. 299.

Dunlop, D. (1971) 'The Problem of Modern Medicines and Their Control', Twelfth Maurice Bloch lecture, University of Glasgow, 11 February, 20.

Farrell, D. (ed.) (1983) *Medicines Review Worldwide – A Patient Benefit or a Regulatory Burden?* Proceedings of the Fifth Annual Symposium of the British Institute of Regulatory Affairs, London: BIRA.

Forrester, J. (1978) 'The Lancet's Analytical Sanitary Commission' *Lancet*, 23/30 December, 1360–2.

Gillespie, B., Eva, D. and Johnson, R. (1979) 'Carcinogenic Risk Assessment in the US and Great Britain: The Case of Aldrin/Dieldrin', *Social Studies of Science* Vol. 9, 265–301.

Griffin, J. P. and Diggle, G. E. (1981) 'A Survey of Products Licenced in the UK from 1971–81', *British Journal of Clinical Pharmacology*, Vol. 12, p. 461

Griffin, J. P. and Long, J. R. (1981) 'New Procedures Affecting the Conduct of Clinical Trials in the United Kingdom' *British Medical Journal*, vol. 283, 15 August, p. 481

Hall, S. (1984) 'The Rise of the Representative/Interventionist State 1880s–1920s' in McLennan G., Held D. and Hall S. (eds) *State and Society in Contemporary Britain*, Cambridge: Polity Press, 7–49.

Hancher, L. (1989) 'Regulating for Competition: Government, Law and the Pharmaceutical Industry in the United Kingdom and France' University of Amsterdam: Unpublished Ph.D. Thesis.

Hay, J. R. (1975) *The Origins of the Liberal Welfare Reforms 1906–1914*, London and Basingstoke: Macmillan.

Hill, A. C. (1935) 'The Changing Foundations of Pharmaceutical Manufacture', *Pharmaceutical Journal*, 4 May, 533–4.

HMSO (1950) Ministry of Health/Department of Health for Scotland and Central Health Services Council, The Second Interim Report of the Joint Committee on Prescribing (London: HMSO), 4.

HMSO (1967a) Cmnd 3410 *Report of the Committee of Enquiry into the Relationship of the Pharmaceutical Industry with the National Health Service 1965–1967*, London: HMSO, 63–71.

HMSO (1967b) Cmnd 3395, *Forthcoming Legislation on the Safety, Quality and Description of Drugs and Medicines*, London: HMSO.

HMSO (1968) Medicines Act 1968, London: HMSO.

HMSO (1972) Committee on Safety of Drugs, Report for Year Ending 1971, London: HMSO, 12.

HMSO (1978) Committee on Safety of Medicines, Annual Report 1977, London: HMSO, 28.

Hodges, M. (1987) 'Control of the safety of drugs, 1868–1968' *Pharmaceutical Journal*, 1 August, 119–22.

House of Commons Select Committee on Adulteration of Food, Drinks and Drugs (1856) Minutes of Evidence, 56–57 and 253.

Howells, W. S. (1941) 'The Pharmacy and Medicines Act 1941: Pitfalls for Pharmacists' *Pharmaceutical Journal*, 18 October 1941, 140–1.

Hurley, R. (1983) 'The Medicines Act – Is it working?' *Journal of the British Institute of Regulatory Affairs* (BIRA) Vol. 2, 3.

Jasanoff, S. (1990) *The Fifth Branch: Science Advisers as Policy Makers*, Cambridge, Mass and London: Harvard University Press.

Jenkins, M. (1987) 'A history of the UK's drug controls' *Mims Magazine*, 56–7.

Jessop, B. (1990) *State Theory: Putting Capitalist States in their Place*, Cambridge: Polity Press, 167–8.

Lang, R. W. (1974) *The Politics of Drugs: A Comparative Pressure-Group Study of the Canadian Pharmaceutical Manufacturers Association and the Association of the British Pharmaceutical Industry, 1930–1970*, Farnborough, England: Saxon House, 63.

Lesser, E. (1977) 'Drug Warnings', *New Scientist*, 26 May, 442.

McLennan, G. Held, D., and Hall, S. (eds) (1984) *State and Society in Contemporary Britain*, Cambridge: Polity Press, 7–49.

McCrea, F. B. and Markle, G. E. (1984) 'The Estrogen Replacement Controversy in the USA and UK: Different Answers to the Same Question?' *Social Studies of Science* Vol. 14, 12.

Mallinson, G. A. (1935) 'National Health Insurance, 1911–1935' *Pharmaceutical Journal*, 4 May 1935, 535–7.

Mann, R. D. (1984) *Modern Drug Use: an Enquiry Based on Historical Principles*, Lancaster: MTP Press.

Mann, R. D. (1988) 'From mithridatium to modern medicine: the management of drug safety' *Journal of the Royal Society of Medicine* Vol. 81, 725–8.

Medawar, C. (1992) *Power and Dependence: Social Audit on the Safety of Medicines*, London: Social Audit, 176–8.

Medicine Control Agency (1991) MAIL No. 68 (July 1991)

Middlemas, K. (1979) *Politics in Industrial Society: The Experience of the British System since 1911*, London: Andre Deutsch.

Miliband, R. (1983) 'State Power and Class Interests', *New Left Review* No. 138 1983, 57–68.

Ministry of Health (1963) *Safety of Drugs, Final Report of the Joint Sub-Committee of the Standing Medical Advisory Committees*, London: HMSO.

Mitnick, B. M. (1980) *The Political Economy of Regulation*, New York: Columbia University Press, 95–109.

Murphy, R. (1988) *Closure Theory: The Theory of Monopolization and Exclusion*, Oxford: Clarendon Press.

Offe, C. (1983) 'The Capitalist State', *Political Studies*, Vol. 31, 669.

Penn, R. G. (1979) 'The State Control of Medicines: The First 3000 Years', *British Journal of Clinical Pharmacology*, Vol. 8, 295–9.

Penn, R. G. (1980) 'The Drug Industry', *British Medical Journal* Vol. 281 6 December, 1563–4.

Penn, R. G. (1982) 'The Development of the Regulatory Control of the Safety, Quality and Supply of Medicines', (Cardiff: M.D. thesis, Welsh National School of Medicine).

PRO (1921a) MH58/241B CSDIP Report (1921).

PRO (1921b) MH58/241B Minister of Health Minute Sheet, 18 February.

PRO (1921c) MH58/241B Letter from Rolf Harris, on behalf of the CSDIP, to the Ministry of Health, 10 June.

PRO (1940a) MH80/21.

PRO (1940b) MH80/21 Letter from M. J. Hewitt, Ministry of Health to De Montmorency, 9 November.

PRO (1941a) MH80/21 Customs and Excise Department, Report to the Chancellor of the Exchequer and the Minister of Health on the Medicine Stamp Duties and the Control of Proprietary Medicines.

PRO (1941b) MH80/21 Minute Sheet, 13 February.

PRO (1941c) MH80/21 Letter from Sir Ian Fraser MP to Sir Kingsley Wood, Chancellor of the Exchequer, 24 January.

PRO (1941d) MH80/21 Medicine Stamp Acts.

PRO (1941e) MH80/21 Letter from W. Eady, Customs and Excise to Sir John Maude, Secretary of Health, 26 February.

PRO (1941f) MH80/21 Letter from J. N. Beckett, Ministry of Health to H. N. Linstead, PSGB, 17 April.

PRO (1950a) MH133/76 Note of discussion on 8 June between representatives of the Ministry of Health and the ABPI.

PRO (1950b) MH133/76 Memorandum from J. S. Walmsley, Secretary of the PAGB to the Ministry of Health regarding the Second Interim Report of the JCP, 14 June.

PRO (1950c) MH133/76 Letter from Sir J. H. Woods, Board of Trade, to Sir William Douglas, Ministry of Health, 20 July.

PRO (1950d) MH133/76 Letter from Sir William Douglas to Sir J. Woods, Board of Trade, 28 July.

PRO (1951) MH58/688 Review of Drug Legislation.

PSGB (1920a) 'Manchester Section' *Pharmaceutical Journal*, 27 March, 308–9.

PSGB (1920b) 'Ministry of Health: First Annual Report' *Pharmaceutical Journal*, 18 September, 288–9.

PSGB (1920c) 'The First Year of the Ministry of Health' *Pharmaceutical Journal*, 13 November, 454.

PSGB (1929a) 'The Trade Outlook II' *Pharmaceutical Journal*, 12 January, 23–4.

PSGB (1929b) 'The Wholesale Drug Trade Association' *Pharmaceutical Journal*, 23 November, 486.

PSGB (1934) 'Control of Drug Distribution' *Pharmaceutical Journal*, 28 July, 117.

PSGB (1939) 'Drugs in War Time' *Pharmaceutical Journal*, 22 April, 404.

PSGB (1941a) 'The Pharmacy and Medicines Bill: Second Reading' *Pharmaceutical Journal*, 12 July, 18.

PSGB (1941b) 'The Pharmacy and Medicines Bill' *Pharmaceutical Journal*, 12 July, 1.

PSGB (1941c) 'The Pharmacy and Medicines Act, 1941: 'The Society and the NPU' *Pharmaceutical Journal*, 29 November, 86.

PSGB (1945) 'The WDTA' *Pharmaceutical Journal*, 17 November, 223.

PSGB (1950a) 'Anxiety for the Future', *Pharmaceutical Journal*, 22 April, 294.

PSGB (1950b) 'Pharmaceutical Industry and Export Drive', *Pharmaceutical Journal*, 7 January, 11.

PSGB (1950c) 'Annual Report of the ABPI', *Pharmaceutical Journal*, 22 April, 301.

PSGB (1954) 'ABPI Annual Dinner: Speech by Miss Hornsby-Smith M.P.' *Pharmaceutical Journal*, 17 April, 312.

PSGB (1956) 'Recruitment by the Industry' *Pharmaceutical Journal*, 5 May, 1.

PSGB (1956b) 'British Pharmaceutical Industry: Speech by Minister of Health' *Pharmaceutical Journal*, 5 May, 239.

PSGB (1959a) 'Trade Association News' *Pharmaceutical Journal*, 9 May, 348–9.

PSGB (1959b) 'Testing of New Drugs', *Pharmaceutical Journal*, 1 August, 1.

PSGB (1960a) 'The Industry Reviews 1959–60', *Pharmaceutical Industry*, 7 May, 401–2.

PSGB (1960b) 'Testing of New Drugs', *Pharmaceutical Journal*, 20 February, 148.

PSGB (1961) 'Evidence by Advertising Inquiry council', *Pharmaceutical Journal*, 25 February, 155.

PSGB (1962a) 'Hot Milk at Bedtime?' *Pharmaceutical Journal*, 25 August, 174.

PSGB (1962b) 'Toxic hazards of new drugs' *Pharmaceutical Journal*, 10 February, 112.

PSGB (1962c) 'Clinical Trials of Drugs', *Pharmaceutical Journal*, 17 May, 429.

PSGB (1962d) 'Drug Toxicity: Debate on Drug Control', *Pharmaceutical Journal*, 1 December, 523–4.

PSGB (1962e) 'Testing of New Drugs', *Pharmaceutical Journal*, 23 June, 552–3.

PSGB (1962f) 'Testing of New Drugs', *Pharmaceutical Journal*, 28 July, 83.

PSGB (1962g) "Magnificent" Export Performance', *Pharmaceutical Journal*, 3 November, 445.

PSGB (1962h) 'Ministry of Health: Interim Advice on Testing of New Drugs', *Pharmaceutical Journal*, 10 November, 450–1.

PSGB (1963a) 'The Industry and the Health Service', *Pharmaceutical Journal*, 4 May, 417–18.

PSGB (1963b) 'Safety of Drugs', *Pharmaceutical Journal*, 13 April, 311–12.

PSGB (1963c) 'Safety of Drugs: Joint SubCommittee's Final Report', *Pharmaceutical Journal*, 13 April, 317–21.

PSGB (1963d) 'Committee on Safety of Drugs: Members and Terms of Reference', *Pharmaceutical Journal*, 8 June, 534.

PSGB (1963e) 'Committee on Safety of Drugs: Assessment of Reports to Begin on Jan. 1st', *Pharmaceutical Journal*, 21 September, 313.

PSGB (1963f) 'Committee on Safety of Drugs: Memo to Manufacturers and Importers', *Pharmaceutical Journal*, 26 October, 433.

PSGB (1964) 'The work of the Committee on Safety of Drugs', *Pharmaceutical Journal*, 2 May, 436.

PSGB (1966a) 'Safety of Drugs: Dunlop Committee Second Report', *Pharmaceutical Journal*, 23 July, 86–7.

PSGB (1966b) 'The Assessment of Safety of Drugs', *Pharmaceutical Journal*, 26 March, 292–5.

PSGB (1967a) 'Safety of Drugs: Committee's Annual Report', *Pharmaceutical Journal*, 15 July, 59–60.

PSGB (1967b) 'The White Paper: Comments by ABPI' *Pharmaceutical Journal*, 16 September, 246–7.

PSGB (1968a) 'The Medicines Bill', *Pharmaceutical Journal*, 10 February, 150–5.

PSGB (1968b) 'Industry, Safety, Sainsbury and the Bill', *Pharmaceutical Journal*, 9 March, 274–5.

PSGB (1968c) 'Medicines Bill: Committee Stage', *Pharmaceutical Journal*, 30 March, 368–9.

PSGB (1968d) 'The Medicines Bill in Committee' *Pharmaceutical Journal*, 23 March, 334–5.

PSGB (1968e) 'Medicines Bill: Committee Stage', *Pharmaceutical Journal*, 30 March, 368–9.

PSGB (1968f) 'Medicines Bill receives cautious approval', *Pharmaceutical Journal,* 24 February, 215–18.

PSGB (1970) 'Medicines Act Reassurance for Manufacturers', *Pharmaceutical Journal* ,17 January, 48.

PSGB (1976a) 'MPs call for Official Inquiry into Eraldin', *Pharmaceutical Journal,* 6 November, 427.

PSGB (1976b) 'CSM asked to Speed Up Procedures', *Pharmaceutical Journal,* 17 July, 46.

Robertson, K. G. (1982) *Public Secrets: A Study in the Development of Government Secrecy,* London: Macmillan, 1–91.

Ronge, V. (1980) 'Theoretical Concepts of Political Decision-Making Processes' in Conrad J. (ed.), *Society, Technology and Risk Assessment,* London: Academic Press, 209–38.

SCRIP (1988a) *World Pharmaceutical News* No. 1279, 3 February, 3.

SCRIP (1988b) *World Pharmaceutical News* No. 1270, 1/6 January, 24.

SCRIP (1991a) *World Pharmaceutical News* No. 1595, 1 March, 8–9.

SCRIP (1991b) *World Pharmaceutical News* No. 1635, 19 July, 2.

Silvermann, M. and Lee, P. R. (1974) *Pills, Profits and Politics,* Berkeley and Los Angeles, California: University of California Press, 48–80.

Smart, R. D. (1981) 'Foreword', ABPI Annual Report 1980–81, London: ABPI, 3.

Smith, T. (1980) 'The Drug Industry: Are the Drug-Regulatory Agencies Paper Villains? *British Medical Journal,* Vol. 281, 15 November, 1334.

Somervell, D. C. (1929) *English Thought in the Nineteenth Century,* London: Methuen, 3–16.

Steward, F. and Wibberley, G. (1980) 'Drug Innovation – What's Slowing It Down?' *Nature* Vol. 284, (13 March), 119.

Stieb, E. W. (1966) *Drug Adulteration: Detection and Control in Nineteenth Century Britain,* Madison, Milwaukee/London: University of Wisconsin Press.

Stieb, E. W. (1970) 'Drug Control in Britain, 1850–1914' in Blake J. B. (ed.), *Safeguarding the Public: Historical Aspects of Medicinal Drug Control,* Baltimore and London: John Hopkins Press.

Thompson, G. (1984a) 'Economic Intervention in the Post-War Economy' in McLennan, G., Held, D. and Hall S. (eds), *State and Society in Contemporary Britain,* Cambridge: Polity Press, 77–118.

Thompson, G. (1984b) "Rolling back" the state? Economic intervention 1975–82' in McLennan, G., Held, D. and Hall, S. (eds) *State and Society in Contemporary Britain,* Cambridge: Polity, 286.

Tweedale, G. (1990) *At the Sign of the Plough: 275 Years of Allen and Hanburg's and the British Pharmaceutical Industry 1715–1900,* London: John Murray.

US GPO (1970) Twenty-second Report Committee on Government Operations, *The British Drug Safety System,* 91st Congress, 2nd Session, Washington DC: US GPO, 37.

Wade, O. L. (1983) 'Achievements, Problems and Limitations of Regulatory Bodies' in Farrell, D. (ed.), *Medicines Review Worldwide – A Patient Benefit or a Regulatory Burden? Proceedings of the Fifth Annual Symposium of the British Institute of Regulatory Affairs,* London: BIRA, 3.

Wheeler, D. E. (1963) 'The President's Statement', ABPI Annual Report 1962–63, 5–6.

Wheeler, D. E. (1964) 'President's Statement', ABPI Annual Report 1963–64, 2.
Wheeler, D. E. (1964) 'President's Statement', ABPI Annual Report 1963–64, 3.
Wilson, G. M. (1962) 'Assessing New Drugs', *New Scientist* No. 297, 26 July, 196.

Index

268 *Index*